ESSENTIAL SECRETS

for ACHIEVING
GREATER SUCCESS
AT WORK

Marshall Cavendish
Business

Illustrations by Edwin Ng
Cover art by Darren Tan
Cover images by iStockphoto
Edited by Shirley Taylor

Published by Marshall Cavendish Business
An imprint of Marshall Cavendish International
1 New Industrial Road, Singapore 536196

Other Marshall Cavendish Offices
Marshall Cavendish International. PO Box 65829, London EC1P 1NY, UK • Marshall Cavendish Corporation. 99 White Plains Road, Tarrytown NY 10591-9001, USA • Marshall Cavendish International (Thailand) Co Ltd. 253 Asoke, 12th Flr, Sukhumvit 21 Road, Klongtoey Nua, Wattana, Bangkok 10110, Thailand • Marshall Cavendish (Malaysia) Sdn Bhd, Times Subang, Lot 46, Subang Hi-Tech Industrial Park, Batu Tiga, 40000 Shah Alam, Selangor Darul Ehsan, Malaysia

Marshall Cavendish is a trademark of Times Publishing Limited

National Library Board Singapore Cataloguing in Publication Data
88 essential secrets : for achieving greater success at work / edited by
 Shirley Taylor. – Singapore : Marshall Cavendish Editions, 2012.
 p. cm.
 Includes index.
 ISBN : 978-981-4351-40-9

1. Career development. 2. Success. I. Taylor, Shirley.

HF5381
650.1 — dc22   OCN770838565

Printed in Singapore by Craft Print International Ltd

88. ESSENTIAL SECRETS

MOTIVATION AND PROMOTION

YOUR SUCCESS AND MOTIVATION

- Becoming a runaway success by Thaddeus Lawrence (page 21)

- Creating a highly motivated life by Kenneth Kwan (page 37)

- How to be a success magnet by Christian Chua (page 49)

BRANDING AND PROMOTING YOU

- Your professional image toolbox by Pang Li Kin (page 64)

- Brand yourself, build your business by Pamela Wigglesworth (page 80)

- Promoting yourself through technology by Sharon Connolly (page 97)

- Mastering the art of media pitching by Andrew Chow (page 117)

SPEECH, LANGUAGE AND COMMUNICATION

YOUR SPEECH AND LANGUAGE

- Voice of a leader by Deborah Torres Patel (page 135)

- Get ahead with global English by Heather Hansen (page 154)

YOUR COMMUNICATION AND INTERPERSONAL SKILLS

- Building great relationships by Shirley Taylor (page 173)

- Communication in four dimensions by Elisabetta Franzoso (page 191)

- Influential networking by Karen Leong (page 208)

INFLUENCE AND SALES

SPEAKING TO INFLUENCE, PERSUADE AND WIN

- Speaking to influence and win by Eric Feng (page 229)

- Persuading with power by David Goldwich (page 244)

SELLING AND WINNING BUSINESS

- Pitching perfectly to win business by Tina Altieri (page 260)

- Perform better, sell more, earn more by Rob Salisbury (page 279)

PRODUCTIVITY AND LEADERSHIP

YOUR PRODUCTIVITY, DECISION-MAKING AND CREATIVITY

- Increasing profitable productivity by Tim Wade (page 299)

- Dynamic decision-making by Tremaine Du Preez (page 319)

- Jumpstart your creative potential by Titus Yong (page 337)

MANAGEMENT, LEADERSHIP AND TEAMWORK

- The corporate jungle by Benjamin Cheng (page 356)

- Timeless management by Bob Feldman (page 370)

- Maximising team performance by Ken Wong (page 385)

CONTENTS

PART 1: MOTIVATION AND PROMOTION

SECTION 1: YOUR SUCCESS AND MOTIVATION

SECTION 2: BRANDING AND PROMOTING YOU

PART 2: SPEECH, LANGUAGE AND COMMUNICATION

SECTION 3: YOUR SPEECH AND LANGUAGE

SECTION 4: YOUR COMMUNICATION AND INTERPERSONAL SKILLS

PART 3: INFLUENCE AND SALES

SECTION 5: SPEAKING TO INFLUENCE, PERSUADE AND WIN

SECTION 6: SELLING AND WINNING BUSINESS

PART 4: PRODUCTIVITY AND LEADERSHIP

SECTION 7: YOUR PRODUCTIVITY, DECISION-MAKING AND CREATIVITY

SECTION 8: MANAGEMENT, LEADERSHIP AND TEAMWORK

INTRODUCTION BY EDITOR

"Don't worry about how we divide up the pie. There is enough for everybody. Let's just build a bigger pie!"

— Cavett Robert,
Founder of National Speakers Association (USA)

When Cavett Robert set up the first speakers association in 1972, he felt that everyone involved in the speaking profession would benefit from growing the number and quality of professional speakers. He referred to it as "making a bigger pie." Most professions are so filled with competition that this thinking isn't rewarded, but to the speaking profession, this ignited an industry boom.

There are now speakers associations all over the world, many of which are part of the Global Speakers Federation. Asia Professional Speakers Singapore, founded in 2003, is proud to be one of these associations. There is a wonderful spirit of caring and sharing at APSS, and our members encourage, support and help each other by exchanging ideas and sharing experiences.

That's what this book is all about — sharing our knowledge, ideas and experience. Our Professional Members are subject experts who have a great deal of knowledge in a variety of topics. They regularly share this expertise, and their speaking talents, by presenting at conferences and conducting training workshops, as well as mentoring and coaching people across Asia and beyond. We felt it was time to make their expertise available to a wider audience by publishing this book.

As Editor, it's been my privilege to work closely with 22 of our Professional Members who together have almost 400 years of experience in speaking and training. I've also learned a great deal in the process.

As you read these 'secrets', I think you cannot help but be motivated and inspired, as I have been. These pages are packed with so many great ideas and insights that will impact your effectiveness and productivity, and ultimately your success.

Cavett Robert had a strong desire to help other people. He left a legacy of a better world through the encouragement of others. In the speaking world we call this attitude 'The Spirit of Cavett' or 'The Spirit of Sharing'. It's been an honour for me to play a part in sharing a wealth of knowledge and expertise with you here. By picking up this book, you have already shown a desire to learn more. The solid advice, personal stories and practical guidelines provided in each chapter will really show you how you can propel yourself to a more successful future. And please, remember to share what you learn!

Here's to your success!

Shirley Taylor.

Shirley Taylor, Editor
APSS President (2011-12)

Special Thanks

I would like to thank Chris Newson at Marshall Cavendish International (Singapore) for giving us the opportunity to publish this book, also their editorial and design team for being so good (and very patient) to work with, and the talented Edwin Ng for his fabulous illustrations. Special thanks to Tim Wade, APSS President (2010-11), for his input and support in this project. Thanks also to the members of the APSS Executive Committee for their valuable contributions, support and friendship during my year as President.

ABOUT APSS – ASIA PROFESSIONAL SPEAKERS (SINGAPORE)

www.asiaspeakers.org

Asia Professional Speakers Singapore (APSS) is an association whose membership is made up of subject experts who are already speaking or training professionally, and others who aspire to become professional speakers or trainers.

Our members are speakers from a wide spectrum of industries and disciplines, who also reach audiences as mentors, educators, trainers, consultants, authors and coaches.

APSS is dedicated to advancing the expertise, eloquence, enterprise and ethics of all its members.

APSS Membership

Membership of an association like APSS is a great way to meet, network and stay connected to other professionals who want to share their knowledge and experience as you all help each other to progress. Membership also helps you to build your network of professionals (and friends) in the business.

There are three levels of membership:

- Professional Members
- Associate Members
- Corporate Members

Some of the many benefits of APSS membership are:

- Monthly meetings, annual convention and special events
- Reduced members' fees for all events
- Free entrance to added-value sessions
- Networking and mentoring opportunities
- Help in growing and sustaining your speaking business
- Connection to the global speaking community
- Automatic membership to Global Speakers Federation
- Eligible to join Global Speakers Network
- Annual subscription to NSA Speaker magazine in pdf format
- NSA's Voices of Experience audio CD in mp3 format
- Option to join special mastermind groups
- Option to attend special members' lunch forums
- Members' rates for international speakers' conventions
- Free registration with eSpeakers.com
- The right to vote at the Annual General Meeting
- Opportunity to be showcased at annual Raise Your Game event
- Receive requests for speakers leads from external organisations
- Profile and photo on the APSS website
- Option to list yourself on GSF (Global Speakers Federation) website

APSS was founded on principles of abundance. We believe that by sharing with each other and caring about the success of our fellow members, we will build a stronger profession. We are a vibrant and dynamic network where members can find support and friendship with fellow speaking professionals.

Your Turn

If you want to learn more about APSS, attend events and monthly meetings, or learn more about becoming a member, please visit: www.asiaspeakers.org

Global Speakers Federation
Advancing the Professional Speaking Community Worldwide

GLOBAL SPEAKERS FEDERATION

APSS is proud to be part of the GSF — the Global Speakers Federation — an organisation of national speaking associations around the world. The GSF currently comprises 10 independent speaker associations representing 13 nations with members in over 20 countries. The Global Speakers Federation provides opportunities for speakers to expand their message by connecting them with colleagues all over the world who can help them enter global markets with greater ease.

Hot Tip

Learn more about the Global Speakers Federation here: www.globalspeakers.net

PART 1

Motivation and Promotion

> **"** *What we do in life echoes through eternity.*
> *If you can't fly, then run.*
> *If you can't run, then walk.*
> *If you can't walk, then crawl.*
> *But whatever you do, keep moving.*"
>
> — Dr. Martin Luther King, Jr.

SECTION 1

Your Success and Motivation

CHAPTER **1**

BECOMING A RUNAWAY SUCCESS
How to be your own source of motivation
in your race of life

by **Thaddeus Lawrence**
Founder
Runaway Success Learning Practice

Thaddeus Lawrence is best known for successfully racing 1,000 kilometres in the hottest, coldest, windiest and driest deserts on earth, a competition rated by *TIME* magazine as one of its Top Ten Endurance Competitions in the world. His remarkable feats in the Sahara, Gobi, Atacama and Antarctica also raised hundreds of thousands of dollars for charities. Thaddeus is the author of *Runaway Success: Life Lessons from Ultra Endurance Racing*, which translates his lessons from the race world into strategies for the real world.

Thaddeus was born in Singapore and has lived and worked in the UK, USA, Thailand and the African continent. His ability to draw wisdom from life's challenges, setbacks, choices and successes makes him suitably qualified to speak about mental peak performance and personal effectiveness. His inspiring stories and racing analogies are packed with lessons and tools to make you more effective at work and successful in life.

Thaddeus is a speaker, trainer and author. He delivers keynote presentations and conducts workshops on resilient mindset, self management, personal mastery and motivation.

Find out more about Thaddeus at: **www.therunawaysuccess.com**
Contact Thaddeus at: **thaddeus@therunawaysuccess.com**

ONE OF THE key elements leading to success in life is the ability to be fully engaged in what we do. A high level of motivation leads to increased enthusiasm and enjoyment in our daily experiences. This results in higher performance levels and a fulfilling sense of accomplishment.

However, many people are unable to drive themselves forward. They give up when success is just around the corner, abandoning their goals and dreams. Others fall victim to the increased demands of work or society, burning out and losing direction. For some, even getting out of bed in the morning becomes a chore.

In this section, Thaddeus Lawrence will share some practical strategies from the ultra endurance racing world to help you stay invigorated and involved in what you do in the real world. While others can be a source of encouragement, you are your greatest motivator and can truly impact your own performance and quality of life.

Thaddeus will help you formulate a plan of action that builds upon your current realities. You will learn to apply proven concepts to your own life and be better able to control your positive states. You will discover how to use what you already have to propel yourself forward.

Secret 1
LIFE IS AN ULTRA ENDURANCE RACE

Can you run 100 metres? One kilometre? 10 kilometres? What about a multi-day ultra endurance race over hundreds of kilometres?

Like most people, you probably answered yes to the first three questions but flinched at the last. "That's mad," you may think, "why go through all that suffering?" In fact, many people would question their own ability to survive such a race.

Well, crazy or not, you are already in the endurance race of life. Life is not a short sprint but a multi-day event. Just when you think you are done, you will have to get up the next day and do it all over again. Your races take place at work, in school, at home. You wear the different hats of a corporate athlete, academic athlete, and domestic athlete.

Life is an ultra endurance race. This is the secret on which all the others are built. I will show you how you can adapt the mindsets and practices of ultra athletes, and turn a life of endurance into an enduring one. If you are keen to stop surviving life and start thriving, here are three key rules you must follow.

Holy Moly!

It is not a question of whether I can, but what is in it for me to want to.

1. Move to the beat of your milestones

Picture this scene: Runners are taking their marks for a 100-metre sprint — their eyes are looking forward and they can see the strip of tape stretched across the finish line very clearly. Their target lies within their range of vision, and this draws them down the straight of the running track.

Ultra racers do not enjoy the same clarity of sight. Their goal is a long way off and it may be several days before they even get anywhere close to their finish line. So what do they do? Instead of getting demoralised by the long distance, they set intermediate goals in the form of checkpoints and stage camps. They get through the race simply by taking it one day at a time and focusing on their daily milestones.

You can do the same with your long-term goals. You are likely to take several years to realise your worthy and meaningful aspirations — completing higher studies, attaining corporate success, securing a comfortable retirement, fulfilling a childhood dream — which are all long-term pursuits. Your staying power and motivation will be greatly enhanced by having a set of short-term objectives.

Breaking down the key components of your goal will provide indicators of your progress within a time frame. Having intermediate goals will help you focus on your immediate steps and help you specify the necessary behaviours to be performed. These small milestone 'wins' will also keep your spirits up and fill you with the energy you need for the long haul.

Hot Tip

Set several short-term objectives. Once you are close to achieving one, start looking ahead to the next one.

2. Learn when to say no

At its essence, an ultra is a series of yes/no questions. Eat now or wait? Short rest or a longer break? Speed up or ease up? Extreme distances magnify every little decision, and one wrong answer can potentially ruin the whole race.

So when the urge to brush aside a small discomfort arises, when the compulsion to compromise on the overall race plan in favour of short-term advancement appears, the most powerful thing an athlete can say is no.

What can you say "no" to? Staying in your comfort zone? Pushing hard in one area of your life and neglecting the rest? See the big picture to get a clear sense of your priorities. Practise self-control so that you are in a better position to realise what you truly desire.

3. Run slow for tomorrow

In endurance sports, 'hitting the wall' is a metaphor for the depletion of glycogen in muscles. When runners hit the wall, they basically run out of energy; the body and mind collapse, draining them of strength and motivation. Some athletes are forced to slow down while others quit entirely. It is not at all a good place to be.

But look all around you and you will see many people hitting the wall of life. Mental burnouts, emotional exhaustion and physical withdrawals are commonplace. If this sounds like you, then you are possibly starting out or operating at a pace that is too fast for you.

The winner in an ultra is not the one who runs the fastest, but rather, the person who slows down the least. Going fast does not mean you will last. Perhaps you need to go a little easier on yourself so that you can get up the next day and do it all over again. This might mean taking a break to recharge, delegating some responsibilities, or learning to say no.

Perhaps you might be protesting, "but I have no choice!" If you find yourself struggling to keep up with essential challenges, then you may want to look at your personal effectiveness. Do you need to develop some of your skills through training and coaching? Or will it help to change your perspective of work and life? If you focus on possibilities instead of problems, you will see the world through more positive lenses. You will enhance your abilities and find the energy to last the distance.

Caution

Ask yourself if you can get up tomorrow and go at the same pace. If the answer is no, then you need to slow down.

Secret 2
IT'S NOT HOW FAST BUT HOW FAR YOU GO

It is easy to separate the novices from the experienced competitors in an ultra endurance race. The seasoned veterans get stronger or at least maintain their momentum as the days wear on. On the other hand, the raw rookies witness a deterioration in their performance and commonly fall by the wayside. Which category do you fall into in your race of life?

Do you adopt a long-term attitude and set ambitious goals but also allow yourself to focus on the present? Do you pay attention to your growth? Are you willing to accept the plateaus of life while keeping a consistent and steady pace? You might even be considered slow by others but you always finish what you started and you finish strong. Does that sound like you?

Or are you the opposite? Do you approach each new task, job or relationship with enormous early enthusiasm only for your interest to fizzle out when the routine sets in? Or do you start off aggressively and then realise you've bitten off more than you can chew? Do you push yourself excessively in pursuit of quick results, only for your performance, relationships and health to experience roller coaster rides of steep climbs and sharp declines?

Life is an ultra endurance race. Success is not about going fast, but going far and finishing strong. This requires you to know a few things.

1. Know your game

Know what you are getting into. It will determine how you train and what you need. Short sprints require a great deal of power and strength. This is why sprinters build muscles to power up and drive themselves forward. Marathoners tend to be leaner. They work on developing their overall fitness and stamina. Ultra endurance racers need something else. The successful ones possess a great deal of mind power and mental control to improve their endurance and resilience.

What is your game plan and what does it require? A salesman and a sales manager have different skill sets. Selling skills and handling objection are important to a salesman while a sales manager needs to learn management techniques and strategic planning. A business leader with excellent corporate communication skills may not necessarily enjoy open and understanding relationships with his spouse and children.

Knowing what you are embarking on will change your responsibilities. How will things change? How will your relationships be different? Your clarity governs your approach and your focus.

2. Know yourself

An athlete has to know when he has over-exerted himself. Sore limbs, muscle fatigue and minor injuries are some of the milder physical manifestations. Other more serious symptoms include disturbed sleep patterns, heart abnormalities and physical collapse. Even a miscalculation in salt intake or water consumption can lead to decreased performance at best or be life-threatening at worst. This is why athletes are always urged to listen to their bodies and respond to its needs by focusing on rest and recovery.

The human body is like a feedback mechanism. Our physical, mental and emotional health are the different ways in which our bodies might protest. Pay attention to your body over a span of time. What do you notice? Do you notice a sudden sprouting of white hair, protracted periods of migraine, or the onset of regular illnesses? Do you observe an abnormally high level of stress, loss of concentration or disillusionment? Or are you in a state of irritability, fluctuating moods and feeling of worthlessness? These are all warning signs from your body that something is not right.

Your Turn

Assess your life by brainstorming about six to eight important areas — for example; career, family, friends, education, money, health, community service and personal growth. Rank each life area on a satisfaction scale of 1 to 10, with 1 being the lowest level of satisfaction and 10 being the highest. Identify the areas of your life with which you are most happy and exercise gratitude. Then identify an area that needs work. What changes are you committed to making to increase your satisfaction in that area? Feel free to choose something that already shows some positive characteristics.

Stop and be honest with yourself. What is it that needs to change? Where in your life might you need to slow down? What do you need to do differently?

3. Know your team

No one runs alone. Even in the most extreme of individual races, there is a whole team of people behind the runner. From his support crew to his personal cheerleaders, from his fellow enthusiasts to his fervent backers; the runner receives a tremendous amount of support that helps him last the distance.

It should not be any different in your race of life. Sure, there will be the naysayers, the detractors, the critics. But how much of their voices should you listen to, as compared to the voices of people who want you to succeed?

Build a team that is aligned with your goals. Find a sponsor who opens doors for you. Get a mentor who advises and develops you. Spend time with the personal champions who stand by you. Establish a trusted network of friends and colleagues who keep you on the straight and narrow. These people are in it for the long haul and will help to get you further ahead.

Hot Tip

Show people how much you care by affirming or complimenting someone on your team every single day.

Secret 3
IT'S NOT JUST ABOUT PRACTISING, IT'S ABOUT THE PRACTICE

Training is a key component of any athletic pursuit. An Olympic sprinter works for years on his technique and strength for a race that will be over in ten seconds. During that short moment every second gives him feedback on how he is doing.

Practising is also a way of life for an endurance athlete. But there are prolonged periods during the long race where he finds himself all alone. The scenery may be unchanging and there is no information on how far he has travelled and how much more he has left. This is the plateau.

Life is a series of ups and downs, but for the most part you find yourself on the long stretch of regular activity with no apparent progress. So keep going until you practise for the sake of practice. The point of running is to run. You love it for its own sake and not because it gets you somewhere. Being fully present is what the practice is all about. Let's take a look at some things you can put into practice.

1. Develop your race ritual

Routine is part of racing. Before the race, runners go through their well-rehearsed preparation. Eating, dressing and limbering up take on a familiar quality. They tuck into the same breakfast, slip on their usual outfits, tune into their customary music tracks, perform their established warm-up exercises, and visualise their race strategy.

These race rituals serve a practical purpose, of course, but they also ready their minds and focus their attention on the event to come. The rituals are the perfect blend of concentration and relaxation, of power and peace. The routine feeds the runners' spirits and readies them for a full immersion in what is to come.

You too can incorporate a daily ritual into your life, a habitual behaviour that prepares you to devote your undivided attention to the challenges ahead. Start by welcoming the day. Lie quietly for a few moments before getting out of bed and put yourself into a positive frame of mind. Smile at yourself and tell yourself it will be a good day ahead. When preparing for sleep, calm your mind through meditation or prayer or by focusing on all the positive things that happened during the day.

Other good habits include sharing in the family meal by eating together on certain days of the week. Practise gratitude regularly and get in touch with what you have in your life. Such simple ceremonies help to keep your work and life on track and your thoughts flowing.

Holy Moly!

Since it takes fewer muscles to smile than to frown, I may as well take the easy way out and smile more.

2. Create newness

Ultra racing can take competitors through some of the world's most stunning and jaw-dropping locations. At the same time, long laborious hours can be spent traversing the same unvaried and colourless landscapes. Such monotony and boredom can be more arduous than the task itself. In such scenarios, it is important for competitors to keep their minds fresh.

We live in the modern world where the need for newness is an on-going obsession. We hanker after new products, innovative ideas, cutting edge technology and fresh conversations. Our entire economic framework and social infrastructure is dependent on all that is the latest and newest. So what happens when we are caught in a life of stagnancy and staleness? We innovate, of course.

Where in your life can you inject freshness? When was the last time you did something for the first time? When did you last learn a new hobby or language? How long has it been since your last date with your spouse? How about taking a different route to and from work? What about finding a new perspective on life? The Chinese word for 'crisis' is made up of two characters signifying 'danger' and 'opportunity'. Maybe it is time you refocused and learn to perceive opportunities in mundane chores.

3. Move in the flow zone

The sense of discovery and growth of self into a new reality is a key part of any optimal experience. Such an experience is characterised by full participation and involvement in an activity. It is where the runner is oblivious to all external conditions and stimulations. Nothing else matters, except the run itself.

But this zone treads a fine middle line between anxiety and boredom. If what you do is too complex for your current competency, you need to increase your skills or risk frustration and anxiety. On the other hand, if you are not engaged in the kinds of challenging tasks that suit your ability, the boredom will lead to disengagement.

Stop and do a self-assessment. Are the skills you possess and challenges you face in sync? If they are, you are in the flow zone and experiencing growth and development. If they are not, either anxiety or boredom may be getting the better of you and you will need to readjust your goals.

Caution

Life events impact stress levels. If you are going through a major life change, get support from your team to help you cope.

Secret 4
WHEN THE TOUGH GET GOING, THE GOING GETS TOUGH

A sprinter forays into the marathon. The marathoner takes on an ultra race. The ultra racer goes the distance in a desert, risks himself in a high altitude race, chases a ridiculous world's first that questions the very core of his sanity. The tough always push a little more, try a little harder and go a little further. When the tough, the courageous and the intrepid start moving forward, they invariably find themselves in the unknown. It is scary. But it is also exciting.

Do not confuse happiness with easiness. It is not the same. What you admire about someone is not his success per se, but his journey. In particular, what grips your imagination and fills you with respect and reverence is his journey of overcoming difficulties, surmounting challenges and prevailing over obstacles. He did not actively pursue happiness; it ensued as a result of his commitment to something big. And it is his triumph over the arduous that makes for a successful life and appeals to our admiration. Here's how you can keep yourself moving forward.

1. Keep moving forward

The purest form of running, and of athletics, is to break through the boundaries of what the human body can do. On an individual level, it is to break through the boundaries of what has previously been accomplished. There is no winning nor losing. For adventurers and athletes, success lies in the journey of the human spirit.

This constant pursuit of growth and discovery is a gift. This is the essence of discipline: not pain or pressure, but learning and illuminating. There is a joke among ultra racers that falling down is progress as long as you fall forward. Here, the label of 'failure' does not exist.

How are you moving forward? Where can you redefine your comfort zone? Assess your career and life over the past year or past five years. Check if you are growing yourself and others or simply being swept along with the tide. Then consciously choose to take inspired action. It does not have to be a drastic move, just a decided small step that can lead to a monumental change.

2. Move with meaning

The first time a runner enters a race, he intends simply to complete it and complete it in one piece. Subsequently he builds up a racing routine and gets comfortable with his chosen distance. Then he establishes targets that he aims to beat in an attempt to better his performance. Then he begins to run for a cause, mentor budding runners, or inspire others through his racing.

In this way the runner works himself up the ladder of survival, stability, success and significance. His goals evolve, and running is the mechanism through which he practices discipline and surpasses limits. There is meaning behind his runs.

Similarly, work is hard when it has no meaning. Work is drudgery when it does not meet a need or serve a stronger purpose. If you find that things are becoming predictable and unattractive, consider how you can challenge yourself. Reset your goals from the achievable and attainable to the ambitious and audacious. Dedicate yourself to a greater cause and make a bigger difference. Listen to your heart and follow its calling.

Your Turn

Look outside your life and think of all the people you admire who are the epitome of what you consider successful. Draw up a list of such individuals, and next to each describe what they do and their areas of contribution. What are the commonalities? There is a reason why you are drawn to them. They could prove to be the starting point for you to construct a knowledge of your own passion and purpose.

3. Get one per cent better every day

A worthy goal is exhilarating. While galvanising us into action, it can paralyse us when we find it too overwhelming. Procrastination, tension and disillusionment set in, and dreams die a slow death. If this sounds familiar to you, just remember that you do not have to get it right every single time. You do not have to perform miracles every day. You do not have to move with leaps and bounds. You just need to get one per cent better every day.

Set yourself a big and meaningful goal, strongly connect with it and then forget about it. It is there and you know where you want to be. Now settle down for the journey, one step at a time, one foot in front of the other.

You know your game and you know yourself. Start each day with just one area in which you want to get better. Then determine an action or series of actions you will take that will move you forward. That's all there is to it. No one triumphs in a long distance race by taking quick sprints or gigantic hops.

Life is an ultra endurance race and there are no secrets to your being a runaway success. But it is not enough that you know it. It is not enough to know how to do it. It is important that you do it.

Success is not merely a cognitive skill, nor is it only an awareness tool. You have to get out there and live it. May you no longer be consumed by endless activity but consciously take inspired action.

Checklist for being your own source of motivation in your race of life:

1. Set intermediate milestones that keep you on the right track and give you the short-term energy you need for the long haul.

2. Keep the big picture in mind and say no to the things and tasks that are not important.

3. Take time out regularly to rejuvenate and reinvigorate yourself.

4. Pay attention to your physical and mental health — they are markers in your life journey.

5. Spend more time with positive and supportive people than with the pessimists who only drain your energy.

6. Establish good, healthy habits that add vigour and vivacity to your life.

7. Pay more attention to seeing the opportunities in your circumstances.

8. Understand your mistakes. When you make a mistake, express what you would do differently next time.

9. Develop clarity and purpose by crafting your personal mission statement.

10. Invest time and money on your self-development.

CHAPTER 2

CREATING A HIGHLY MOTIVATED LIFE

How to constantly motivate yourself and
find success in all that you do

by **Kenneth Kwan**
Motivational Team Strategist
Deep Impact Pte Ltd

Kenneth Kwan is a Motivational Team Strategist who speaks to hundreds of leaders, professionals and public audiences. He has been featured as a speaker in Learning and Development Summits for HR professionals. In addition, Kenneth has trained or spoken to over 6,900 individuals to achieve their peak potential and instilled a deep desire for them to grow by themselves.

Kenneth's high-impact training and unique ability to get entire groups of people to change their behaviour quickly have resulted in them reaching their peak performance levels and achievements. He advocates that the mindset, rather than typical skills training, is the first place to start. This translates into better alignment of organisational values, greater team spirit, higher revenues and the building of trust.

Kenneth was born in Singapore and has spoken in seven countries. He established Deep Impact Pte Ltd, which has helped organisations improve their performance through team-building and training programmes.

Kenneth is an international motivational speaker and trainer in the areas of team building, team training and personality profiling.

Find out more about Kenneth at: **www.DeepImpactOnline.com**
Contact Kenneth at: **kenneth@deepimpactonline.com**

INTRINSIC MOTIVATION IS necessary in order for a person to succeed in life. It is the fuel that helps to propel a person towards a goal, stay focused and disciplined to achieve it.

However, there are some people who feel that it is over-rated while others believe it is absolutely important to have it. The question is *how* do you make it work for you? How can you use your own personal motivation to achieve the results that you want in your life?

In this section, Kenneth Kwan will share the common misconceptions about motivation and also the theory behind motivation. Kenneth will share powerful tips on how you can stay motivated and constantly work towards getting better results in your life.

Secret 5
IT'S WHAT YOU SAY TO YOURSELF THAT COUNTS

I'm sure you will agree that personal motivation is really important for things to happen in your life. It is the 'why' that keeps you moving and fuels your drive to succeed. However, most people suffer from a lack of motivation. That is one reason why so many people choose to attend motivational talks.

But do motivational talks really work? Or are they designed to spur you in the heat of the moment and then fizzle out after a couple of days? Why is it that some people swear by such talks and say that they changed their lives, while others come out saying it was a fun programme but nothing really changed for them? Let's take a deeper look at whether motivational talks actually work, and whether you can keep yourself motivated to achieve peak success in your life.

Before we carry on, ask yourself a few questions:

- What do you usually say to motivate yourself? Are they words that empower or disempower you?
- What emotions do you feel when you wake up? What about when you are at work? Are they negative or positive emotions?

Interestingly, most people wake up in the morning with very little motivation about what they are going to do for the day. Negative emotional states such as boredom, lack of motivation or energy, a sense of dread, fear, worry, unhappiness, procrastination and general laziness are very common, and they tend to outweigh the positive states. It is because of the constant repetition of such states that people feel unmotivated and have no desire to want to do more in life or at work.

Challenges at work also make it very difficult for people to feel motivated at all. For example, focusing on negativity or having colleagues that pick on your every mistake will make you lose motivation. Many workplace environments do not help. There are so many places where mediocrity is tolerated, giving the impression that staff members only need to do just enough to get by; and that doing more is met with disdain. There is no spirit of excellence within such an organisation, and it leads to people being content just cruising around in their jobs.

How words will affect you

Being just 27 years old when I first entered the training industry, many people warned that the industry did not favour young trainers and preferred speakers with years of corporate experience. However, I knew that it was not

Asking good questions will give you good answers.

so much a question of 'can it be done?' but rather 'how can it be done?' Asking resourceful questions on the 'how' helped me tremendously in getting the answers I needed, so I focused on getting the right strategy to become an effective trainer.

I knew that I had to use words that empowered me, words without self-doubt. I had to tell myself, "I am energetic, dynamic, fast, humorous, expressive and connectable." I focused on what I had that gave me an advantage over other trainers rather than what I did not have.

My story is an example of the power that words have over our lives. We must be very careful about what we say about ourselves. If we constantly tell ourselves we are bored, we will get bored. If we tell ourselves that something cannot be done, our minds will refuse to think of ways to do it. It is important to constantly check ourselves and make sure that the words we speak are able to empower us and draw us closer to our goals. Constantly think of possibilities and you will be able to find ways of achieving your goals. As Henry Ford once observed, "If you think you can do a thing or think you can't do a thing, you're right."

Caution

The words you choose to say to yourself today have a profound impact on you. It will definitely mould your attitude and mindset. Choose your words carefully and safeguard against what you will hear in life.

Secret 6
MOTIVATION STARTS FROM WITHIN

Many participants have asked me why some people change and others don't. In every crowd, there will always be people who are transformed by what I say, but there will be some that will walk away asking, "What time is lunch?"

It is important to know that every individual is at a different point in their life. We have two camps of people. In the first camp are those who are hungry and ready for a change. They will listen to every single word and try to make it applicable to their lives. They seek to make a connection between what was taught and decide that they need to change their lives. In the second camp are people who are not prepared to make changes to their lives. They might say that what was taught was good but they are not ready for the change. The effort, time or money it takes to create a breakthrough is just too much. In addition to the people in the second camp, there are people who are not self-aware. They do not know what they really want in life or they just don't wish to think too much about their present circumstances.

No one can force you to make a decision, but the decision you make before you leave the hall after hearing the message will have a profound impact on your life.

Understanding motivational theory

According to motivational theory, assuming that there are two people, person A and person B, A cannot motivate B. B can only motivate him or herself.

Then what is the purpose of person A? And what is the purpose of a motivational speaker?

A motivational speaker instills desire and helps people to examine where they currently are in their lives. This would help them to form future goals and make decisions for their future. Once people hold a certain desire, they will be clear about what they want in their lives, and change happens. When people reach an internal conviction on what they should be doing next, it will help to propel them to do something significant for themselves.

The very first place in motivation is to create desire. Without desire, nothing can happen. Nothing actually moves. It cannot be just any 'want' that someone might have for this moment; it has to be a strong desire. Better still, a compelling desire is even better. The bigger the goal, the more compelling the desire needs to be. The more compelling your desire, the more ways you will naturally find to make things happen in your life.

Many people just 'want' things to change but are not willing to put in the effort or invest in the cost that comes with it. This group of people will not get what they want because it remains a 'want'. Whatever we want in life comes with a price. This price could be your time, money, sleep, self-denial in the things you eat or drink. When it comes to crunch time, the question is will you pay the price to get what you desire? This is why desire is so important.

Misconceptions about motivation

Some people who have attended motivational seminars felt that the motivation only lasted for a while, and that they revert to their old patterns and habits after a week. After a couple of months, the seminar would be a distant memory.

This is where most people fail.

Remember the motivational theory I explained earlier? Person A cannot motivate B. Only B can. This means that B has to take personal responsibility for his own motivation. Remember, A can only help create a desire in B to want to make things happen in his life. Therefore B has to ensure that he constantly stays motivated in what he desires to do.

It is a folly to think that motivation will last your entire life. It is also a folly to think that a motivational talk will make you motivated for the rest of your life.

Motivation is something that you have to constantly work on. You must motivate yourself It's just like eating. You can't just eat one day and be filled for the rest of the week. Are you getting your daily dose of motivation?

Holy Moly!

Go on a positive intentions diet. Fast from negative intentions.

⚟ *Secret 7*
SUCCESS COMES FROM DOING THE RIGHT THINGS

Motivational programmes are not cheap. Some of them can cost several thousand dollars. The worst thing you can do is to pay for them and produce no results in your life. How do you actually prepare yourself and ensure that you get the most out of it?

1. Empty your glass

The first thing you need to do is to empty your glass. Empty your previous experiences and treat each new experience as a fresh one that you will be curious about.

It is important not to approach the programme saying that your current experience is right and you will not learn anything new. Once you do that, your mind will automatically shut down and refuse to receive any new information. Remember too that new information does not change a person. Most people do not change simply because they know about something. For example, most people know that they need to eat less, eat healthily, lose weight, exercise more or even sleep earlier, but how many people do it? This shows that cognitive understanding of what you should be doing does not necessary lead you to taking action.

2. Decide that you will be in the front

I mean this literally, in that you should sit at the front of the audience. This is because the front of the audience is always hungry and more energetic compared to the people behind. People at the front tend to participate in everything, so they learn and experience much more. People sitting behind may not benefit as much.

3. Revisit what you have learnt

After you learn something important, it is vital to revisit what you have learnt. Many people don't do this. It is often not a matter of how much you know but how much you act on what you know. One of the things that helped me actualise the principles learnt was to constantly revisit the information learnt. I have read through some material at least five times. Reading once will not be enough. I want to synthesise the information and ask what other aspects of my life I will need to work on. This relentless pursuit of learning and self-reflection has helped me to acheive the results that I wanted in life.

Know your strengths

Being motivated is one thing. However, most people often neglect an important point, which is how to stay motivated. One of the easiest ways to stay motivated is to find out what your strengths are and stay in that zone. You will need to be self-aware of the things that you can do well, and try to stay clear of areas in which you are literally weak. Once you can be self-aware, you will tend to do things that will make you more happy and successful.

'Talents' and 'strengths' are two different terms altogether. 'Talent' is the ability to quickly pick up a certain skill. This natural advantage means that people with talent are predisposed to learn a particular skill faster than others. 'Strengths' refer to what you can do really well. If you have strong vocals and can sing in front of people, you can consider singing as one of your strengths.

However, having talent does not equate to being strong at something. If you wish to be a professional sprinter, you will first need to have talent. Having talent means that you should be able to run fast naturally and qualify for selections. However, you will need to work extremely hard on your talent and be willing to take the long gruelling hours of training to make sprinting your strength.

Notice that professional athletes work very hard and strive for excellence in their training. They keep trying to beat their best times, and will put in the hours and the effort to be the best in their field. They gradually become stronger in their skill, and that is when people consider that particular skill to be their strength. It's important to remember that nothing will ever become a strength if you do not put in the hours of hard work.

The interesting thing about being strong in a particular skill is that it can help you to pick up other related skills. For example, if you know how to play the guitar well, you will tend to pick up other string instruments relatively quickly.

The good news is if you are not naturally talented in doing something, you can compensate with a lot of hard work to eventually make it your strength. However, this takes a lot of determination and constant practise.

By continually working on your strengths and compensating your weakness, you will tend to stay motivated in what you do. Remember that people are motivated by what they can do well in, not areas in which they are weak. Therefore, it is good to constantly work on your strengths, not on your weaknesses.

Your Turn

Make an inventory to list down of your talents and strengths. Ask your friends and family to help you identify what you are good at. Work on those consistently and measure your own improvement.

Secret 8
TO STAY MOTIVATED, YOU MUST TAKE CHARGE AND STAY IN CONTROL

So what can we do to constantly motivate ourselves and get better results in our lives? Remember that motivation requires constant effort, and you must make a conscious decision to motivate yourself every day. Here are six points to help you be more focused and motivated:

1. Identify your motivational points

You have to identify what makes and keeps you motivated. You need to constantly ask yourself what things in life make you really excited. Is there something that propels you forward? Is it money, a sense of purpose, happiness, your faith or relationships? Finding your motivation points is very important. This is the first thing you need to establish.

2. Master your habits

Motivation is a desire, but the discipline to do what is important is influenced by your habits. You need to control the things you do on a habitual basis, because you could be motivating yourself but not supporting your new belief system with your habits. If so, you will not stay motivated.

A friend of mine wanted to be more disciplined in her life but likes to snooze after waking up. After hitting the snooze button, she falls back to sleep for a little while. That 'little while' then becomes half an hour and she finds herself arriving to work late every day. This habit of snoozing disempowers her and affects her own self-belief that she can achieve whatever she sets her mind to. Every time she wants to change a new habit or do something that is beneficial for her, she is not sure if she can actually do it because she is so conditioned to believe that she cannot control herself because of her snoozing habit.

Hot Tip

Always watch your habits. Your habits actually affect your self-belief about yourself. It is important to constantly reinforce good and empowering habits.

3. Raise your standards

Human beings are constantly seeking to improve and work on new things. If you stagnate in doing a same task for many years, you will soon be tired. By raising your standards, deciding that you want to do things better, faster and with excellence, there is a sense of pride and excitement in what you do. Major results only occur when you choose not to live life aimlessly but with a greater sense of purpose and excellence.

4. Mix with highly motivated individuals

The company you keep is really important. Listen to what they say and how they speak. Are they using empowering words or are they complaining about many things or people around them? Once you start being engaged in trivial details, you will soon realise that is endless and pointless. Listening to people who constantly talk behind others' backs, draw lines or simply refuse to do more because they are not paid for it will not spur you to reach your potential. Remember that empowering people empower other people.

5. Perpetual self-learning

Another area that you might want to consider is to surround yourself with good books, videos or movies. Read to get inspiration, and focus on reading books that will help you grow in your personal development. Most people only have a limited amount of time to read, so choose to your reading wisely as it will influence your daily thoughts. Similarly, watch movies that inspire you towards achieving greatness. Some inspirational movies are great because they influence your thoughts and help you to grow to be highly motivated.

6. Beware of your physiology

The way you move, walk or talk will affect your physiology. People who have low self-confidence tend to speak softly, look downwards and even slouch. Your physiology affects your psychology, so be conscious of it. Do you notice how you feel more confident when you are better dressed? Or that when women wear their stilettoes, they suddenly feel more desirable? Even colours play a part in affecting our physiology. Research shows that a woman dressed in red is usually deemed to be more attractive. If you take care of your physiology, you will usually feel more confident. People who are more motivated tend to move faster. Just the simple act of walking briskly with a sense of purpose will help you feel more motivated.

Checklist for staying motivated and getting better results in life:

1. Identify what makes and keeps you motivated.

2. Take active steps to safeguard your emotional state.

3. Intentionally invoke positive emotional states daily.

4. What are your motivational points? What will make you stay motivated?

5. Take personal responsibility for your motivation and do not to allow external circumstances to affect it.

6. List down two disempowering habits you need to get rid of immediately.

7. Raise your standards. Decide what you want to be excellent in.

8. Mix with highly motivated individuals who empower you consistently.

9. Develop a habit of reading books that will inspire and challenge you.

10. Watch your physiology and notice how it affects your self-esteem.

CHAPTER 3

HOW TO BE A SUCCESS MAGNET
Easy ways to achieve success quickly and effortlessly

by **Christian Chua**
Founder
Christian Chua Training Academy

Christian is a leading authority in the areas of behavioural profiling, body language and motivation. He is the author of seven highly successful books including the popular *How to be a Success Magnet* and *Making a Fortune while Sipping Coffee*.

Christian spends a lot of time making keynote speeches and conducting workshops for organisations around the region. When on the platform, he is able to engage with his audience immediately and his presentations are always easy to understand, thought-provoking and revelational.

He is constantly appearing in the media for his expert opinion and his sought-after articles.

Christian was President of Asia Professional Speakers Singapore from 2008–9.

Find out more about Christian at: **www.christianchua.com**
Contact Christian at: **chrix@starhub.com.sg**

I DEFINE SUCCESS as simply achieving the goals that you set out for yourself. If you set a goal and are able to achieve it, you will feel a sense of success. You then set new goals and strive towards new successes.

In the same way, success isn't about achieving goals that society deems important but means very little to you. If you strive for wealth, prestige and other achievements so that society can give you a pat on the back, then you simply live a life that was prescribed by society. If you do things so that in the eyes of society they could say that you are successful, I call that having a false sense of success.

Having financial stability is one of the most sought-after goals for many people. However, there are others who don't strive to become exceedingly rich at all. Not everyone wants to make money beyond the threshold of need, especially at the expense of their health, family and leisure.

Some people really want to be exceedingly rich because their inner being is craving for it. They thrive on being recognised so they focus on being financially superior to others. When they achieve this goal, they are happy. For most people, success can be categorised in many other ways — for example, financial success, social success, family success, spiritual success, even being healthy and happy can be a success.

In this section, Christian Chua will share some powerful tools to help you to achieve success systematically. He will equip you with the right attitude and skills that you can instantly apply in your daily life to bring you much closer to the success you desire.

♀ *Secret 9*
YOUR FIRST IMPRESSION OPENS AND CLOSES DOORS OF OPPORTUNITIES

I call this secret 'The Approachability Factor'.

As the saying goes, you never get a second chance to make a good first impression. When looking at a stranger, it takes only a few seconds before you start forming an impression of him or her. You may form an impression from the way he dresses, the expression on his face, or perhaps his body language. Guess what? People are doing exactly the same to you.

Consciously or subconsciously, people judge us by our outward presentation. The clothes we wear express who we are and perhaps how much we care about how we look. The expressions on our face show whether we are having a good day or a bad day. Our body language tells others if we are in a rush, tired, or simply not in the mood to interact with anyone. These signals we send out allow others to know if we are ready to engage them or not.

If you are at a social gathering of a hundred people and you know that you can only meet a handful of new people, how would you decide who to spend your time with? You will probably base your selection on the impression that people have on you. In the same way, when you are one of the hundred people in that room, everyone else is making those same decisions about whether to get to know you or not. People will look at your face, your overall presentation, your body language and other non-verbal signals to decide if you are on their list of people to approach.

In short, we are continuously being noticed and judged.

Always dress presentably

Imagine this scene: You're dressed in very casual clothes, with unkempt hair, no make-up, slippers instead of shoes, rushing into a shop. There, you bump into the person who interviewed you for a new job the previous day. What sort of impression do you think that will give? Not a good one, right? Of course, many people dress casually when they are not working, but some people take it to extremes. If you do this and then meet someone important, you are not likely to project a very good image, and the person is not likely to hire you.

When you are well-groomed you will send a message that you are conscious about yourself and conscious about the people around you. You will probably be more refined in your mannerisms and your consideration towards others.

Hot Tip

Many unscheduled meetings could turn into opportunities. Make sure you always look presentable.

The power of the smile

Did you know that your smile is one of the most powerful first impressions that you can leave on others? It is the number one feature that makes you attractive. Most people have a naturally great smile. It is far-reaching and piercing. It turns unhappiness into good cheer and invites friendship and kind feelings. People feel comfortable when they are welcomed with a smile.

A smile may have many meanings. For instance, pleasure, friendliness, a welcome and even amusement. It is part of a universal body language that doesn't need any further interpretation. Unfortunately, many people are not generous or ready to give something that costs them nothing.

When we visit a new country, the friendliness of the people we meet affects our decision as to whether we like the country or not. When we are served at a retail outlet or at a restaurant, we prefer service with a smile. In any industry, customers like to be served with a ready smile.

Holy Moly!

My ready smile can be the deciding factor on whether people like me or not.

Sales people are encouraged to smile when they are speaking with their clients on the phone. It has been proven that clients can sense the difference in the tone of the conversation when a person is smiling and when that same person isn't smiling. Some people have the tendency to smile less when they speak on the phone because they feel their smile cannot be detected over the telephone. However, this isn't true, and the absence of that extra friendliness makes a difference.

When we are introduced to a new acquaintance, the trick to making a warm connection lies within the first few seconds after being introduced. Give a smile that is broader than usual. The stranger does not expect a warm smile from you, and because they don't expect it, it comes across as a warm and pleasant surprise. This connection will allow you to gain the other person's interest much more quickly than a lukewarm introduction. Your approachability factor lies largely on the signal you continuously send out. Whether you are at the food centre, in school, or at the train station, people will decide if you are a person they want to approach.

If you have a permanent frown or a down-turned smile, you are projecting that you are in a bad mood and want to be left alone.

Be conscious of your approachability factor. It's the first step towards being a success magnet.

Caution

There's a saying: 'Don't judge a book by its cover'. Unfortunately, people do this all the time.

Secret 10
YOUR SUCCESS IS DIRECTLY PROPORTIONATE TO YOUR LIKEABILITY

I call this secret 'The Likeability Factor'.

Networking is one of today's buzzwords. Experts know that you cannot succeed alone, and you need help from others to succeed. The more people you know, the greater your opportunities will be. In business, I often hear sales managers tell their sales executives, "It's a numbers game. The more cold calls you make, the higher your chances of closing a sale." Well, I would like to add a bit more to that. It is not just about how many people you call, but really, how many people end up liking you after your call.

After forming a good first impression with your approachability factor, we will now focus on what happens after a person meets you. Your likeability factor.

So what makes a person likeable? Here are some elements that I consider to be very important. Check them off if you believe they apply to you:

- Do you greet others warmly and with respect?
- Do you offer a generous smile?
- Do you avoid high-risk questions and being too nosy?
- Are you a good conversationalist?
- Are you able to adapt to any topic when having a conversation?
- Do you have good sense of humour?
- Do you avoid being obnoxious?
- Are you polite and non-judgmental?
- Do you treat everyone as though they are special?
- Are you positive, encouraging and motivating?
- Do you allow others to have their say instead of giving your opinions all the time?

When people like you, they will go out of their way to do things for you, help you when you need it, put in a good word for you when you most need it, and even support you emotionally during a crisis.

Likeability factor in career and business

Many people focus on their ability and less on their likeability. Ability is the competency in a job or when providing a professional service. So people spend a lot of time developing their ability, graduating from one reputable school after another. People in business focus largely on their products, but many neglect the vital part of the business, which is having likeable sales people that bring in massive sales.

There is no point in having a good product if people don't like dealing with you, particularly when you are working in the service industry. When you patronise a restaurant, visit the hair stylist or go retail shopping, you expect people to treat you nicely. One rude remark is all it takes to make someone think, "I am never going back to that place again." No matter how good the food at the restaurant or how great the hair stylist is, you will never return to that place again.

In a job interview, your credentials simply help you to qualify for the position, but they do not guarantee that you will get the job. One other factor is whether you fit the profile that the employer has in mind. Ultimately, to be employed, the interviewer needs to like you.

Are you a people magnet?

Visualise yourself as a popular person. People readily like you, they love what you do, they enjoy listening to you when you speak, and they like being around you because they feel invigorated after speaking with you.

When you are at a party, people are attracted to you. You always gather a small crowd around you wherever you go. You get invited to many social outings and are presented with many business opportunities. You have lots of friends and you are well liked in the workplace. Strangers seem to feel comfortable breaking into a conversation with you wherever you go.

Hot Tip

'Ability' coupled with 'likeability' greatly increases your chances of success! That would be sensational wouldn't it? Some people say life isn't a popularity contest. But seriously, would it be better for people to like you or dislike you?

Would you rather spend time with people you like or dislike? Would you rather have lunch with people who have attractive personalities? Would you rather associate with people who are interesting, polite, humorous, sincere and kind, or with people who have a repulsive character? I think the answer is obvious.

Hot Tip

Many people network to develop business. Rather, when you build relationships, the business will develop spontaneously.

Secret 11
BEING RECOMMENDED IS THE MOST EFFECTIVE MARKETING TOOL

I call this 'The Recommendability Factor'.

One of the best ways to open the doors to new opportunities is through a recommendation.

If a product you are selling is good and your customers recommended it to their friends, they have practically sold the product for you. If you provide a service, a good word from a reference makes selling a lot easier. If you are looking for employment and you were highly recommended to the employer, you have a greater chance of getting an interview than if you were not recommended.

The question is: How can you get yourself at the top of other people's recommendable list?

Unfortunately, many people have a long list of people they can recommend to others, so you are in competition with all these people for that recommendation. The recommendability factor is the quality you possess that makes a person willing to risk their reputation to promote you to others.

Do you have the recommendability factor? Are you on the top of people's recommendable list when opportunities arise?

Regardless of the industry you are working in, regardless of the types of opportunities you are seeking, there will be people you know who can introduce you to others who can help to fulfil your objectives.

The trick is to get yourself on the 'recommendable' list of the people you know. Let me explain a little further. Let's say you are working in the financial services industry. It is very likely that a person knows an average of two to four people who have careers in the financial services industry. If someone wishes to purchase some financial products and asks one of your close friends to recommend a financial advisor, are you the first person he would recommend?

In order to be on the top of a person's 'recommendable' list, you need to understand that the worst fear of recommending you to others is that the person's reputation is at risk.

If you do a bad job or eventually fall out of favour with the customer, the customer will return to the person who recommended you, saying, "Why did you recommend this person to me?" Not only does that person now think poorly of that sales person, but they may also have changed their impression of the one that made the recommendation.

Holy Moly!

Recommendations could be greater than all my marketing campaigns when attempting to achieve sales.

To be on the top of other people's recommendability list, here are some great attributes you need:

Top qualities to make you recommendable for business:

- Reliability (deliver what you promise and deliver it on time)
- Competency and quality (being professional and meeting the quality standards expected of you)
- Likeability (adaptable/flexible/well-mannered)

Top qualities to make you recommendable for regular social opportunities:

- Sincerity
- Reliability
- Likeability (Charisma)

Top qualities to make you recommendable for more sophisticated social opportunities:

- Good dress sense
- Great social skills
- Intelligence
- Sincerity

These qualities do not exclude any other necessary qualities you may have in mind. However, without these qualities, you may wonder why some opportunities did not come your way.

As you would expect, different opportunities will require different qualities. Sometimes we wonder why we were not recommended for a certain job or invited for a social outing even by a very close friend. The fact is that people risk their reputation when they recommend you or even bring you to a social function. It takes more than being a good friend to be recommended to opportunities.

If you find that your peers are more recommendable than you, I suggest you reflect on the reasons why you are less recommendable. Note your flaws and correct them. You could sometimes be abrupt, insensitive, boring, or irritating. You may have poor grooming habits, or you might just be obnoxious or arrogant. Being aware of these factors is a great starting point for making improvements.

Work on your weaknesses and apply the other skills that are suggested in this book. If people do not feel comfortable recommending you, take it as strong feedback. Reflect on why this may be so and be aware of the changes you need to make.

Your Turn

Be aware of what people are saying about you. This could really decide whether opportunities will be opened to you. If you do not like what people are saying to you, ask yourself what you would like people to say about you and ask yourself, "How do I get them to say nice things about me?"

Secret 12
INVEST IN FRIENDSHIP AND YOU WILL YIELD GREAT RETURNS

I call this 'The Lovability Factor'.

The lovability factor is all about how you are able to delight the people that you come into contact with, to a point where they feel that they either owe you something, or that they want to go out of their way to do something for you.

Imagine you are travelling in your car in the rain. You notice that there is a person at the side of the road changing his flat tyre. What if you stopped your car, got out and held an umbrella over the stranger as he changed his tyre? Would he be grateful to you? Sure he would.

But what if you don't have an umbrella with you? If you step out of your car and help him change his tyre in the rain anyway, how do you think the stranger will feel? Grateful? I think he will feel more than just grateful. Perhaps the word would be 'indebted'. He will feel indebted to you.

After you have both finished changing the tyre, I seriously doubt your new friend will just say thank you and take off. He will probably ask to exchange name cards and propose a coffee on another occasion.

Now, let's say during your next encounter with this person, you discover that he has a vital link that you need. For example he may be in HR or a director of a business. If you ask him for a favour, eg to link you up with a person or a business, this is when he will say, "Of course I will help you". This important connection could make a significant shift in your life. It could be anything, a link to a link to a link that makes you millions of dollars. It could be a link to a link that results in you meeting your future spouse. It could be a link that leads you to curing a medical situation you have been praying for. Whatever it is, it will make a big difference and be a milestone in your life.

Many of our milestones are filled with links and connections that people are a vital part of.

If we could increase these opportunities in our lives, opportunities that result in many more vital links, we will certainly speed up our journey towards the success we are seeking.

How do we find or create such opportunities in which we could delight the people that we meet? Delight happens when a person is pleasantly surprised — pleasantly surprised by your action because he didn't expect to receive what he did. In the first case of the person changing his car tyre in the rain, he certainly didn't expect that anyone would go out of the way to help him.

I often ask people in the insurance business, "When you give a calendar as a gift to your clients at the end of the each year, does your client say 'Wow! I am surprised, I am really grateful!'?" Probably not. A calendar is something they expect every year. In fact, if you didn't send him a calendar on a particular year, he would ask you "Hey! Where is my calendar?" So such gifts are not so much of a delight than a requirement in the case of this business.

But what if you did something like this — sometime in the middle of the year, for no apparent reason, you drive to your customer's place armed with a box of tarts and simply present them to him. He might ask, "What is this for? What is the occasion?" You say "It is just a way of saying how much I appreciate your business, and how much I appreciate your friendship."

When you do things that your customer least expects, you bring his emotions to the 'delight' level. When you delight people, they have a greater tendency to reciprocate the kindness.

Hot Tip

Build relationships. Don't just make acquaintances. Real opportunities happen when you build meaningful relationships. Check out more on building relationships in Chapter 10.

When you first meet a person, you meet his outer person. The outer 'crust' is a hard protective layer. He is cautious and will be careful about how vulnerable he wants to be.

As he gets to know you better, he reveals more of himself. He begins to trust you. As he finally decides that you are a good person, he connects with you fully and opens his core self (or inner person) to you.

When you build a meaningful friendship with someone, when you reach the core, that is where most opportunities lie and that's when they will share meaningful opportunities with you.

Hot Tip

It is better to build relationships with three people than to give out 300 meaningless name cards.

Be open to meeting people. You never know, the next person you meet may become your faithful friend.

Checklist for being a success magnet

1. Put effort into how you look.

2. Care about what people think of you.

3. Take pride in your dressing.

4. Try to make people like you.

5. Make people say positive things about you. What people say about you can affect the level of opportunities you receive.

6. Be careful with your choice of words and tone of voice.

7. Plan how you communicate. It makes a huge difference.

8. Make sure you are a risk worth taking.

9. Bring out your positive qualities so that people can instantly associate you with them.

10. Go out of the way to help others and they will reciprocate by going out of the way to help you.

SECTION 2

Branding and Promoting You

CHAPTER 4

YOUR PROFESSIONAL IMAGE TOOLBOX
How to transform yourself from forgettable to memorable

by **Pang Li Kin** *AICI CIP*
Founding Director
Potenxia Unlimited

Pang Li Kin is a leading Certified Image Professional (CIP) in Singapore recognised by the Association of Image Consultants International (AICI). She is author of *Professional Image: Your Roadmap to Success*, part of the ST Training Solutions Success Skills series. As the President of the AICI Singapore Chapter, Li Kin is one of the driving forces behind the development of the image industry in the region. She is also a Certified Coach by Results Coaching Systems and is an appointed Success Coach with AICI globally.

Li Kin has 25 years of experience in business development, leadership, training and coaching. Her global experience spans 20 countries worldwide, and she works with individuals and corporations to enhance their image through their communication, appearance and interpersonal skills. Her clients include professionals, executives and business owners in both the public and private sectors.

Li Kin is an author, speaker, trainer and coach. She holds a Bachelor of Social Sciences (Hons) degree (University of Singapore) and a Masters of Social Planning & Development (University of Queensland).

Find out more about Li Kin at: **www.potenxia.com** and
www.potenxiacoaching.com
Contact Li Kin at: **likin@potenxia.com**

EVERY TIME YOU meet someone, you store an image or impression of the person in your brain. To make it really simple, let's call this a 'box' of that image. This 'box' is then stored in one of two rooms in the brain: the positive room or the negative room. In a matter of seconds, the brain processes that image and stores it in the positive room when the impression is positive, and in the negative room when the impression is negative. This is why first impressions count – you can make or break a first meeting depending on where your image is stored. It is also much harder to move from the negative to the positive room, which means that good first impressions must be lasting as well. It makes sense, then, to create your image in a 'box' that consistently remains in the positive room.

In this section, Li Kin will show you what you need in your professional image toolbox to transform your image from being forgettable to memorable, so that you stay in the positive room all the time. You will learn how to create an image that reflects your best qualities through your look, your sound and your behaviour.

Secret 13
IT'S WHAT'S INSIDE THAT COUNTS

When you receive a gift from someone, you are delighted not so much in the box itself, but what's inside the box. The same goes with your image: when someone is attracted to you, they are curious to know who you are inside. If not, they may forget you the next day. If you wish to be memorable instead of easily forgettable, then start with an examination of what's inside your box.

Here are three steps to get started:

1. Determine what's inside your own box

If you want people to appreciate you for who you are, they must be able to see your best qualities in a matter of seconds upon meeting you. How is this possible? Let's look inside your box and see what ingredients make up the brand called YOU. Think of yourself as a gift, and if people were receiving you as a gift, what qualities would you like them to associate you with? Create three attributes that describe you at your best and make them your brand values.

Your Turn

Ask people who know you or work with you to list three attributes to describe you at your best. Narrow down to the three most common attributes that align with yours. This way, you have brand values that represent you and what others think of you.

2. Weed the 'forgettable' and replace them with 'memorable' attributes

What makes a brand forgettable? Nothing really. Brands are forgotten when they don't do or say anything that reminds you of their positive attributes. They are like products you see on the supermarket shelf with 'no brand' on the packaging. It's the same with your image. Now that you have the three brand values, the next step is to see if you have any negative attributes that need weeding out. Make a list of three attributes that describe you at your worst. If you need help, ask a really close friend who will be honest with you.

Compare the two lists, the positive and the negative, and examine which attributes have helped to put you in people's positive room, and which have left you in their negative room. How can you weed out those negative attributes and replace them with the positive ones? If not addressed, the negatives can be overpowering and kill the very positive attributes you have worked so hard to achieve.

Holy Moly!

It is easier for people to remember my negative attributes than my positive ones. I need to be aware of the negative impressions people have of me so I can replace them with my positive attributes.

3. Revamp your personal brand

When companies embark on a branding exercise, they focus on three elements: the packaging, the communication and the consumer experience. You can do the same with your personal brand. With your three brand values obtained in Step 1, you can now decide how to present this image in your box. The three elements that affect the branding of your box are:

- Packaging (how you look)
- Communication (how you sound)
- Behaviour (how you act and relate to people)

The three elements that make your toolbox memorable.

Review your three brand values, and see if they are consistent with these three elements. Ask of each attribute:

- Do I look like my brand?
- Do I sound like my brand?
- Do I behave like my brand?

Let's make this easier by using an example. Supposing your brand values are 'Inspiring, Progressive, Energetic'. Check the following:

- I look inspiring, progressive and energetic
  (eg: I am creative and up-to-date)
- I sound inspiring, progressive and energetic
  (eg: I communicate with positive energy)
- I am inspiring, progressive and energetic in my work
  (eg: I focus on the vision and future)

If you have not checked all three entries here, this means there is a gap between your brand values and what you are projecting. Do you wear clothes that are outdated and dull (your packaging)? Do you sound cynical when someone suggests a new idea (your sound)? Are you resistant to change and believe that your way is the best way (your behaviour)? If your answer to any of these questions is 'yes', you may be projecting the opposite of inspiring, progressive and energetic. This means that the inside of your box (who you are at your best) is not reflected in one or more of the three elements. If that's the case, it's time for a revamp. Now look at your brand values and identify the gaps.

○ *Secret 14*
YOUR PACKAGING IS THE FIRST THING PEOPLE NOTICE

Successful brands spend millions of dollars on their packaging. Why? It's not because consumers don't know what they offer and the quality they stand for. It's because the packaging must reflect the substance inside. Look at the example of Tiffany's blue box and white ribbon packaging. It has become a global branding that represents Tiffany — no one would dare present you with anything but Tiffany in that blue box. The packaging tells you what's inside.

This is the same with your packaging. Look at yourself in the mirror. Does it tell people who you are inside? Are your best qualities reflected in your appearance? Open your wardrobe. Does it represent the brand called YOU? Let's take a look at those three brand values you created in Secret 13. Read those words out loud while standing in front of your wardrobe. Do these words resonate with what's in your wardrobe? If not, you've got some work to do.

Here are three ways to make your wardrobe speak for your brand:

1. Use the right colours to convey your brand

Successful brands are easily recognisable by their colours: Tiffany is blue; Coca-Cola is Red; Google is multi-coloured. It would be almost criminal to see these brands use their competitor's colours. If you want to reflect your best, you would want to wear the colours that work for you. Ignoring this step would be like wearing your competitor's colours!

To find your best colours, you could consult an image professional who is trained in colour analysis. Once you know your best range of colours, you can then decide which hue best represent your brand values. Use this colour guide to help you select the best colour(s) for your brand:

Red: Dramatic. Bold. Dynamic. Energetic. Passionate.

Blue: Trustworthy. Loyal. Dedicated. Dependable. Conservative.

Green: Amiable. Gentle. Peace-loving. Steady. Calm.

Yellow: Cheerful. Fun. Optimistic. Easy-going. Friendly.

Hot Tip

If you are a relaxed and fun sort of person, you don't need to wear a full yellow outfit every day. What you can do is to add a touch of yellow where it is appropriate (and if it works for your skin type). It can be in an accessory, tie, or in the prints or embellishments.

2. Let your clothes do the talking

While colour is the first thing people notice in a packaging, it is the design that appeals or repels. This may include the look as well as the materials used. In the case of the Tiffany box, the simple blue box with a satin white ribbon represents a classic and high quality look. There is no text on the box that says 'Tiffany'. The packaging speaks for itself.

The same goes for your dressing. Let's take a peek at your wardrobe again. What are the styles like? What kind of quality of fabrics? How do they co-ordinate to tell a story about who you are? Do they convey your brand? Does it appeal to the right people? Use this office style guide to select the clothes to match your brand:

For Men

Jacket suit:	Professional. Powerful. Distinguished. Respected. Credible.
Shirt with tie:	Professional. Responsible. Trustworthy. Credible. Dependable.
Shirt without tie:	Mature. Steady. Practical. Informal. Approachable.
Short-sleeved shirt:	Informal. Casual. Relaxed. Friendly. Approachable.
Polo T-shirt:	Casual. Hands-on. Flexible. Spontaneous. Easy-going.

For Women

Skirt/pant suit:	Professional. Powerful. Distinguished. Respected. Credible.
Blouse and skirt:	Mature. Responsible. Trustworthy. Credible. Dependable.
Blouse and pants:	Practical. Informal. Approachable. Steady. Supportive.
Sheaf dress:	Classic. Graceful. Confident. Polished. Proper.
Flowing dress/skirt:	Feminine. Gentle. Fun. Approachable. Romantic.

Caution

When matching your clothes to your brand, it must also be appropriate for your work and office environment.

Prints also tell a story about your brand, and when combined with the style and colour, they can create the impact you want. Here's a guide to help you match prints with your brand values:

Stripes:	Formal. Conservative. Professional.
Checks:	Approachable. Informal. Sporty.
Floral:	Gentle. Romantic. Supportive.
Geometric:	Dramatic. Dynamic. Driven.
Animal:	Energetic. Fun. Bold.
Paisley:	Classic. Elegant. Refined.

3. Make a statement with accessories

Your accessories give the finishing touch to your packaging. They also tell a story. When you add your own touch with well-chosen accessories, you create a unique look. When you wear the same accessory with a different outfit, you create another unique look. Not only do accessories help you make a statement about yourself, you can also save money by investing in a few great pieces that can go with many outfits. When choosing accessories, you need to consider two elements:

- Scale (or relative size): Match the scale to your facial features. If you have relatively big eyes, the scale of your accessories can be larger.

- Shape: Match the shape to your facial features. If you have relatively sharp or angular features, the shape of your accessories can be similarly shaped.

With your packaging in place, you are ready to look at the next element in your toolbox — the way you sound. In the next secret we'll examine how your communication can make you memorable for the right reasons.

Secret 15
YOUR SOUND REFLECTS YOUR TRUE VALUE

Do you often wonder what's in a gift box before opening it? First, you look at the packaging, size and shape and try to make a guess. When that fails, what do you do? Yes, you shake it! By the sound of the gift inside, you could perhaps make a better guess of what it is.

The same goes for our image. When we speak, people store a memory of this 'sound' in their box and recall what kind of a person you are. Based on their impression of your packaging, the box may also capture a composite of how it matches your sound. If one is positive and the other negative, the negative image will remain longer in the box. For example, if your packaging conveys a professional and authoritative figure but you sound timid and shy, people will remember you as timid and shy more than professional and authoritative.

Holy Moly!

Looking good is not good enough. I need to sound good too! If I'm going to be memorable, I need to invest as much in my communication as in my appearance.

Here are three ways to create a memorable 'sound':

1. Speak with impact

The saying, "Empty vessels make the most noise" has some truth in it, as my teacher used to say to our chatty class. She had no intention of making us into great orators; she merely wanted us to be quiet. When it came to English lessons, we would learn how to read and write properly according to a set of rules. Many of us scored distinctions in English, but why did so few of us make great orators? Speaking with impact, is not just about using the language proficiently, it is about getting the result you want when you speak. Perhaps this is one important lesson still missing in our language classes?

To speak with impact, one sure-fire way is to lower your pitch. When you end a sentence on a lower pitch, you sound more confident and powerful. A high pitch creates excitement and is useful for that purpose. Use a low to medium pitch to project credibility, and switch to a high pitch only for special effects.

Your Turn

Try reading this sentence ending on a high pitch and a low pitch: "I am excited to speak to you today on the power of communication." Notice how your pitch might go up a little on the second syllable of the word "excited" or the first syllable of "power" but not throughout the sentence. Aim to end off the last syllable of "communication" on a strong low pitch.

2. Write with clear intent

How does writing have anything to do with the 'sound' of your brand? Lots! Take a moment now to read this paragraph aloud. What 'sounds' can you hear from reading? While most people do not read out loud, our subconscious mind does, and we can hear the underlying messages as if they were spoken. If you want your reader to 'hear' you clearly and get the message you intend, then review all your written communication to see if you are writing with clear intent or just rambling. Follow this guide to writing with clear intent:

- Start with your purpose – keep to one or two lines.

- Set the context to tell the reader what to expect (for example: 'I propose two options').

- Present only the information related to your purpose – do not digress from the main point.

- Tell the reader what action or result you want from them. If there's no action, say so.

- Do not include unrelated information, or you run the risk of the reader remembering the last bit they read and ignoring your main message.

3. Manage your silent messages

Have you ever received a gift box that makes no sound? You can only make two guesses: that it is empty, or the gift is made of very light material like feather or fabric. Just like this gift box, people can guess what is inside your box (or not) even if you don't make a sound. They do this by reading your body language. These silent messages can help make or break your image, depending on how well you manage them. Take a look again at your brand values and review what body language can best project these values effectively. Use this quick checklist to help manage your silent messages:

- **Gestures**: How do your gestures support your brand values? Do you use repeated gestures that are meaningless or do you use gestures to convey your message?

- **Facial expressions**: Do your facial expressions support your true emotions? How can you use positive facial expressions to convey the messages you intend?

- **Proximity**: What messages do you send when standing too close or too far from your colleagues, clients or people you've just met?

Secret 16
YOUR BEHAVIOUR SEALS THE IMPRESSION YOU MAKE ON OTHERS

According to Chinese custom, it is impolite to open a gift upon receiving it. I remember Christmas Eves when my children would receive Christmas presents from aunts and uncles and were not permitted to open them till the next day. To them, it's not good enough to have a beautifully wrapped gift if you don't know what's inside.

This brings us back to Secret 13 — that it's what's inside the box that counts. Once you have mastered this secret, and worked on Secrets 14 and 15, you will get the final stamp of approval when people look inside your box to see how you behave. This secret is about how your behaviour, both at work and at play, matches the brand values you so carefully crafted earlier.

Here are three behavioural traits to make your box consistent with your brand values:

1. Be authentic

How would you feel if someone gave you a gift that is a 'fake' brand? Would you rather have something else? When it comes to your behaviour, this is the same feeling if you project yourself as one thing, and when people get to know you, they discover that you are not 'real'.

To be authentic is to be sincere and honest about who you are, and how you project this image. Take a look now at your brand values, and check it against what messages you are trying to convey in your packaging and your sound. Do they all match up or is it made up?

Check your authenticity in two areas

- **Decision-making:** Do you make decisions that are consistent with your brand values? Or, do you confuse people with decisions that seem to contradict who they think you are? Let's say, for example, your brand values are 'Efficient', 'Responsive', and 'Reliable'. You will be authentic if you make decisions in a prompt and responsible manner.

Hot Tip

If you need more time to make decisions, always ask for it up front. Do not give excuses like "I'm busy". Instead, give reasons that reflect your authentic brand values, for example, that you want to be more thorough.

- **Action-taking:** Your behaviour is often judged by what you do, or do not do. The key question here is: does your action or inaction match your brand values? If your brand values are 'Thoughtful', 'Considerate', and 'Graceful', people may not expect you to act quickly or rashly.

2. Be civil

I am sure most of us are taught some manners at home or in school, so I will not give you another lecture on how to be civil. There is no strict right and wrong behaviour. The key point here is how does your civility match your brand values?

Again, let's look at your brand values and review this checklist to see how you are doing:

- **Relationships**: How do you show civility in your relationships to reflect your brand? If one of your brand values is 'Empathy', you would be expected to show respect for people's feelings. Your relationships with people would always take them into consideration, and others would come before self.

- **Public manners**: In public, people don't know what your brand values are. The question for you is: How does your civility in public convey your brand values? What impression of your behaviour would affect the public's perception of you? How can you extend your civility in public so you are true to your brand? If one of your brand values is 'Friendly', are you consistently friendly to everyone you meet, from the bus driver to your company CEO?

3. Be polished

Being polished is not for high society alone. It is a behavioural trait that can be learnt. When you are polished, you stand out from the crowd. When you are not polished, you stick out like a sore thumb. Look at your brand values and ask yourself: how do you wish to stand out and what areas need polishing? Here are two essential areas to consider:

- **Etiquette**: This includes the way you meet and greet, your table manners, how you socialise, your observation of customs, and respect for diversity. While there are universal rules on etiquette, each society, culture or group may have their local rules. Etiquette is about how you represent your brand best through the way you carry yourself.

Caution

Regardless of how polished you are in your dining etiquette, do not insist on being served according to your standards when visiting another country. Being polished is also about respecting another culture's etiquette.

- **Respecting time**: The way you show respect for other people's time will convey an impression of what your brand value might be. If you are perpetually late, people may associate you with being disorganised. If your brand value is 'Efficient', you will have to work very hard to change that perception.

With polished behaviour, you have put a final touch to make yourself truly memorable. This is what we call a lasting impression, and this makes your professional image toolbox complete. To make your image work for you, you need to master all the secrets in your toolbox: the brand values you stand for, your packaging, your sound and your behaviour.

Checklist to transform your image from forgettable to memorable:

1. Determine three attributes that best describe who you are, and make them your brand values.

2. Review your wardrobe to see if it reflects your three brand values.

3. Discover the colours you need in your wardrobe to convey your brand values.

4. Identify the styles that you need to upgrade your wardrobe and better reflect your brand values.

5. Identify the accessories that can help you make your brand stand out.

6. Create an impact in your speech by lowering your pitch.

7. Write with a purpose and make your intent clear to get the results you want.

8. Match your brand values with your behaviour at work and at play to reflect you at your best.

9. Show respect to others by behaving civilly both at work and in public.

10. Polish your etiquette both at home and abroad to consistently reflect your brand values.

CHAPTER 5

BRAND YOURSELF, BUILD YOUR BUSINESS

Sell more to prospects when you create
a brand perception and brand blueprint

by **Pamela Wigglesworth**
Founder and Managing Director
Experiential Hands-on Learning

As founder of Experiential Hands-on Learning, Pamela Wigglesworth is passionate about helping SMEs and entrepreneurs shorten their learning curves and accelerate their business results.

A resident of Asia for over 21 years, Pamela and husband John moved from Hong Kong to Singapore in 1995. Pamela began training and teaching in 2001 while simultaneously running another business. She eventually founded Experiential Hands-on Learning in 2008. In addition to training, Pamela teaches Entrepreneurship at a business school and contributes to the Textile Fashion Federation as a business mentor.

Pamela is an American corporate trainer and international keynote speaker. She conducts in-house training on branding, low budget marketing communications and presentation skills.

Find out more about Pamela at: **www.experiential.sg**
Contact Pamela at: **pam@experiential.sg**

BRANDING IS ABOUT perception and satisfying the needs of the consumer or client. A brand symbolises how people think about your product or service. Branding helps clients and prospects in decision making by creating a perceived knowledge of what they are going to buy *before they buy it*.

Perception is the belief the client and prospective buyer holds in his mind about your product or service. People buy one product or another based on the perceived benefits or solution they believe the product will offer them. For most consumers, the perceived benefits are subconscious.

In this chapter, Pamela Wigglesworth will share how understanding brand perception and crafting your personal brand blueprint will help you to sell more to clients who are interested in what you have to offer.

Identifying your target audience, knowing your brand personality and positioning are just some of the components of the branding process, otherwise known as the brand blueprint. The brand blueprint is what provides the building blocks of a successful brand.

Just as an architect needs to have a blueprint to provide direction on how to build a structure, you need a blueprint that outlines to your prospects what your brand can offer.

Secret 17
YOU WILL SELL MORE TO CONSUMERS WHEN YOU DEVELOP A BRAND PERCEPTION

What comes to mind when I say the word 'brand'? Most people automatically associate a brand with a well-known product or service. However, even the smaller products, services and businesses are brands — and that means you are a brand too. There was a time when a product or service was only considered a brand if the public referred to it by the brand name. Two examples of this are asking for a soft drink by requesting for a 'Coke' rather than a 'cola' or asking for a 'Kleenex' instead of a 'tissue'.

I was in a drug store in Australia and asked the woman at the counter, "Where are the Q-tips?" She looked very confused. I asked again, "You know, Q-tips?" She was completely puzzled. I realised that she didn't understand me because she was not familiar with this product by its brand name. It also occurred to me that I wasn't able to articulate what I was looking for (cotton swabs), because growing up, we never used the term 'cotton swabs', we always said, "Grab the Q-tips," using the brand name as the item description. This type of strong brand identification is what leads new businesses to think they are not yet a brand.

A brand is an identification or mark that differentiates your business from others. Remember though, that a brand symbolises what other people think about your business.

Holy Moly!

My brand is the unique value of my company's products or services in the minds of my customers or prospects.

Having a clearly defined brand perception will help you to sell more to your prospects. The question is, do consumers know what your brand stands for? What is *your* brand perception in the marketplace?

Let's take a closer look at this and how it relates to you as a brand.

1. What does brand perception have to do with me?

You're probably wondering what 'brand perception' means and how does it help you to build your personal brand? In a nutshell — everything! Branding is based on the principles of perception and satisfying the needs of the consumer. It's about communicating your message to the consumer more effectively so they immediately associate what your business has to offer with their needs.

Perception is the feeling or idea that consumers have in their hearts and minds about you. It's your job to create the perception of brand 'YOU' in your customer's minds. You can do this by taking what it is that you do best in terms of your product or service, and then designing the brand perception around that.

2. Craft your brand perception

Now that we know that perception is important, just how do you go about creating your personal brand perception? It's easy. We use the five senses — sight, sound, smell, touch, taste. Perception is the process by which we receive information through our five senses and assign meaning to it. For example, visual clues like the colour pink and a script font on letterhead or advertisements could create the perception of a female-owned business or one that caters to women. Famous Amos cookies and BreadTalk know that by allowing the aroma of their baked goods to waft through the mall, you will perceive the goods as fresh and tasty, and this will bring on the desire to make a purchase. Through the senses, customers have a perceived idea about your brand before they buy from you.

3. It's not what you do but the consumers' perceived results that matter

People don't buy products or services. They buy results. A woman buys facial soap not because she wants a clean face, but for the results she believes it will bring her. That could be soft, radiantly clear skin. She also believes that if her face looks great, she will feel great, and she might get noticed or stand out in a crowd. Ultimately, if she stands out in the crowd, she just might attract that special someone.

Now I'm not advocating that soap companies are saying that you'll get a new partner as a result of using their product, but some get pretty close. If you pick up a bar of Lux soap, for example, it doesn't say 'soap' anywhere on the packaging. It says 'beauty bar'. Everything about the packaging creates the perception that you will have radiant skin – the product name, the colours, the picture of a beautiful woman with flawless, whitened skin.

Let's look at how this relates to a service business. If you own a small three-person Public Relations (PR) company, rather than refer to yourselves as small, you could call yourself a boutique PR agency. This description implies intimate and classy. The consumer perception might be that smaller equates to greater attention to detail. The results consumers believe they will receive are far superior service and better results than they would achieve using a large firm.

Brand perception can also be created with a product name and pricing. What comes to mind when you read the words Häagen-Dazs? Is your mouth watering already? Häagen-Dazs has established itself as a premium brand of ice cream, sorbets and frozen yogurt. From the name, most people assume that it is a European brand, but it actually originated in the Bronx in New York, USA. Creating a unique name, using only the finest ingredients and selling his original three flavours of ice cream at a premium price, Reuben Mattus was able to create a perception of a premium quality, international brand of ice cream and to charge a higher price than the everyday brand of ice cream.

Holy Moly!

I need to walk in my prospect's shoes. I must find out what results he or she is hoping for. If I share the perceived results in my branding, I will sell more.

Your Turn

Review your product or service. List the benefits that your product or service offers. Then look at it again and list the perceived results the consumer believes he will achieve by using your product or service. When marketing your message, focus on the perceived results, not the benefits.

Secret 18
YOU WILL GAIN MORE BUSINESS WHEN YOU DEVELOP A UNIQUE SELLING PROPOSITION ANSWERING YOUR CONSUMERS' WANTS AND NEEDS

I can already hear you asking, what is a Unique Selling Proposition (USP)? How am I going to gain more business if I don't know what that is? Well I'm glad you asked. The fact that you are asking this question means you're serious about increasing your business. The concept of the USP is used by thousands of marketers to develop benefit messages used in advertising, branding and promotional materials.

Your USP is a benefit statement that is unique to your products or service and important to the consumer. In essence, the USP becomes a promise that your customers, clients or prospects will receive this unique benefit only by using your product or service. In some cases, USP is also referred to as a 'brand promise'.

This benefits statement is not to be taken lightly. You are virtually making a promise to the consumer that when they buy from you, they will always receive your unique benefit. It's important that you keep that in the back of your mind when developing your USP. In a nutshell, the concept of the USP is to create a 'pick-up' line that will have your customers favouring you over your competition.

What defines a benefit and what does it mean for our target audience?

Before moving on to what makes you special, let's first take a closer look at what defines a benefit. First of all, each product or service has special features (also known as attributes). For your product to resonate with your customers, you will need to identify your product features in terms of what is most important to the customer.

The benefit emphasises what the product or service can do for the target audience by translating a product feature or attribute into something that benefits the end user (your client).

To effectively craft a USP, you need to uncover the true benefits as perceived by your customer. What is it that attracts them to you?

The DNA of a USP

A USP helps to maintain 'top of mind' awareness for existing and potential clients. To help illustrate this, let's look at the USP of a well-known brand: What brand comes to mind when you read, "When it absolutely, positively has to be there overnight"? Did you answer Federal Express? Sure, they are a courier company like many others, but their USP makes a promise that your package will arrive as scheduled by including the words, "absolutely, positively".

1. Who are you and what makes you special?

So what is your USP? What is so special about your brand? There are thousands upon thousands of brands for consumers to choose from. As a business owner, you need to have a clear idea of what you have to offer your target market. What problem do you solve? What want or need do you fulfil? What are the features or attributes of your product or service that the consumer will view as a benefit and therefore want to buy from you?

Caution

Identify the one or two things that are unique to you that will distinguish you and that you can promise your target audience that you will always deliver. If there is the possibility of someone offering the same things, then you don't have a clear USP.

2. Establish your brand personality attributes

Every brand has a personality, whether people realise it or not. Just as every individual has a personality, so does your product or service. Think about it. What is your personality type? Do you tend to be loud and extroverted or are you quiet and soft-spoken? Have you noticed how people with big personalities also tend to be a bit bold with the way they dress too? I'm not talking about someone wearing colourful and crazy patterns that make them look like a clown. I'm suggesting that people with outgoing personalities might wear brighter colours — ladies might wear bold jewellery or men a unique, conversational tie.

Part of creating your brand also involves creating your brand personality attributes. The closer you match your brand personality to that of your target market's needs, the greater the chance they will buy from you. Brand attributes are human characteristics that can be associated with the brand.

- Virgin Atlantic Airlines conveys an energetic, aggressive, passionate personality.

- Apple is recognised as being innovative, stylish, hip, casual, and hassle-free.

Think about what human attributes can be associated with your brand so that consumers can easily align themselves with your goods and services.

3. Develop brand icons that reflect your brand personality

When most people hear or think of the word 'icon', they may think of a pop icon or the little logos on your desktop that represent different pathways to places within your computer. These are different kinds of icon. In the case of brand icons, we are referring to the different aspects that are related to your brand.

Brand icons will vary from product to product, and are specific to each brand. Let's look at some standard icons that just about every brand will have. The first and most important brand icon is your name. According to Al Reis and Jack Trout, authors of the book *Positioning: A Battle for Your Mind*, "In this positioning era, the single most important marketing decision you can make is what to name the product." I couldn't agree more, so do bear this in mind when you are considering your own brand name.

The font you use and the colour of that font are also brand icons. The key is to use a font and corresponding colour that reflects the brand personality of your product and service.

Notice how kindergartens use primarily colours and big chunky fonts to spell out their brand. They immediately communicate to the consumer the type of business they are in. We see colourful primary colours and automatically think of children, fun and playfulness. As a parent, you can easily align yourself with the school thinking that it's a place where you would want to send your child.

Logos and mascots can also be brand icons. Golden arches and Ronald McDonald can be spotted by children immediately. To them, these icons are associated with 'Happy Meals' and toys.

Take time to think about an appropriate font and the colours you select to ensure they are in line with your brand personality attributes. Make sure they create the desired perception in your target audience's mind.

♀ Secret 19
YOUR BRAND WILL GROW WHEN YOU IDENTIFY YOUR TRUE NICHE AND TARGET AUDIENCE

When speaking to start-up businesses, I often ask the questions: Who is your target market? Who are you are selling to? Many respond with, "I sell to everyone" or they indicate a range of customers across various age groups. That's mass marketing.

My response to any individual or company who says they sell to everyone is: if you try to be everything to everyone, then you're nothing to no one. Your brand will only grow when you can clearly and concisely state who your target audience is. You need to identify your niche market, which focuses on a specific segment of consumers.

A niche (rhymes with rich) can be defined by a consumer's demographics and psychographics such as age, gender, marital status, income level, social status, lifestyle and hobbies. It can also be determined by consumer wants, needs or preferences.

1. Break the 'Jack or Jane of All Trades' myth

If it is your intention to profitably promote your brand, then you must steer clear of trying to be a Jack or Jane of all trades. Selling to the masses is expensive, and you simply don't have the time, manpower or financial resources to market to everyone. The narrower the niche, the wider the opportunity.

You can effectively sell a single product or service to more than one niche market. The secret is to develop different marketing strategies aimed at each market, with an emphasis on the features, attributes and benefits that meet the underlying needs of each market. By having a separate marketing strategy, you are then able to adapt everything from product features to all aspects of the marketing communication mix to that specific market.

Holy Moly!

I can actually save time, save money and even make more money by focusing on one target market rather than attempting to reach out to the masses.

2. Specify your ideal customer based on your USP

When I suggest you specify your ideal customer based on your USP, this is really referring to your target audience. I've talked a lot about the target market but I've never really defined what that means.

The target market refers to the people that you are selling to or hope to sell to. To effectively sell to your target audience, you need to have a clear understanding of who they are. This is where demographics and psychographics come into the picture.

The details of your ideal audience could be segmented by gender, age, marital status, nationality, education and income level. You can also include their interests, hobbies, social standing and lifestyle.

Your objective must be to develop a succinct profile of your target audience so that you can then solve their problems and meet their wants and needs with the products or services you offer. Knowing your ideal client allows you to cost-effectively market to them whenever and wherever they are.

3. Learn what your prospects' greatest challenges are

There are both rational and emotional reasons why people make a purchase. People buy products or services to solve an immediate problem or to fulfil a need or want. You've just identified your specific target audience based on their demographics and psychographics. With knowledge of the target audience, you can now learn what are their underlying needs and wants.

Hot Tip

A quick and easy way to get detailed information about your ideal target audience is to use secondary research information. Secondary research is information completed by someone else. For example, find a magazine they would buy and then contact the publication and request a media kit. The media kit will have a detailed analysis of the demographics and psychographics of their readers. You too can use this information to define your audience.

This is the time to probe. What are the greatest challenges they face? Are their needs currently being met by the competition? Are they happy with what is available in the market? Is what they need available at a price they feel is reasonable and value for money?

When you take the time to learn more about your prospects' greatest challenges, you can then serve their needs. This will translate into more business for you.

Secret 20
GREAT BRAND POSITIONING WILL HELP YOU TO SELL TO THE RIGHT MARKETPLACE AT THE RIGHT PRICE

I know you would like to be selling in the right marketplace and at the right price, so it's important to understand how your business compares with your competitors. Your role as a marketer or business owner is to develop a strategic approach to creating a sustainable competitive advantage. This is called 'brand positioning' and it's not as difficult as it sounds.

Positioning or a position is how the consumer defines your brand in the marketplace. The goal is to position your brand in the mind of the consumers and help them to understand the benefits your product has to offer in comparison to the competition. In layman's terms, you need to establish a place in your customer's mind relative to your competition.

Every product has some sort of position. It's up to you to communicate to consumers a consistent message about your product and where it fits into the market.

1. Differentiate yourself. Find your sweet spot in the marketplace

It's up to you to develop the brand positioning for your product or service. This can be achieved by asking some questions based on what is happening around you. Start by asking questions like:

- What does the marketplace for the type of product/service I offer look like?
- What are the other products like?
- Where are the products being sold and at what price?
- What are the gaps in the marketplace or holes in my particular category?
- What's most important to my target audience?

After answering these questions, take it a step further to determine if you can find an unmet need or one not adequately being served by your competition. (I'll talk more about that in a moment). Do you do something unique and beneficial that sets you apart from your competition and gives you a competitive advantage? Are you able to improve on a product's weakness and the product's appeal?

Let's look at an example. A brand known around the world and positioned as a premium brand is Singapore Airlines. Their brand positioning is based on a product/service differentiator. They're known for their innovation, best technology and excellent customer service.

Find your sweet spot in the marketplace.

2. Determine your price value positioning

Price is one of the elements in the 4Ps of marketing. Your product price, or the fee you charge in conjunction with where you sell your products or services, plays an important role in your value position. Your value position is basically the perceived ranking of your product or service in the marketplace.

If you are new player to the market, you can establish a price value in the mind of your target audience based on where you sell your brand. Products sold in high-end department stores by association will be perceived as having a higher value. The value perception of the high-end department store is high price, high quality. The value perception of a discounter is low price, low quality. At the onset of your brand development, your value perception should also be considered when creating your USP.

Hot Tip

When it's time for you to decide your product pricing or fee structure, check out competitors who offer similar products or services. Look at where they are selling their goods and services, and use that as a benchmark for your own product pricing.

3. Observe the competition to further carve out your positioning

Differentiating yourself is an important element in establishing your positioning. If starting a new product or service, you don't need to build a new mousetrap from scratch. The key is to find out how you can improve an existing mousetrap.

The best way to carve out your own position is to look at what the competition is offering in the marketplace.

- What is the quality of their product/service?
- Where are they in the market in terms of price?
- What is their level of customer service?
- What are their hours of operation?

One of the reasons for looking at the competition is not so you build an entirely new product or service, but to find out how you can improve on certain aspects of a product or service. Take hours of operation as an example. In the late 1990s, I operated a ladies boutique in a shopping mall that was in between two major hotels. The shopping mall stores did not open for business until 11.00 AM. I observed daily the number of tourists who aimlessly walked around the mall in the early morning hours looking for something to do and purchase. Most of them had arrived into Singapore early that morning, but could not get into their rooms right away, so they came to the mall to stroll and kill time.

To accommodate these potential shoppers I changed my hours of operation from 11.00 AM to 9.00 PM to 10.00 AM to 8.00 PM. As a result, my sales increased dramatically because I gave people a place to go. It was also a great benefit to my regular local customers with small children. They could come in to shop while the kids were at school and still be home in time before the kids got back from school.

I didn't have to change my product one bit. I simply made it convenient for my customers by shifting my hours of operation by one hour. Oh, and since the mall was empty from 8.00 PM to 9.00 PM so I also stopped paying my staff to stand around for one hour when there were no customers, also increasing my profitability.

What can you learn from your competitors that will allow you to position yourself as the brand that does things differently in a manner that it becomes a plus for the consumer? By simply tweaking one or two things and doing them better than your competition, you can create your brand's positioning in the marketplace.

Build your business when you build your brand blueprint and sell more to clients and prospects.

Your Turn

When you look at your competition, what elements of their business work well? What elements are not so great? Of the items that they are not executing well, is this something that you might be able to do better? In what area could you excel over your competition?

Checklist for building a great brand

1. Identify the wants and needs of your ideal target audience.

2. Establish a clear picture of your target audience demographics and psychographics to design your brand around them.

3. Determine how your product or service can help solve the target audience's problems, wants and needs.

4. Establish who your ideal customer is. Be as specific as you can when listing the demographics and psychographics of this person.

5. Craft a brand perception that will become synonymous with your products or services.

6. Develop your Unique Selling Proposition (USP) that draws your target market's attention by addressing their wants and needs.

7. Create three to five brand personality characteristics with which consumers can easily identify and align themselves.

8. Find your sweet spot in the marketplace and differentiate yourself from the competition.

9. Find out what your competition is doing and figure out how you can improve on what is already out there without having to fully reinvent the wheel.

10. Position yourself in the market with the right price and in an appropriate location in line with your value position, and your customers will be more likely to find you.

CHAPTER **6**

PROMOTING YOURSELF THROUGH TECHNOLOGY

Hone your online image and gain exposure by
leveraging social media and information technology

by **Sharon Connolly**

CEO
Maximise Group Training and Consultancy

Sharon Connolly is a leading educator on personal image and visibility. She speaks, trains and coaches individuals on how to look their best and increase their chances of success by becoming more visible, including projecting a powerful image online. Sharon frequently appears on television and radio, and writes for magazines, websites and blogs. With her simple, down-to-earth training methods and straight-talking advice, Sharon has helped thousands of people hone their image and improve their success in business and relationships. She has a popular YouTube Channel with over 200,000 visitors.

Sharon started her own IT training company in the UK in 1995 teaching Microsoft products to corporate clients. In 2001 she made what seemed like a 'crazy' decision to retrain as an image consultant. Ten years later, that decision has proven to be very smart as she is now uniquely placed to advise clients how they can look good in person and also exploit social media and technology to consistently promote themselves and increase their chances of success.

Sharon moved to Singapore in 2009 with her husband and two teenage children. She continues to deliver training and personal coaching on image, personal branding and IT.

Find out more about Sharon at: **www.maximisegroup.com**

Contact Sharon at: **sharon@maximisegroup.com**

CREATING AN IMPACT and consistently promoting our brand values are vital for continued success. Getting the best opportunities can actually be more about visibility than ability. Chapter 4 in this book discusses how you can create a positive personal image, and Chapter 12 details how to increase your influence by networking. While these two aspects are essential to your success, it is also essential that you continue to reinforce and practise these strategies online.

Most of us spend many hours a day communicating from our computers. It's important to make sure that we are using every communication touch point to promote our brand values and increase our network.

We all use the Internet extensively to find products, services and people. The advice in this chapter will help you to define and promote your online presence. Whether you want to promote your own business or services, or become visible to head hunters to advance your journey up the corporate ladder, enhancing your online presence is essential.

Sharon Connolly will share tips on how to define your online brand and how best to promote your products, services or self through online channels.

⚿ Secret 21
THE MORE ACTIVE YOU ARE ON SOCIAL MEDIA, THE MORE OPPORTUNITIES YOU WILL GET

Join in the conversation! There are many social media platforms such as Facebook, Twitter and LinkedIn that will help you connect to companies that you would like to work with, people that inspire you, and products that excite you.

I've had many TV, radio and media opportunities because of posts I've made on social media. It is an excellent platform for self-promotion. It doesn't cost you anything, apart from your time. If you frequently blog, tweet, comment and add value with companies and people you aspire to be involved with, your voice will be heard. Your contributions may even be requested in the form of articles, guest blogs, and other things. Consistency and tenacity are essential though.

Let's examine a few of the many social media platforms you may wish to use.

Facebook

You would have had to have been hiding under a very big rock for a long time to not be aware of Facebook. However, if you think it's just a fun tool to connect to friends and family, then you are missing the boat. Just take a look as some of these amazing facts about Facebook:

- There are more than 500 million active users.
- 250 million active users access the site via a mobile device.
- 50 per cent of active users log on every day.
- The average user has 130 friends.
- People spend over 700 billion minutes per month on Facebook.
- More than 2.5 million websites have integrated with Facebook, including over 80 of comScore's* top 100 US websites.

* comScore is the global source of digital market intelligence

Here are three things to consider when using Facebook.

1. Facebook fan pages

If you have your own business then I suggest you set up a separate fan page for your business. The difference between your fan page and your personal profile page is that you do not get updates from all your friends. Also on your fan page people connect to you without you having to give permission. Rather than becoming your 'friend', fans will choose to 'like' your page. If you allow them to do so, they can write comments and posts on your wall. The number of friends allowed on your personal page is limited to 5,000, but you can have an unlimited number of fans on your fan page. If you have a business and want to nurture a long-term relationship with your customer base, a fan page is definitely the way to go.

2. Facebook groups

A Facebook group is a great alternative if you belong to an association or want to connect with people who have similar interests or goals. Groups can be exclusive with membership by invitation only, or they can be open so that anyone is allowed to join. Groups are better for viral marketing (that means spreading your message to lots of people very quickly), but they do lack some of the technical opportunities of fan pages. However, you can easily send all your current friends a message asking them to join your group and then communicate to all group members with a private message. Choose Facebook groups to communicate with a select group of your existing friends or a discussion group.

3. Your personal Facebook profile

A recent Microsoft survey found that 84 per cent of recruiters had rejected potential candidates because of inappropriate social media profiles. Think about how your posts and photographs align with your personal brand. If you are a lively party person, your fun and outgoing nature may enhance your potential success in a sales role, but it would not create the right impression for a studious lawyer. Do remember that reputations can be ruined very easily with an inappropriate comment or photograph on your profile.

Hot Tip

Work colleagues can sometime feel offended if you decline their friend request. Consider adding them as a friend, but allowing them to see a limited version of your profile. Research the 'mailing lists' options to do this.

Twitter

Originally created by journalists to get up-to-the-minute news blasts out to a wide audience instantly, Twitter is now a powerful instrument in your professional success toolbox. If you have a business, it will help you promote your products and services if you have a Twitter profile and send out regular tweets. (A tweet is an online broadcast of up to 140 characters of text.) On Twitter, you 'follow' (connect with) brands and people who inspire you. In turn, if you have a something of interest to contribute you will attract your own 'followers'.

You may want to follow industry leaders, speakers, trainers, anyone who inspires you. You will discover links to interesting articles, blogs, videos, personal development material. The important thing to remember with Twitter is that you must consistently contribute and add value. Once you do this, opportunities will come to you.

LinkedIn

LinkedIn is your online curriculum vitae or resumé. It's a site for professional connections loosely based on the concept of six degrees of separation. The idea is that everyone is, on average, approximately six steps away from any other person on earth.

Here are few tips on how to maximise your LinkedIn profile.

- Firstly, have one! It's the primary business connection software tool used by recruitment companies and employers.
- Ensure that your profile is up-to-date.
- Have a professional headshot. If you don't have one, you need one.
- Collect testimonials. If you give a good presentation, if you worked on a client account or delivered a great project, then ask your connections for testimonials.
- Join discussion groups related to your industry and contribute often.
- Promote your profile by answering questions in the knowledge base.

Secret 22
TO BUILD CUSTOMER RELATIONSHIPS YOU NEED ONLINE MARKETING

When a customer visits your web page, what is it that you want them to do? It would be great if they landed on your page and immediately picked up the phone and booked your services or ordered your product. The truth is we like to shop around and browse before we make a decision, and your potential customer often leaves your site without purchasing, continuing to research before committing to buy. Depending on the service you offer, your customer may take months or even years before finally deciding on a purchase.

Smart business owners and website designers know that in order to do business with us, our customer has to trust us, and for that to happen we need to form a relationship with them. Getting your customer to sign up for free newsletters, fact sheets or e-books is a great way to stay in touch, build trust and create a relationship with your potential customer.

Regular informative communication with your prospects increases your chances of a sale or referral.

Hot Tip

Make sure what you send is not sales literature. Aim to inform, educate and advise your prospects. You need to be generous with your expertise by adding value or your reader will simply hit 'delete'.

Auto responders

One of the easiest ways to manage prospect communications is with an auto responder package. Popular examples of these are Icontact, Constant Contact and MailChimp. These are subscription-based services that will completely manage your CRM (Customer Relationship Management). Your website provider may also have CRM software included in your package.

The exact process will vary depending on the program you choose to use. A lot of online help and tutorials are available online, but briefly here is what to aim for:

1. Use the CRM package to create a user form. Decide what information you would like to store about your prospect. An email address will be compulsory but you can also gather more information at this stage if you wish.

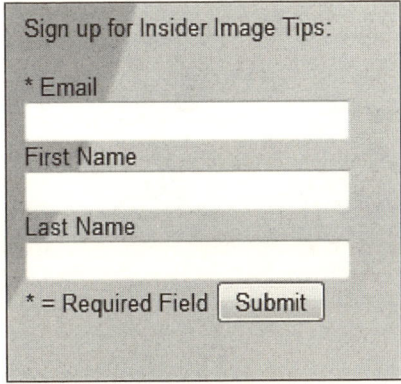

2. Specify a mailing list that the form feeds information into.

3. Set up auto responders for that mailing list. An auto responder is an email or newsletter to automatically be sent after a selected time period. For example, you may send the first auto responder as soon as the prospect fills in the form, thanking them for subscribing and advising them that they will be receiving regular updates from you. The second auto responder could go out seven days later, the third another seven days after that, and so on

The content and frequency of your auto responders will depend on your business, but it is said that it takes around seven communications from you for your prospect to begin to feel valued and begin to trust you as a supplier.

The great thing about auto responders is that they work automatically without you being there.

Ah thank you Jeeves, I deserve my Cosmopolitan. I've sent out 27 newsletters in the last 15 minutes.

Your CRM software package will have lots of pre-designed templates you can use, or you can get your graphic designer to create something consistent with your branding. As well as EDMs (Electronic Direct Mailers) you can also use your CRM software for surveys and managing your mailing lists.

Your CRM software will also give you powerful tracking information. Tracking software will allow you to see which of your prospects have read your emails, whether they clicked on any links you may have provided, or if they forwarded the email to another person.

Another great thing about CRM software is that it will handle your 'unsubscribes'. If someone no longer wishes to receive emails from you, CRM software always provides an unsubscribe link so that they can permanently remove themselves from your mailing list.

Article marketing

If your EDMs are full of handy hints and interesting facts, article marketing is another great way to share your expertise with a larger audience.

There are many article directories online, such as www.ezinearticles.com. These directories have a high page rank, which is a score given to a website with great content and lots of visitors. When you include links to your website in your articles, the inbound links from such highly-ranked pages will help your website climb up the search engines too.

A well-written article could be picked up by a journalist or blogger and distributed to a wider audience. Ensure that all your articles contain your contact information and a short profile, and state that you should be given credit by anyone who wants to use your article.

Hot Tip

The key to successful article marketing is often a catchy headline, so spend time getting this right.

Blogs

A blog (web log) is a type of website. A blog differs from most websites because its information is not static. New information is added frequently, often daily. A blog is sometimes more like an online diary. Often administered by a single person, a blog also invites feedback, comments and interaction with visitors.

You can create a simple blog in minutes and it's free to set up. The most commonly-used software packages are WordPress and Blogger (by Google). Easy to use templates make setting up a simple blog a breeze. More complex features (often called widgets) can be added for more interaction and complexity. Blogs are often ranked highly by the search engines because they are up to date and content rich. A blog is like a welcome mat to your website. As well as interacting with your customers, it's also a great way for you to direct traffic to your website and encourage people to sign up for your newsletter.

Secret 23
YOU MUST BECOME YOUR OWN GOOGLE SEARCH ENGINE SPECIALIST

You probably get emails daily from companies that promise you the prestigious number one spot on Google search pages. Don't be tempted by their promises. No one can guarantee you placement on Google, or any other of the search engines. You could invest a lot of money in something that doesn't actually bring you any new business or additional revenue, plus there is a lot you can do yourself to help you get nearer to those coveted top spots.

Decide what people will search for

The most important step is to identify the correct search phrases. Notice I say phrases, not words. These days Internet users are very specific on what they are searching for. Let's say that I'm searching for a course to help me with my writing skills. Shirley Taylor at ST Training Solutions has the perfect course for me, but unless I've used this company before, or someone has recommended it to me, I will not be searching for Shirley Taylor or ST Training Solutions. I am more likely to search for 'writings skills course for admin staff in Singapore'. Most Internet researchers are very specific. If I key in 'writing skills', the results that I get are not accurate enough. I might get information about pens and paper and becoming a novelist. If I want a relevant list of results, I need to enter more specific search criteria.

ST Training Solutions could fairly easily get to number one on the Google list for anyone typing in 'Shirley Taylor', but as I previously mentioned only existing customers and referrals will use this as their search criteria. ST Training Solutions would like to attract new business from potential delegates who wish to improve their writing skills, so it is important that they can be found by someone typing in a phrase similar to 'writings skills course for admin staff in Singapore'.

We call this a 'long tail search string'. If you want to compete for those valuable search engine top spots, you need to craft long tail search strings for every page of your website that you would like to get listed. That's right! Not just one for your whole site, one for every page that you would like potential customers to visit.

Holy Moly!

When it comes to search engines, you need to think of each page of your website as an individual site.

Do your research

Before you start writing dynamic long tail search phrases, it's a good idea to research your competition. Google is not the only search engine but it is the most popular one, so let's focus that one first. Visit the 'adwords keyword finder' tool at https://adwords.google.com.

In the box provided, type in the search phrase you are thinking of using. You may have to verify that you are a 'person' not a 'computer' by completing the 'Captcha code'.

Find keywords
Based on one or more of the following:

Word or phrase (one per line)	Website
writing skills course in singapore	

If you are targeting customers in a particular geographic region, be sure to select that region. It will default to United States, and you can remove the location if you are offering a global service.

You will see a list of similar or related search strings displayed as below.

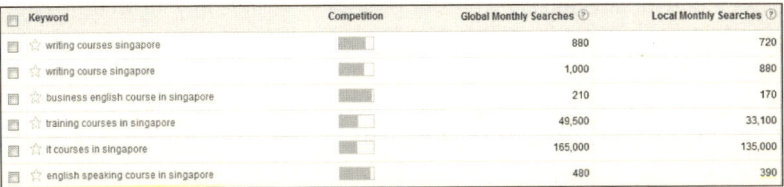

Keyword	Competition	Global Monthly Searches	Local Monthly Searches
writing courses singapore		880	720
writing course singapore		1,000	880
business english course in singapore		210	170
training courses in singapore		49,500	33,100
it courses in singapore		165,000	135,000
english speaking course in singapore		480	390

The final column shows you how many people each month in that region type that exact search phrase into Google. 'Training Courses in Singapore' has a lot of traffic (33,100) but those visitors will have trouble finding what they are looking for so they would most likely refine their search and submit another phrase. We see that people are searching for 'Business English courses in Singapore' but the number of local monthly searches for that phrase is fairly low (170). More importantly, the companies fighting for that business is high. 'Business English courses in Singapore' would not be a good search phrase because the competition for that phrase is high, but the number of actual searches is low.

By researching and experimenting with different phrases, make sure you look for a search phrase that has a high number of monthly searches but a low number of competitors searching for that phrase.

Take a look at this as an example

Keyword	Competition	Global Monthly Searches ⑦	Local Monthly Searches ⑦
communication skills training in singapore	-	-	-
communication training in singapore	▨	390	260
communication skills course in singapore	▨	73	73
communication course in singapore	▨	590	480
singapore communication training	-	-	-

Looking at these results, we can see that if we use 'course' instead of 'training' we get more visitors. We also see that although our course is on 'communication skills', people searching for these courses in Singapore do not include the word 'skills' in their searches.

For each page on your website that you would like browsers to visit, you need to create a long tail search phrase, or a number of relevant search phrases. Do make a note of any popular words or phrases to include in your website copy at a later stage.

Next you must ensure that your long tail search phrases are in the text on that page. Google works hard to ensure that the sites that come to the top of the page are extremely relevant to the search string. So make sure your long tail search string, and any other high potency key words and phrases, are scattered through the text on your page. This sometimes means you have to be a little creative with your narrative and can't write exactly what you would prefer, but you need to balance elegant sales prose with search engine placement.

Be careful not to repeat your key phrases too many times. Google will penalise you for repetition!

Page description and title

National Speakers association

About 6,260,000 results (0.35 seconds)

► **National Speakers Association** > Home
www.nsaspeaker.org/
National Speakers Association, is the leading professional association for speakers.

It will also pay dividends if you put your search string in the page description and page title. When your website designer creates each page of your website, he or she should specify a title a short description for each page. By including the search phrase in the page title, this will help your page ranking.

Choose a clever URL

The URL (uniform or universal resource locator) is the address of your page. Savvy web designers use the search phrase as part of their file structure in the web page, or even as the domain name itself. In the example below, when we search for success skills books, the listing with the number one position has 'successskills' in the url.

success skills books

About 65,600,000 results (0.10 seconds)

ST Training Solutions - Success Skills Series » **Success Skills books**
stsuccessskills.com/books.html
E-mail Etiquette by Shirley Taylor, Present for **Success** by Alison Lester,
Communication: Your Key to **Success** by Shirley Taylor and Alison Lester, Powerful ...

SEO (Search Engine Optimisation) is a *huge* subject and the goal posts are forever changing, but I hope in this secret you have learned a few things you can do to help get your page higher up the listings without spending money.

○ *Secret 24*
IF YOU WANT TO GET NOTICED AND REMEMBERED ONLINE, YOU NEED A GREAT VISUAL IDENTITY

In my previous secrets, I've talked about using technology to reach out to your client base. I've given you ideas about ways to contact your clients and potential clients with regular newsletters, auto responders and via social media. It can take up to 12 touch points to get a potential customer to trust you, and it is more effective if those touch points are in various mediums, such as newsletters, hard copy mailings, print advertisements, radio, etc. Your challenge is to create stunning material that reflects your corporate identity.

Before you create a newsletter, print out a flyer or even send an email, it's important to plan and design your visual identity. Your communications will be fighting for attention among a sea of other emails and mailers, so you need to stand out, and you need to be consistent.

Each time someone sees a communication from you, it should be instantly recognisable as coming from your organisation. Make a strategic plan for your choice of

- Typefaces
- Corporate colours
- Style of graphics
- Page layouts

You must plan a general look and feel that personalises and makes all your communications instantly recognisable. Ideally you will enlist the help of a graphic designer to create your visual identity, but if you need to do this yourself then this chapter tells you how to give your communications a glamorous make-over.

Typefaces

The typeface is the style of lettering you choose. You might be more familiar with the term 'font' but there is actually a difference. The typeface is the name of the lettering and spacing designed by the typeface designer, for example Arial or Times New Roman. The font includes variations on that typeface such letter size or attributes such bold or italic. It's important to decide on the typeface for your brand and use it consistently.

Always use a business typeface. Typefaces such as comic sans or lucida handwriting are not good choices; they look childish and are also difficult to read. First decide if you want to use a serif or a sans serif typeface. A serif typeface has little 'feet' at the bottom of letters. Serifs are more classic, and refined. Serif typefaces are easier to read quickly as the eye is led from one letter to another. A sans serif font does not have the 'feet' at the bottom of each letter. The look is crisper, cleaner and more modern but not as easy to read. You won't find newsletters and magazines writing in serifs, except perhaps for titles.

> Examples of a serif typeface
> Times New Roman, Book Antiqua, Calisto MT

> Example of a sans serif typeface
> Arial, Helvetica, Gill Sans MT

Designers often mix and match, perhaps choosing a serif for headings and a sans serif for body text. The choice is yours, but make a decision and stick to it.

Colours

Plan and stick to your corporate colour palette. If you have a logo, you can base your colour strategy around this, but it is a little more detailed than just saying "I like to use red". Think about the psychological effect that your colour choices will have. Red is passionate and strong but could also be aggressive. Blue and purple have a more corporate feel to them. Yellow and orange are more playful and fun.

Think about the combinations of colours you will use. Search online for 'colour wheel' and you will learn how opposing colours on the colour wheel will stand out and create more impact, and how complimentary colours will create a more elegant look and feel. Decide on colours for typefaces, headings, backgrounds, tints (a tint is a background colour that we can type over). Ideally you will find the pantone (www.pantone.co.uk) colours and the RGB colour codes on your computer so that your colour choices are perfect in print and online.

Use of graphics

When advertising or presenting using slides you might want to use pictures to convey your message. Plan a style for your graphics too. Never use clip art, as this immediately makes you look like an amateur. Browse through stock photography sites. I use www.istockphoto.com and www.fotolia.com. These are sites where you can find reasonably priced professional pictures. Ask yourself whether you should use studio pictures that have white backgrounds, or would your brand be better complemented by black and white shots?

For example, the slides from my presentations are immediately recognisable to my audience as part of my brand, as the colouring and style is consistent with my website. My photograph is on my business card and wherever possible I choose a bright graphic that is a metaphor for the point I am making on the slide. I use this branding in print advertising, as part of my YouTube campaign, Facebook fan page, in fact wherever I can.

 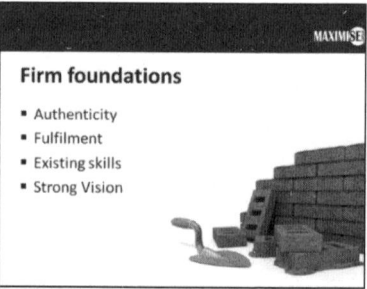

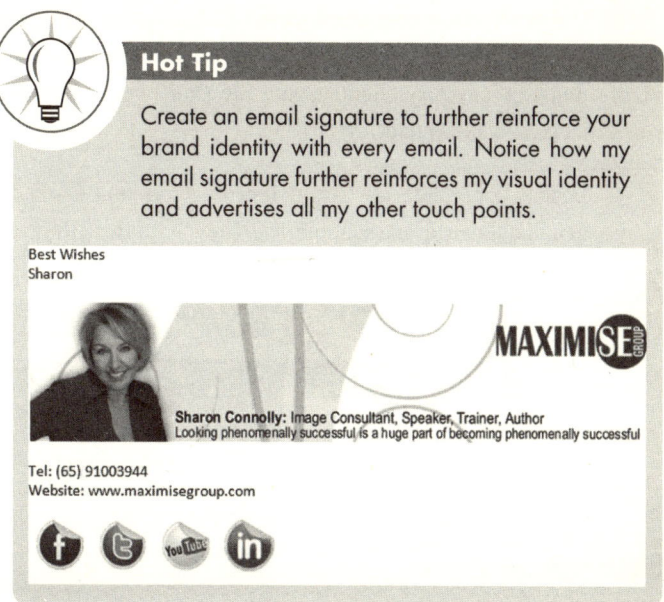

Hot Tip

Create an email signature to further reinforce your brand identity with every email. Notice how my email signature further reinforces my visual identity and advertises all my other touch points.

Best Wishes
Sharon

MAXIMISE GROUP

Sharon Connolly: Image Consultant, Speaker, Trainer, Author
Looking phenomenally successful is a huge part of becoming phenomenally successful

Tel: (65) 91003944
Website: www.maximisegroup.com

Tips for professional layout

As I mentioned earlier, ideally you will enlist the help of a graphic designer to set up your visual identity, but if you are doing it yourself, here are some more tips for perfect presentation.

1. Do not use CAPITAL LETTERS. In an email this is seen as shouting. Capital letters are hard to read and they look unprofessional. Apart from when you want to EMPHASISE one word in a sentence, you should never use capital letters. Instead, use a larger, heavier font or a different colour.

2. Never underline. Underlining was initially used when typewriters could not produce bold or different sizes of text. Underlining is never used in professional graphic design. Underlined text on a computer indicates a hyperlink. Underlining when there is no hyperlink confuses the reader.

3. Use plenty of white space. A great headline and in an impactful typeface will stand out much better if there is not too much text. Don't cram too much on one page. Reduce your message and surround it by space to increase your impact.

4. Design your page on a grid layout. Keep text boxes, pictures and headings lined up and symmetrical. They should lead the eye to important messages.

Hot Tip

I recommend further reading at www.bamaga zine.com. A little extra knowledge can completely transform your material.

Checklist for promoting yourself online

1. Check your Facebook security settings and make sure you are aware of what information you are showing to your friends. If necessary, create lists to restrict inappropriate content.

2. If you have your own business, create a Facebook fan page to collect followers and help promote your business.

3. Ensure your LinkedIn profile is up to date and be sure to collect testimonials whenever you can.

4. Have a procedure for storing contacts that you collect from networking. Follow up with these contacts regularly.

5. Register with a contact management service and create at least seven auto responders to handle new enquiries effortlessly.

6. Create a blog and update it regularly. Alternatively be an active contributor on other blogs and forums in your area of expertise.

7. Create a twitter account and tweet regularly.

8. Follow peers and competitors in your industry. Share their tweets with your followers and they are likely to do the same for you. This will raise your profile and reach.

9. Establish an online visual identity and use it consistently throughout all your marketing material.

10. Create a great email signature that promotes all the ways you can be found online.

CHAPTER 7

MASTERING THE ART OF MEDIA PITCHING
How to manage your public relations like an expert

by **Andrew Chow**
Managing Director
IdeaMart (S) Pte Ltd

Andrew Chow is a certified life coach, entrepreneur, speaker and author. He has spoken at many conferences to business leaders in Southeast Asia and civil servants in the Middle East and North Africa. Andrew's insights on social media strategy, media management and personal branding have made him a choice selection for workshop leaders. His dynamic presentation style and thought leadership make him a frequently sought-after keynote speaker. Andrew also won much positive feedback from business associations like Singapore National Employers Federation (SNEF), Singapore Chinese Chamber of Commerce (SCCCI), and campuses like Singapore Institute of Management (SIM) and Management Development Institute of Singapore (MDIS).

Andrew had more than 180 interviews and features about him or his business since late 2005 on Channel News Asia, News 8, 938LIVE, *The Business Times, Zao Bao, Berita Harian, Today, The New Paper, My Paper,* STOMP, *Female, Her World, Peak, Shape, Lifestyle,* etc. He was also the business coach on Effective Media Management for Singapore's leading radio station 938LIVE — 'Positive Business Minutes' and 'A Slice of Life' programmes. On social media, Andrew founded several social networking portals with over 10,000 profiles.

Andrew founded Ideamart (S) Pte Ltd in 1994, and won the Spirit of Enterprise Award in 2008 and the Successful Entrepreneur Award in 2010. Graduating from Thames Valley University, Andrew is also a Certified Trainer, Assessor and Developer for WSQ courses under Singapore Workforce Development Agency (WDA).

Find out more about Andrew at: **www.ideamart.com.sg**

Contact Andrew at: **andrew@ideamart.com.sg**

MEDIA RELATIONS IS both an art and a science. Knowing your basics and adding some creativity and flair are really essential for all businesses.

If you want a head start in gaining publicity, it's essential to understand what constitutes news and know what the media and press want. Having good publicity about your product and branding will always enhance the public perception on their value.

There are basically two types of news — hard news consists of basic facts and figures, while soft news covers news of human interest. The press usually prefers news that is unusual, current, local, abnormal, sensational and socially impactful.

The press and media are powerful stakeholders of your business. The press prefers to develop a story while the media prefers to explore different angles. For example, there is no story if you announce to the press that your company is celebrating its twentieth anniversary this year. However, if your company plans to donate $20 million to charity to celebrate its twentieth anniversary, it will be a big story!

In this section, Andrew Chow will share his experiences and give you four powerful ways to help you pitch to the media and the press. This will enable you to manage your public relations efforts like an expert. You will learn how to carry yourself professionally and yet still be personable to the host and the audience you are addressing. No media management tips would be complete without talking about crisis management. You will learn how to answer the most pressing questions journalists may ask in a crisis situation.

♀ Secret 25
PUBLICITY BEGINS WITH YOUR KEY MESSAGE

Many business owners treat the media as a platform for low-cost marketing for maximum reach. Nothing can be further from the truth. There are some basic rules of how any media in the world will operate. Here are four things I know the journalist won't do for me.

1. He will not protect my business if I am in a crisis.

2. He won't advance my business if I am doing well.

3 He won't help me to say what I want to say.

4. He won't include everything I tell him.

How can you connect with the media through public relations? The answer lies in your key message. This is what the media is interested in evaluating if their readers, viewers or listeners are to find your message useful.

Prepare your key message as a press release

Just like notes in a conference that participants can take away, key messages will be the focus point for the media. A key message is usually communicated through a press release.

A press release brings your key message to the attention of the press and broadcast media, and in turn the public, generating publicity.

Hot Tip

Write your press release exactly the way you want it to be reported or featured. That will include an interesting title as a headline too.

Here are some guidelines to help you with your press releases:

- **Include basic information.** The release should answer the questions: who, what, when, where, why and how. Get your story across early. If your first sentence or paragraph is obscure, complicated or boring, journalists probably won't bother reading on.

- **Keep the release concise.** One printed A4 side if possible, and no more than two. Avoid jargon, acronyms and abbreviations unless they are generally well-known by your target audience. Include quotations. Draft them yourself if need be, but always get them approved!

- **Don't make misleading statements.** Make sure your subject and style suit the target audience. For events, give a precise timetable and location, including clear information on any opportunities for photos and interviews in a 'Note to Editors' at the end of the release.

- **Give the release a short title.** The purpose is to attract interest, so make it clear and self-explanatory. Brainstorm several interesting headings and select one with the maximum impact for your story. Put the date on the release. Always include a contact name and phone number, an email and web address for further information. Use double or 1.5 lines spacing to make the release easier to read. Check spelling, grammar and punctuation.

Your Turn

Brainstorm a list of unique selling propositions about your business that the press and media have not reported or featured. For each pitch, create a possible story or angle for each media on your list. Send out a press release and follow up with a call to discuss further.

Unfortunately, not all press releases will be taken in their entirety by the editors and producers.

Here are some scenarios that may happen after you submit a press release:

- Your press release is thrown into the trash. Every reporter has hundreds of emails and faxes of press releases. Usually editors get to decide what is newsworthy. Unless you know the reporter personally, it will be a waste of time to send a press release to his mailbox. Make sure you have an interesting headline and put it on the subject line of the email. If the reporter finds it interesting, they may read it.

- The press release is printed but contains incorrect information. It is always a good idea to ask partners to proofread your press release. The common mistakes are usually made over figures and dates.

- Part of your press release is printed, but your competitors are quoted too and they downplay your points. The media will always try to maintain objective reporting and would seek the opinion of others in your industry to make the article more balanced.

- Part of your press release is printed, but analysts are quoted who change your story. This is similar to the previous point, and this time your key message may be diluted.

- Part of your press release is printed, but your point is not included. This may happen when the media is already doing a story and your press release merely provided them with some illustrations and examples to strengthen their point.

We all want our stories to be featured in the press and reach out to as many as possible. One great method of doing this more effectively is to write your press release the same way you want it to be printed or featured. It saves the journalists and editors much editing time.

Holy Moly!

There is no such thing as 'big' or 'small' companies in the media or press, only 'featured' or 'unknown' ones.

⚟ Secret 26
POSITION YOURSELF AS AN INFORMATION RESOURCE CENTRE TO THE MEDIA

Who should you be helping? It is always more effective directing your pitch to the editors as they decide what is newsworthy information. Journalists are usually assigned different stories, though they can recommend your story if they are approached. The equivalent in the media will be the producers of radio shows and TV programmes.

When is the best time to pitch? The best time to approach a journalist isn't just before he is due to submit his stories. It is advisable that you send your pitch through email and follow up with a call. Unless your story is about an event, it may take a few more days before the journalist gets back to you. If you are pitching for a story in a magazine, try doing it three months before the intended date of issue. Magazines have long story-writing, editing and production times. They are generally more suitable for human stories rather than angles.

What should you include in your press release? Ensure it has all the supporting information. Always include the key personnel's contact preferably with their LinkedIn profile. Photo, drawings and other visual information should be included from a social media file sharing site. This will enable the journalist to conduct further background research to your story. If your story is an upcoming event, ensure you have briefed the different participants on the possibility of being interviewed.

Caution

Even if one producer or editor has rejected your story, pitch it again to another. It's all about timing and the window of opportunity when you build rapport with the media.

How to be more effective in media pitching?

- **Use pictures.** If a picture is worth a thousand words, a great picture is worth a million. Invest in good photography if you want your pictures to be used. Invest in a good makeover picture of yourself if you would like the editors to include your photograph in the story. A glamorous shot usually works.

- **Exercise exclusivity.** Some members of the press will only cover your story if they are promised an exclusive coverage. If you feel that the readership base of the particular press is your target audience, offering exclusivity may be a good idea. An important note is to have integrity. If you offer one media your exclusive story, do not offer the same to another unless the first has officially rejected you. Prepare other exclusive story angles for different press and media to maximise your chance of more comprehensive coverage.

- **An insider's story usually works.** If your pitch is about an event, inviting the journalist to participate may produce a story based on an insider's feedback and evaluation. The advantage of this approach is that you can offer this to various members of the press. If you have an event, and some of your advocates volunteered to be interviewed by media about their experiences, this would be an excellent story too. Always brief your advocate about how to handle media questions. Set your 'out-of-bounds' markers for possible answers.

- **Be creative or controversial.** Always be creative in your story. Journalists receive hundreds of press releases daily. Most of them end up in the trash if there is nothing unique about the pitch. In 2007, I organised the first ever 'Love Boat' experience for 120 singles in Singapore. One of the popular TV channels followed us for three days because I offered them three creative angles of the same event. One of them was five competitors in the dating industry putting down their competition and co-organising my mega event. So the angle of 'from foes to friends' was both creative and controversial.

- **Offer your insight from survey and observation of current trends**. The easiest way to produce hard news is to conduct a survey and present your new findings. This is effective in positioning your company as the leader of your industry. New insights and findings will never cease to amaze the media. If you discover something that no one found out before, you will have yourself a great story!

Hot Tip

If you believe the media is more likely to cover a pitch from a popular public relations agency, then all the established companies with great PR budget will be on the media every day. The media will not give preference to any big names. They want big stories!

How to handle yourself if you are going through a media crisis?

No company will ever be fully prepared for any crisis in their business. The key is to develop a standard contingency plan to keep the public informed through the media on how they handle the crisis.

There are ten questions a reporter will want to know in a hard news situation:

- What happened?
- Why did it happen?
- Was anyone injured or affected by it?
- Could this have been prevented?
- Has this ever happened before?
- Currently, what are you doing about it?
- When will the problem be solved?
- How will you prevent this from happening again?

- Did you know this was going to happen?

- What would you like to say to those affected?

In an extreme crisis situation, the CEO or the chairman of the company should preferably be the main spokesperson in order to project an honest and open attitude. When dealing with reporters from the tabloids, you must ensure you handle tricky questions carefully. Never release information that you heard 'off the record'. It will be published. Avoid being put into a situation which you have to answer 'Yes' or 'No'.

Caution

Stay away from using 'off the record' comments to the media. It will be printed even if your name is not associated with it.

♀ Secret 27
BE PREPARED TO BE IN THE LIMELIGHT

If you are going to be successful in managing publicity for your business, your personal branding on radio and television must stand out. Having a voice of authority on radio and visual presence on television will connect you with the host and the audience. For most businesses, the brand personality rests on the personality of the owner – you.

Preparing for a radio phone interview

- Before the interview, prepare both long and short answers for a list of suggested questions. Ensure you have the right phone volume. Switch off call waiting on your phone. Arrange your notes on your desk so that they can be easily accessed. Perform mental and physical relaxation exercises. Have a glass of water nearby.

- During the phone interview, speak in a normal conversational voice, and display enthusiasm. Be creative by providing useful information, revealing new information, or using memorable words or phrases. Limit your answers to less than five sentences. Avoid using filler words ('umm', 'well', 'like', 'you know', 'really', etc). Concentrate on the interview process to anticipate the upcoming moments. Do not speak too much, and leave room for the interviewer to ask questions. It's his show after all, not yours. Make your 'sales pitch' only at the end of the interview. Repeat all numbers, addresses, URLs, etc.

- After the interview, send the producer and host a written thank you note. Follow up on any promises made on-air to listeners. Remind the producer of your interest in being a guest again.

Preparing for a live radio talk show

Treat it like a normal conversation. There will be commercial breaks, traffic reports, weather updates, etc. In between breaks, continue to chat with the host, as he/she may discover more interesting pointers and ask you again when the show is live again. Remember that only your voice is connecting with the listeners, so put some emotion and feeling into it. Continue to gesture with your hands and allow reasonable body movement in the studio just like when you are having a conversation with someone. Avoid going into the usual question and answer mode. You can answer a question with another question and exchange roles with the host creatively if you know him/her well.

Preparing for a television interview

Beware of your dress code. Do not wear bright white, weather map blue, or chrome key blue. When you are booked for a studio appearance, find out the colour of the set and dress so that you don't blend in. Do not wear contrasting patterns. Wear bold, fashionable ties, but not ones that distract. Do not wear shiny fabrics or anything that glares. Do not wear bracelets. Women should wear pearls instead of shiny necklaces.

- **Gestures and body movement.** Use gestures economically to make points. Too much body movement can be distracting. Every movement is body language and some of it is not good. Leave your body open and quiet. Both men and women should cross their legs when seated.

- **Have the right posture.** Be in a 'state of readiness'. Don't slump shoulders or lean back. Keep your torso erect. Request pillows to help you sit erect if necessary. Men should unbutton their jackets when seated and remove their tie clip and pens from their shirt pocket.

- **Maintain eye contact.** Don't wear glasses if you can help it. If you have to wear glasses, make sure they have non-glare lenses or learn how to hold your head effectively. Energy comes from your eyes, so be careful with eye movement. It's usually best not to move your eyes. You will need long stretches of eye contact. Only look at the person who is interviewing you. Hold your eye contact there after you finish a statement.

- **Watch your tone.** Use the right volume to make points and create variety. Listen to yourself before you go on. Slow your speaking rate and enunciate carefully.

Publicity relations 2.0 = mass media + social media

The mass media faces stiff competition from social media. While the mass media may give you the authority, it is social media that gives you the authenticity.

Social media interaction is online social conversation from any content generated by people using different tools or media. They are not one-to-one or one-to-many conversations. Rather, they are many-to-many. Social media has resulted in a fundamental shift in the way we communicate.

The stakeholders involved in such conversations can be your customers, your donors, your volunteers, your employees, your investors, your critics, your fans, your competition or anyone who has Internet access and an opinion. The conversation isn't organised or controlled but organic and complex, speaking in a human voice.

Your social media presence can help you in all stages of marketing, self-promotion, public relations, and customer service. The mass media will pick up your story and may feature you without you pitching to them.

Hot Tip

Combine the authority of the mass media with your authenticity on social media to create the powerful hybrid publicity for your business.

Secret 28
MANAGE YOUR PRESS CONFERENCE LIKE A PARTY

You should only organise a press conference if you have subject matter that is sufficiently interesting for the media. Press conferences are appropriate to mark a major event or announce important news, where the ability to see results at first-hand, or to question the personalities involved, will bring added value for journalists. Handle questions from every member of the press appropriately, just like having different special friends in your party.

Another justification is to give a general briefing about a topic of current or emerging interest. This may not necessarily produce a great deal of immediate press coverage, but will provide journalists with a contextual framework for future announcements. Nevertheless, it's always preferable to provide a news angle that will justify the time spent in attending such an event.

Press invitation — revealing and concealing

The objective is to get the media and press to know the agenda without having too much information. Your invitation for the press conference should be interesting enough to make them curious but not enough to feature your story. Here are some guidelines to follow:

- If you are launching a service, mention its usefulness without revealing the process.

- If you are announcing a major event, mention the name and the target group without details of date, registration, etc.

- If you are presenting an award, give details of the award category without the names of the winners.
- If you are managing a crisis, give general guidelines without mentioning the exceptions.
- If you are forming a new association or group, give a description of its objectives, but leave out details like the founding members and future plans.

Timing is everything

You should send out your invitation 10 days before the press conference. Beware of long holidays. My invite for a press conference on 9 January 2008 was sent on 27 December 2007. Many media journalists were on leave and didn't get the information on time.

There will always be other press conference or stories on the same day. The press will decide which story to cover, and you have no control over the media response to the conference. Be positive and work without those who are present. Incidentally, 9 January 2008 was also the day for the launch of Terminal 3 at Changi Airport. Many local and foreign media were at Changi Airport covering this big story. I still managed to have a respectable group size of 10 different press and media.

RSVP

Just like a party, you must include RSVP on your invitations so that you can prepare enough copies of your press kit for all the people who turn up. Prepare name tags and collect business cards at the reception. Some journalists will ask you what other media will be there. They won't be going to your press conference if they are looking for exclusive stories. Send them the press kit via courier two hours after the press conference ends.

Press kit

Like in all great parties, everyone goes home with a gift, which in this case is your press kit. At the conference, ensure your press kit has the same presentation material and pictures (both hard and digital copies). It should also carry product samples, and souvenirs if applicable, and remember to include profiles of key personnel. A comprehensive contents page is always useful to help journalists see a snapshot of what's in the kit. Prepare a list of special jargon used too, as you cannot assume the press will understand your jargon or special codes used in your industry.

At the conference

Always prepare enough seats and wireless microphones. Make sure there are ample copies of press kits at the reception to be given out as the journalists arrive. Ensure names of speaker/presenters are displayed on a long table in the front. If there is any performance or demonstration, a designated space should be prepared. Go through your meeting agenda, ensure you cover every point in the invite. Any questions and answers should be after the presentation is over.

Managing questions and answers

Maintaining private conversations in a party is always better than group talk. During my press conference in 2008, I issued three awards to my partners and presented details of a month-long celebration of love for 'Romancing Singapore' all within 45 minutes. I was anticipating a spirited crowd asking many questions on the several stories that were mentioned. No one asked a single question!

To my pleasant surprise, the fun began when we had lunch. Four of five members of the media began to ask me many questions privately. Remember, the media looks for angles while the press picks up stories.

Some journalists will want to cover certain aspects of your story and usually like to speak to you exclusively. There's always friendly competition among the members of the media too and no one wants to report what can be found elsewhere.

Some members of the press will come to look for other stories not on your agenda, so try to provide some insights or comments within your limit as much as you can. You may answer them in a different way but ensure your message is consistent.

Your Turn

Organise fun social events like a cocktail party to replace a traditional press conference. Your other business stakeholders, Internet bloggers, social media practitioners, freelance writers and press/ media journalists are all invited to network. Be social and yet professional, and make sure your image is communicated first at your event.

Media relations is like dating, the more you know each other, the better you can communicate and understand each other.

Checklist for mastering the art of media pitching

1. Create a database of all suitable media and press contacts related to your business.

2. Maintain friendship with the media by being an information or resource centre.

3. Write your press release in exactly the same way you want it to be published.

4. Ensure your press conference has substantial new information to be released to the media.

5. Make your interview on radio sound like a conversation instead of a question and answer session.

6. Maintain good posture and mind your body language on television. Every movement will be magnified.

7. Share your contents, and do not sell your expertise. The media dislikes marketers on their platforms.

8. Prepare long and short answers to any pre-arranged questions.

9. Face the media yourself if you are handling a crisis. Do not hire a Public Relations agency to manage that for you.

10. Engage the media on a regular basis to ensure publicity is a way of life in your business.

PART 2

Speech, Language and Communication

> " There are four ways, and only four ways, in which we have contact with the world. We are evaluated and classified by these four contacts: what we do, how we look, what we say, and how we say it."
>
> — Dale Carnegie

Your Speech and Language

CHAPTER

VOICE OF A LEADER
How to speak with energy, credibility and confidence

by **Deborah Torres Patel**
Director
Expressing You Pte Ltd

Deborah Torres Patel has performed for millions of people on radio, TV, Broadway and international concert stages since she began her professional singing career at age four in America.

Deborah has shared the stage with legendary entertainers like Sammy Davis Jr., Kool & The Gang, Whitney Houston and Michael Jackson. She worked with Broadway Theatre directors Martin Charnin 'Annie' and Pat Birch 'Grease', and her voice-overs have been awarded at 16 International Film Festivals. She is honoured to partner with Success Resources, the largest personal development seminar organisers in the world, and has shared their speaking platforms with renowned experts like Anthony Robbins, Robert Kiyosaki, Blair Singer and T. Harv Eker as well as world leaders like former British Prime Minister, Tony Blair.

For the past 27 years Deborah has dedicated herself to teaching hundreds of thousands of personal and professional clients in 66 countries to communicate with confidence, power and authenticity.

Her popular public programmes and in-house corporate trainings focus on leadership communication, speaking and singing voice, presentation skills and public speaking.

Deborah was a Founding Member of APSS.

Find out more about Deborah at:
www.expressingyou.com and www.deborahtorrespatel.com
Contact Deborah at: deborah@expressingyou.com

NO MATTER WHO you are or what you do, the ability to present yourself and your ideas powerfully has never been more important than in today's 24/7 digital information age. Speaking well can influence others' views, close a deal, motivate your team, enhance your business, and elevate your reputation.

Everyone knows the importance of exercising the body, but few people realise that the voice needs exercise too. Most people spend way too much time sitting in a front of a computer and are not aware of how to quickly transform stagnant, sedentary energy so they can motivate themselves and others into immediate action.

In this section, Deborah Torres Patel will share simple strategies to help you become a dynamic communicator. She will also share practical exercises to dramatically increase your energy, effectiveness, credibility and confidence.

Deborah will give you practical tips to get your point across with fewer words and more impact in any language. You'll learn how important it is to look, sound and feel like an inspiring leader who speaks with an authentic voice that puts people at ease and powerfully reflects who you really are.

⚷ *Secret 29*
HIGHEST ENERGY ALWAYS WINS

Take a look around your workplace. Do the leaders in your organisation have high energy? Are they confident and credible? Do they lead by example? Is their communication style effective? Do they have good posture and carry themselves well? Is their voice powerful? Are they calm under pressure?

The stress of round-the-clock communication has taken a huge personal toll on work life balance. It's also had an impact on the physical health and energy levels of a large majority of the world's working population.

Unfortunately, there is no magic pill we can take to achieve well-being and balance in today's demanding digital age. However, I'd like to share some very quick and effective ways for you to increase your energy levels within a very short time, and help you to shift from an unresourceful state to a resourceful one in a matter of seconds.

Why would you want or need to do this?

There are a multitude of challenges that weigh on us every day. The ability to efficiently release stress and tension is essential to our effectiveness. As a leader, when the stakes are high and the moment is brief, you may need to motivate and inspire your team, impress your superiors or close a deal. The more energy you have, the easier it will be to accomplish your goals.

Shake it out!

To prepare for an important phone call, meeting or presentation, to quickly release anger or frustration, or if you've been sedentary too long, here is one fast exercise that can help you to increase your energy. If you are at work you will want to head to some place private to perform this exercise, like an empty meeting room, hallway or even a washroom.

Don't pout! Shake it out!

138 88 ESSENTIAL SECRETS

It may sound strange but the fastest and easiest way to eliminate tension in your body is to stand up somewhere where there is enough space for you to move around quickly, and shake out your entire body. Shake your head, arms, legs, hands, feet and body as fast and as wildly as you possibly can. Simply shake for three to 10 seconds and you'll be amazed at the amount of tension that will be instantly released. Your body will feel energised and alive.

If you are in a place where you can make noise, you can add spontaneous moaning sounds or vocalise on an open "Ahh" vowel sound simultaneously as you are shaking out your body. This will also help you to release vocal tension.

Caution

Don't force or strain your voice. Make little to no effort; simply allow your body to naturally make sound as you shake it out vigorously. Check out Deborah's video at this url: www.expressingyou.com/88secrets.

Neck and shoulder exercises

Most people spend a lot of time sitting in front of a computer or driving. Both of these activities place a lot of strain on our neck and shoulders. It really helps if you take some time throughout the day to free as much tension as possible from these important areas.

Neck and shoulder stretches are absolutely essential and not to be skipped. Even if you work in a structured environment with people around, no one will think it strange that you take the time to stretch your neck while having a break from your computer.

Here are some simple neck and shoulder exercises for you to try:

- Stretch your neck — up, down, side and side (allow two to three deep breaths in each direction as you stretch).

- Stretch your neck as far as you can, looking up, so that you get a good stretch in the front of your neck.

- Stretch your neck forward with your chin towards your chest while clasping your hands together on the back of your head, elbows forward, allowing the weight of your arms to deepen the stretch. This is a great stretch for the back of your neck.

- Stretch your neck to the right side with your right ear towards your right shoulder. Place your right hand on the left side of your head above your left ear, allowing the weight of your right hand and arm to deepen and further intensify the stretch.

- Repeat the same exercise on the opposite side.

- Neck rolls. Perform slow neck rolls in both directions – clockwise and counter clockwise. Take your time to breathe and work out the kinks in your neck.

- Shoulder rolls. Perform slow shoulder rolls rotating your shoulders in a circular motion, stretching as far as possible in each direction (clockwise and counter clockwise).

Your Turn

Deborah has made a video to show you neck and shoulder exercises. Check it out at this url: www.expressingyou.com/88secrets.

You will find a lot of benefits from releasing tension in your body. You will have a greater range of movement and physical expression, which will help you to be more relaxed and open, and then normally your mind and spirit will follow. As a result, your physical and mental energy will naturally increase.

Being able to generate a high level of energy any time you need it will make a significant difference in your performance.

Secret 30
WHEN IT COMES TO VOCAL POWER, EASY DOES IT

If you are like most people, you hardly ever think about your voice. You are probably not aware of the fact that if your voice sounded better, you could increase your income and dramatically improve the quality of your life. Why? Getting anything you want in life requires communication. When it comes to voice, which is critical to your communication, there are three simple keys to unlock your vocal power.

Key #1: Breathing

If you have ever watched a baby breathe, you would have noticed his tummy area or diaphragm effortlessly moving in and out with each breath. As we get older, most adults lose touch with their natural ability to breathe deeply and fully. Breathing from our diaphragm gives us real vocal power.

Without being overly scientific, your diaphragm muscle naturally creates suction that draws air into your lungs when you breathe.

Just like when you were a baby, the diaphragm should naturally do the work for projecting and controlling your voice. The good news is no matter what your breathing is like now, at one time you were able to breathe perfectly.

Holy Moly!

I was born with perfect breathing. My body innately knows how to breathe.

To re-experience diaphragmatic breathing, simply place your hand on your stomach with the middle of your palm on top of your belly button. Imagine that your tummy area is like a balloon. When you inhale, allow it to expand by filling it with air. When you exhale, simply release all your air and allow your tummy to return to its normal position.

Your Turn

Now, look into a mirror large enough to see yourself breathe from the waist up. Watch yourself as you take a deep, full breath. Pay attention to what your chest and shoulders are doing when you breathe.

If you lifted your chest or shoulders much when you inhaled, you're probably only getting only a small amount of air to support your breath and you are barely using your diaphragm.

As a result, your breathing will be shallow and the tension in your shoulders will eventually create more tension in your neck and jaw areas, which are critical to having a relaxed voice. To sound better, you must relearn how to breathe using your diaphragm.

Contrary to what you would think, it is more important to focus on the way you breathe out than the way you breathe in. Aim to exhale your breath completely before inhaling again. When you have exhaled all your air, your body will naturally inhale.

If it is difficult for you to feel your diaphragm move, simply lie down on the floor and place a medium size book on your tummy. The weight of the book will make it easier for you to feel what's happening in your diaphragm. When you inhale, continue to imagine your tummy filling up like a balloon, and push the book up towards the ceiling. When you exhale, simply let go and release your air and diaphragm. This will automatically bring the book back down. Practise this book exercise until you are more in control of your breathing.

Your Turn

Deborah has made a video to show you how to breathe with a book on your tummy. Check it out at this url: www.expressingyou.com/88secrets.

Ideally you should breathe fully using your diaphragm all the time, not just when you are using your voice. Breath is the fuel for speaking. Your breath should always support your sound when you speak. This means you should only be speaking when there is a solid even flow of air coming out of your mouth and when your diaphragm and tummy area is coming back in as you exhale.

Hot Tip

Yoga and swimming naturally help you to improve your breathing. Both these forms of exercise train you to have better control of your breath.

Key #2: Relaxation and release

It is faster to warm up your voice when you first release tension in your body as we did in secret one. Most people experience vocal tension specifically in the tongue, jaw, face, neck or shoulders and are normally unaware of how much that consistent stress impacts their verbal and non-verbal communication.

Speaking should feel effortless. However, when speech isn't enunciated clearly, consonants are dropped off at the ends of words. If you experience vocal fatigue or lose your voice quickly, it is a sure sign of tension and lack of breath support.

You should *always* warm up before an important call or presentation. When you warm up your body and your voice your mind will become clearer. Your energy will also flow more freely, which makes it much easier to think on your feet.

Hot Tip

Making funny faces using all of your facial muscles will help you to release tension in your tongue, jaw and face. This will help you look, sound and feel more at ease.

To loosen up tense places ... make lots of funny faces.

Your Turn

Deborah has made a video to show you a quick warm up for speaking to release vocal tension and warm up your voice. Check it out at this url: www.expressingyou.com/88secrets.

Caution

Do not strain your voice when you warm up, and don't force your pitch too high or too low. If you feel pain, you are doing something incorrectly.

Key #3: Arc and focus

My dear friend and mentor Arthur Samuel Joseph of Vocal Awareness, a well-respected voice coach to many celebrities, created the arc focusing technique.

Imagine you can see your voice leaving your body, lifting and soaring upwards as if your sound could fly. This will naturally place your voice in what Arthur calls the 'nasal edge'. Imagine your sound extends beyond your nose into and through the shape of an arc.

When you speak, simply imagine that you can see your voice move up and through on an arc as in this diagram.

The ARC

Caution

When visualising the arc, don't tip your chin up or down. Keep your head level in a natural position with your chin and parallel to the ground.

In my experience, the arc focus moves from your upper lip, diagonally up to your nose and outward from your eyes focused directly to where you want your sound to go. For example, to direct your sound and fill a room, visualise your voice soaring to the back of the room you are in, or if you are outside, directly to where you want your voice to travel to. You can create a stronger connection when speaking to someone face-to-face if you direct your sound to the eyes of the other person.

♀ Secret 31
ADDING LIFE TO YOUR WORDS WILL BRING YOUR WORDS TO LIFE

What you say vs. how you say it

Most people are concerned or often nervous about 'what to say' but the reality is that 'how you say it' is far more important. The way your voice sounds and the way you use your body leaves a much stronger impression on others than the words you choose.

For decades, research has revealed that the words we speak statistically only account for about seven per cent of what makes you a credible communicator. The remaining 93 per cent has to do with the tone of your voice (38 per cent) and your physiology (55 per cent), which includes your breathing, gestures, body language, the way you walk, dress, sit and stand, your posture and presence, and even your eyes and facial expressions.

Long before you begin to speak, people are forming opinions about you. Additional judgments are created within the first three to five seconds of hearing your voice. Once that initial impression of you is made in people's minds, it is very hard to change.

For this reason, even a well-rehearsed and beautifully crafted presentation can go badly wrong if the messenger is not in alignment with his or her message. When your physiology and your words don't match, you appear inauthentic, and on a subconscious level this will make people have doubts about you, or worse, distrust you.

Reading out loud

Whenever you are speaking, it is important that your words come to life. One of the best ways to practise being a more exciting, dynamic and authentic speaker is to read aloud.

Read slowly, focusing on one word at a time. Attempt to make each word look and sound like the meaning of the word. Each sentence you read will have key words that can be stressed for maximum impact. In most cases the key words will be obvious to you.

Your Turn

Read this sentence out loud in front of a mirror where you can see yourself from the waist up stressing the underlined key words and making them look and sound like what they mean:

"The global trend is up."

- Did you find yourself naturally gesturing with your words?

- Did you gesture using one or two hands?

- Was your body stiff or without movement?

- Did the word 'global' look and sound round like the shape of a globe?

- Did you make a decision about the specific meaning of the word 'trend' or did you combine it with the word 'global' or with the word 'up'?

- When you said the word 'up', did you naturally look up or gesture your hand or arm in an upward direction?

You probably have never asked yourself so many questions about how you say things or what your body is specifically doing when you speak. I'm not asking you to act out every single word, or be overly dramatic like a bad actor. However, when you make decisions about key words, if you visualise their meanings and embody your specific interpretation of the words, you will be perceived as a more dynamic communicator. You will also look and feel more confident, credible and charismatic.

You will be amazed at how much more engaging you will become when you are connected to the words you speak (the message) and you will quickly discover that you (the messenger) have come to life.

Hot Tip

Read aloud five minutes a day until you become really comfortable bringing your words to life. Take your time. Savour and experience each key word. Most importantly, have fun!

To find out if your reading is exciting and dynamic, read a story to a young child. If your reading captivates them, they will pay attention and hang on to your every word. If they look bored and get distracted, you need more practise.

With practise, embodying the words you speak will eventually become second nature. You will discover how simple it is to speak with confidence and conviction, and that in turn will help you inspire others into action. One of the first places you can test how well this simple reading technique works is on the telephone or on a conference call.

Quick telephone tips

No matter what your voice sounds like, these two telephone tips will add energy and confidence to your voice and presentation:

- **Stand up**. If you want to get your message across with power and conviction, stand up and embody the words you are speaking. If circumstances make it difficult for you to stand, sit alert with your back erect, feet on the floor and with your buttocks towards the front of your chair.

- **Script it**. Scripting your voicemail, important calls, notes or your presentation slides will make you sound more articulate and self-assured. If you have a habit of using verbal fillers like 'uhm' while searching for words, scripting what you say will help you to practically eliminate them.

Remember, it's not 'what you say' but 'how you say it' that is remembered most. When you script your calls, you no longer have to worry about 'what to say' because chances are that you, or someone on your team, would have invested time in crafting your message.

Therefore, all you have to do in the presentation portion of your telephone call is read your notes out loud and embody them. Simply focus on bringing your words to life just like you practised in the reading aloud exercise, and you will sound natural, intelligent and in control.

If you take just a few minutes to draft a simple script or write out your notes in bullet point form next to your slides, this will work wonders to create a better impression. It will also give you confidence and will leave people with a positive experience of who you are.

As you have learned by now, your voice reveals a lot about you and makes a big difference in the way you are perceived.

Record your voice to track your progress

Want to test it out? Simply record yourself speaking on a topic before and after scripting. You will be amazed at what you hear when you play back the two different recordings.

The best way to track your on-going progress is to record yourself. Simply commit to improving one presentation at a time.

Caution

Most people find it hard to listen to the sound of their own voice. The quality of the way you sound will only be as good as the quality of your audio recording device, so don't judge yourself too harshly.

Secret 32
YOUR ATTITUDE AND ACTIONS SPEAK MUCH LOUDER THAN WORDS

Leaders are defined by their capacity to lead effectively, and actions speak louder than words. People are constantly making decisions about you based on the way you look, sound and move.

Your physiology affects how you are perceived and has a lot to do with the impressions people hold of you. Physiology includes your breathing, gestures, body language, the way you walk, sit and stand, your posture and presence, and even what your eyes and face are doing.

Merriam Webster's dictionary defines the word 'presence' in several ways. Among the definitions are:

- One that is present
- The bearing, carriage, or air of a person
- A noteworthy quality of poise and effectiveness

There are many books written on the topic of presence, and many health professionals can improve your physical stature. However, here are some practical tips to perk up your posture and put your best voice forward:

- Stand up straight and tall with your feet about shoulder width apart.
- Chest raised, heart forward, shoulders back, relaxed and down.
- Hold your head level with your chin parallel to the ground, not tipped up or down.
- Distribute your weight evenly between your feet.
- Be aware of your centre of gravity. Be centred whether still or moving.

With good posture and diaphragmatic breathing, your chest and shoulders shouldn't move much when you breathe. Your stomach should simply go out when you inhale and in when you exhale, as we discussed in secret 30.

Eliminating ineffective gestures

There is a lot that I could say about gestures. Most people's bad habits go away quickly when they are connected to and are visualising the meaning of their words and ideas.

However, there are a few things I'd like to caution you about:

1. Pointing at people with one finger when you speak can alienate your audience.

    When most people use pointing gestures, it's to show conviction of thought. However, in some instances a finger-pointing gesture is perceived culturally inappropriate. Speakers using finger-pointing gestures are also considered to be lying, or they can look like they feel cornered and need to defend themselves. If possible, don't use a one-finger pointing gesture to emphasise. Use your entire hand instead.

2. When you use identical or parallel gestures with both hands at the same time, people usually perceive you as uncomfortable.

    It's so important that you are natural when you speak. The right side of your brain controls your left side, and the left side of your brain controls the right side. As a result, in normal conversation, our hands normally move independently of each other.

    If you look uncomfortable, people will subconsciously be uneasy with you, which means that in most cases they don't want to look at or listen to you for very long.

    There is no need to over gesture. If you don't know what to do with your hands and arms, simply drop them at your sides.

The whole point of making sure your words sound like what they mean is to put more personality, emotion and passion into your voice. When you are really comfortable with your body and connected to the words you say, your gestures will naturally be in alignment with your images and with practice will become second nature.

3. Do not walk backwards when you speak, or shift your weight repeatedly from side to side. Both habits make you seem tentative.

    Even if you are excited about your presentation or making a point, moving backwards tends to weaken you in front of an audience. The forward backward, forward backward repeated movement when speaking is also very distracting.

    Another form of distracting movement is shifting your weight from side to side. What happens is that people will stop paying attention to what you are saying and merely watch you move back and forth.

    If you want to move when you speak, by all means do. If you move for a purpose or with intent as a result of being connected to what you are saying, you will look natural. Most people get into the forward and back or side-to-side stepping habit because they really want to move but don't think they should be moving. Give yourself permission to use the whole room and walk around during your presentation if you like. You will appear in command and demonstrate confidence.

Communicating with intention

To embody a strong leadership presence, you must communicate with intention and walk your talk. For example, if you want the people you are leading to be more confident about moving forward, you need to appear more confident yourself. Everything about you has to represent confidence.

To appear more confident, walk with excellent posture. Your chest will be up, your shoulders back and down yet relaxed, your head held high, and your chin in a natural position. Have a look of confidence in your eyes. Focus and walk directly to where you are going with a confident, energetic stride that communicates to people around you that you are in control. Confident people are even more attractive when they are warm to others, and they naturally smile when making appropriate eye contact.

Hot Tip

One of the fastest ways to improve your confidence and look like a leader is by employing a professional image consultant.

The way you dress also has a lot to do with how others perceive you. For example, if you want to be a CEO, ask yourself, "Would a CEO or Chairman of the Board wear this to work?" If the answer is yes, you are on the right track. If you come up with a no answer, or if you are unsure, you may need to re-think your wardrobe.

Hot Tip

The easiest way to lead with heart is to speak from your heart.

I'm not advocating making yourself vulnerable to others in the business battlefield. However, true confidence communicates that you are secure enough with yourself that you don't need to be overly guarded. Authentic leadership is a delicate balance between your heart and your head, as well as your humanity and your expertise.

Checklist for developing the voice of a leader

1. Manage your energy levels with simple stress-reducing exercises. When in doubt, shake it out!

2. Do neck and shoulder exercises to release built up tension throughout the day whenever you need to, especially if you drive or work on a computer.

3. Breathe fully at all times. Your breath is your fuel for powerful speaking.

4. Warm up your voice and body before every important presentation.

5. Direct your sound by visualising your voice soaring on an arc.

6. Read out loud to practise bringing your words to life.

7. Visualise and embody your key words for maximum impact.

8. Stand up to get more energy and expression in your voice on an important call.

9. Script important calls or presentations to reduce verbal fillers and sound more articulate and confident.

10. Walk your talk. Your attitude and actions speak much louder than words.

CHAPTER 9

GET AHEAD WITH GLOBAL ENGLISH

How to speak English clearly and effectively
in international settings

by **Heather Hansen**
Director and Lead Trainer
Hansen Communication Lab Pte Ltd

Heather Hansen is a speech and language expert specialising in International English pronunciation. She is creator of the online training portal, *English Pronunciation Lab*, and author of the book *Powerful People Skills*, part of the ST Training Solutions Success Skills series.

Originally from the United States, Heather has lived and worked in six countries. She moved to Singapore in 2006, and since then has worked with a wide range of professionals from leading organisations in the region.

Heather is a speaker, trainer and author in communication and interpersonal skills. She runs customised in-house programmes as well as one-on-one training, helping professionals to speak more clearly, correctly and confidently.

Find out more about Heather at: **www.hansencommlab.com** and
www.englishpronunciationcourse.com
Contact Heather at **hh@hansencommlab.com**

ENGLISH HAS UNDENIABLY taken its place as the leading language of international commerce. One third of our planet speaks some level of English. In China alone, there are more people learning to speak English than there are native English speakers around the world. The statistics are overwhelming.

The English that is now spoken in international business differs greatly from the native English variety you learned to model in school. Both native and non-native speakers need to learn the new rules of speaking English appropriately in international settings.

In this section, speech and language expert Heather Hansen will show you how English is being used in international business, and how you can get ahead at work by speaking English clearly and confidently. She'll show you how to adapt your language to the people you speak with and how not to get lost in translation. She'll help you focus on the areas of spoken English that really matter so you can be understood by everyone, everywhere, every time.

Apply Heather's practical tips during meetings, teleconferences, presentations, office conversations or any other time you need to speak English clearly and effectively.

Secret 33
NO ONE OWNS THE ENGLISH LANGUAGE

Languages are funny things. They aren't even 'things', actually. They are living, breathing organisms, growing and changing every moment, depending on how people use them. English is a perfect example.

For centuries, English has been developing and changing. From what is considered to be its very beginnings in the 5th century AD, when Germanic tribes invaded Britain, to today, English has gone through many phases. From Old English, to Middle English, to Early Modern English and today's Modern English, we can hardly recognise the language as it was originally spoken and written.

After 16 centuries, you would think that the language would be done evolving! But even today, we see continued developments. New words are added to the dictionary every year as our world changes and technology advances. People use the language differently depending on location and background.

The way we use English differs so greatly that much of our identities are tied up with the language. English speakers can usually identify each other based on accent, vocabulary and usage. We know if someone is from the UK, the US, Australia, Canada, or even Singapore. Some of us can even pinpoint the exact city or region a person is from within those countries, simply based on how the person speaks.

So what happens when all of these different varieties of English meet? Modern business environments, coupled with amazing technological advances, have brought us all closer together. English is the primary language bridging team members from all over the world.

Who does English belong to?

It's hard to estimate just how many people in the world speak English. There is no official global data charting languages and their users. In a study by leading linguist, David Crystal, published in 2003, he estimates that there are about 400 million native-English speakers in the world, while 1.2 billion people speak English as a second or foreign language. Today's estimates now put non-native speakers closer to 1.4 billion.

Native speakers have long claimed ownership of the English language. We are, of course, the ones who introduced the world to English through our conquering, colonising, and missionary efforts. We speak the language naturally and fluently as a birthright. Lucky us! It's now up to the rest of the world to learn this fantastic language and speak it in a way that we can understand.

What a dangerous mentality! As much as native speakers like to believe that they have ownership over the English language, modern statistics prove that this certainly is not the case. In fact, David Graddol, teacher and researcher for the British Council, found that a huge 96 per cent of global conversations in English include at least one non-native English speaker.

And there lies the secret – no one *owns* the English language.

When you really understand the truth of this statement, you may notice your relationship with the English language change.

For native English speakers it means we need to take more responsibility for our communication. We can't assume that it's the non-native speaker's job to learn to speak English in a manner that is considered acceptable for us. We need to be open to variations in the way people sound and the grammar and words they use. We need to try harder to understand.

Non-native speakers, you aren't off the hook! Your perspective needs to change as well. You can no longer view native speakers as gate-keepers of the English language. Non-native speakers can teach English just as well as native speakers (and in many cases, much better). You can have confidence and pride in your foreign accent. There is no 'model' accent or variety of English. Assuming you are understood by others, the way you speak is just as valid as the way a native speaker speaks.

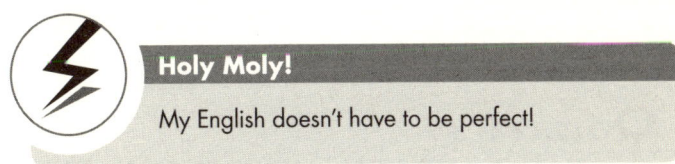

Holy Moly!

My English doesn't have to be perfect!

Your accent isn't your problem

You don't need to change your accent to be better understood. What you need to do is focus on speaking clearly, confidently and with pride in whichever accent you might have, because that accent is a big part of who you are!

Caution

Do not confuse accent and clarity. Your accent doesn't need to change. We (non-native and native speakers) simply need to put more effort into speaking clearly in international environments.

As the different varieties of English blend together, we are now seeing an international variety of English emerge. Linguists have been studying global English for over a decade, and are finding that important patterns emerge when we interact on an international level.

Proper grammar and pronunciation are not as important as they used to be. It doesn't matter so much how the message is articulated as long as the message is understood. Some would argue that this is a negative and that everyone should speak 'properly'. On the other hand, in our fast-paced business environments, isn't it more important that business gets done?

There are ways that we can ensure that our messages are understood by everyone, everywhere, every time, even if the English we use isn't perfect. Let's take a closer look at these important secrets of successful international communication.

Secret 34
NATIVE AND NON-NATIVE ENGLISH SPEAKERS HEAR ENGLISH DIFFERENTLY

Most of my clients are confused when they come to me seeking help to change the way they speak. They can't understand why some people can understand them perfectly, while others can't seem to understand a word they say. They tell me that non-native speakers from the Asian region understand them very well, but native speakers always have trouble. Non-native speakers from Europe, depending on where they are from, can also have difficulty. How can there be such a big difference?

First we need to know how people hear and understand languages. Language is a matter of conditioning. As we grow up, we learn from speakers around us – mainly our parents, teachers and friends, and also television, radio and other forms of media. Our ears become tuned to the variety (or varieties) of English speech we hear, as well as any other languages we come into contact with.

Growing up in northern California, I mostly heard the common accent and variety of that region. When I went off to University (also in northern California) and became friends with kids from southern California and other parts of the US, we would joke about the differences in slang and the pronunciation of some words. I can even remember some heated debates about whether soft drinks should be called 'soda' or 'pop'.

As I began to travel the world, I had more contact with British dialects of English, Australian and Canadian English, plus all different non-native accents in English. Some varieties were easier for me to understand than others because they were similar to the sounds of my native dialect. Others were so different that I could hardly understand them.

When I studied abroad, I noticed that non-native speakers could often understand each other better than I could. How could that be when I was the native speaker?

I didn't know (and in fact, the linguistic evidence was just being gathered at that time) that native and non-native English speakers hear the language differently. Certain parts of the language that are very important for native speakers don't carry any importance for non-native speakers. This is why you can speak to some people and have no problem at all, but others still won't understand you.

The first person to begin documenting this was a Frenchman living in Japan and working for IBM, Jean-Paul Nerrière. He began studying the way non-native speakers communicated, and eventually developed a new form of English called 'Globish' (pronounced as 'Globe-ish'). This 'new' language is a simplified version of English, and includes exceptions to what we consider 'proper' grammar rules and pronunciation. The most important feature of

Globish is its vocabulary list of 1,500 base words, from which an additional 5,000 words can be built. Globish begs the speaker to speak simply, using words everyone can understand.

Why native speakers don't understand

1. Most native speakers grow up hearing only native English

To most non-native speakers, what seems to be such a huge advantage can actually be why native speakers have more trouble internationally. Of course there are exceptions, but most of us grow up hearing only our own dialect of English, plus a commonly accepted 'standard' variety used in various media. This is how our ears have been tuned. When the day comes that we meet different varieties of English, we aren't very prepared for how they sound.

Non-native speakers, on the other hand, often tune their ears to several varieties of English. English language courses are now making students aware of both British and American English. For learners in international settings, they get to hear their classmates' accents in English as well. For students growing up in countries where English is an official language (but not necessarily a native one), they hear their own country's version of English along with international varieties in the media.

Holy Moly!

Non-native English speakers actually have a better ear for English than native speakers!

2. Native speakers communicate with the nuances of stress and intonation

In addition to the actual words used, native speaking listeners subconsciously focus on the stress and intonation of those words to fully understand a speaker's overall meaning. Although word stress is still a grey area in linguistic research, studies are beginning to show that word stress is more important to native speakers than non-native ones.

Speaking from my own experience, I'd have to agree. Living in Singapore, my biggest problem understanding locals has been the differences in word stress. Someone once told me to write something in my 'ca-LEN-dar', and I honestly had to write out the sounds in my head and read the word back to myself before I could figure out what was being said.

My non-native speaking husband, on the other hand, came home from work just a few short months after moving here, telling me he had to write a couple of 'pur-CHASE' orders that evening. He had no problem understanding the local English and adopting it himself.

Why non-native speakers don't understand

1. Their English proficiency may not be high enough

The obvious reason why some non-native speakers won't understand you is that their level of English is too low. If you know that a person has very limited English, you can accommodate them by simplifying your vocabulary and using very basic grammatical constructions.

2. You speak too quickly

Many non-native speakers have not reached a level of English proficiency that does not require them to translate in and out of their native tongue. I've met many people here in Singapore who have grown up with English in school, but still translate back to their native languages when they communicate. If you speak slowly and group your messages together in easily digestible chunks, you will be much easier to understand.

3. You use idioms or culture-specific analogies

Native speakers use idioms and culture-specific analogies ('miss the boat', 'touch base', 'home run', 'shake a leg', etc.) without thinking. We often don't even know the history behind these phrases or why we say them. They're just things we say! It's unreasonable to assume that non-native speakers understand these hundreds of phrases, many of which are specific to the native speaker's country of origin or national sports. Even among native speakers, many words and phrases can have a completely different meaning in other native-speaking countries!

Hot Tip

Always consider the linguistic background of your listener. If the person is a native speaker, pay attention to the way you stress your words and speak as clearly as you can. If the person is a non-native speaker, watch your pace and choice of vocabulary. The goal of communication, after all, is not only to speak, but to also be understood!

Secret 35
THERE ARE ONLY THREE AREAS OF SPEECH THAT REALLY MATTER

To communicate well in international settings, there are only three areas of your speech that you need to master: almost all consonant sounds, the difference between long and short vowels, and how you group your messages into chunks. Let's take a look at each of these areas in turn.

Consonant sounds

If you want your words to sound crisp and clear, you need to make sure that each of your consonant sounds is pronounced correctly. There are a number of sounds that are commonly confused. The first group of sounds are voiced and unvoiced pairs.

These pairs of sounds are produced in the same way, i.e. your lips, tongue and jaw are in the same position. The only difference in their production is whether or not you use your voice.

Voiced	Unvoiced
D (duck)	T (tuck)
B (bop)	P (pop)
Z (buzz)	S (bus)
G (bag)	K (back)
V (very)	F (fairy)
J (junk)	CH (chunk)
ZH (confusion)	SH (Confucian)

Your Turn

There are two great ways you can *feel* the difference between voiced and unvoiced consonants.

1. Try reading the words above with two fingers covering the front of your neck over your larynx (voice box). Do you feel the vibration when you say the voiced sounds? You shouldn't feel any vibration when you make unvoiced sounds.

2. Place the palm of your hand a couple inches away from your mouth. When you say the unvoiced sounds P, F and K, for example, you will feel a lot of air on your palm. Compare this to when you make the B, V and G sounds.

Depending on your native language, there may be other sounds you find difficult. If you don't have an English sound in your native language, you will change the sound to the closest sound you know in your own language.

Asians are known for having difficulty with the R and L sounds, whereas Indian English speakers and many Germanic language speakers will have trouble with W and V. Also commonly confused are the sounds M, N and NG. In the next secret I'll be sharing with you some ways that you can practise your pronunciation and begin distinguishing between these challenging sounds.

The careful reader might be wondering why I haven't mentioned the terrible TH sound. This sound is hard for just about every non-native speaker to produce. The good news is, studies have shown that an inaccurate pronunciation of TH does not stop a listener (native or non-native) from understanding you. This does *not* mean that your constant mispronunciation of TH as D, T, S, Z, or F won't totally annoy a native speaker, because for many it will, but they should still be able to understand what you're trying to say.

Short and long vowels

Vowel sounds are made up of two elements: their quality and their quantity. Vowel quality refers to the way a certain vowel sounds. For example, think about how the *'i'* is pronounced in the word 'sit' versus how the *'ea'* is pronounced in the word 'seat'. The quality of the vowels is different; they have different sounds.

The quality of your vowels isn't so important in international communication as long as you are consistent. If I use the short *'i'* in 'sit', I should also have a short *'i'* in 'pit', 'mit' and 'kit'. My listener will quickly tune their ear to my vowels and should be able to understand me easily.

However, even if you're being consistent with the quality of your vowels, you could still run into some trouble if your production of a certain vowel sound overlaps with the pronunciation of a different vowel. Your sounds still need to be unique (just like the consonant sounds).

The quantity of a vowel refers to the length of the sound. You may not have noticed, but we sometimes lengthen vowel sounds in order to make neighbouring consonant sounds clearer.

For example, if a word ends with a voiced sound (D, B or Z, for example), we will stretch out the vowel that comes before it. This is how we can distinguish whether the final sound is voiced or unvoiced. Compare the pronunciations of these words. You should be stretching out the vowel sound before the voiced consonant endings (the first words in the pairs), while the vowels followed by unvoiced sounds are short and crisp.

cab - cap   *mad - mat*   *eyes - ice*

bed - bet   *advise - advice*   *hob - hop*

Caution

Inaccurate pronunciations of vowel sounds can lead to very embarrassing situations. Consider the ramifications if you were to pronounce the long 'ee's in these two words as short 'i's:

BEACH   SHEET

Please sit in your sit and fasten your sit belt.

Chunking your messages into logical thought groups

The final way you can ensure that your message is always understood is to group your words into smaller chunks of information, separated by pauses or a change in tone. If you speak in one long, uninterrupted stream, it is harder for the listener to understand your meaning and figure out which parts of your message are the most important.

Consider this paragraph:

> "Last year was a record-breaking year for our company.
> Our profits were higher than ever before, and I'm happy
> to announce that we have continued this growth into the
> first quarter of this year. The success of this company
> would not be possible without the dedication and
> commitment of all of you. For that I thank you."

This important message grows in feeling and becomes easier to understand when we group the information into smaller thought groups and emphasise important words. There is no right or wrong way of doing this, so don't worry if you read the paragraph differently. Depending on what you feel is most important in your message, you might choose to emphasise different parts by grouping the text another way. Here is how I would read this text (with emphasised words in capitals):

> "Last year // was a RECORD-BREAKING year // for our
> company. Our profits // were HIGHER than EVER before,//
> and I'm HAPPY to announce // that we have CONTINUED
> this growth // into the first quarter // of this year. // The
> SUCCESS of this company // would NOT be possible //
> without the DEDICATION // and COMMITMENT // of all of
> YOU.// For THAT // I THANK you."

Chunking your message, instead of just speeding through it, serves two purposes. It allows your listener to digest what you've said, and you can direct your listener's attention to the most important parts of your message.

Secret 36
IMPROVING YOUR SPEECH CAN BE FUN AND FULFILLING

There are plenty of reasons not to spend time working on your speech. I regularly hear the excuses from my clients. "I just don't have time to focus on this," "I'm too old to change anything anyway," and, "The misunderstandings I have aren't that bad" are pretty common arguments.

What many people forget is that there are fun and interesting ways to raise your awareness about how you and the people around you sound. You can also make progress with your pronunciation in as little as 15 minutes each day. In fact, I suggest you don't practise in intervals longer than 15 minutes, because as your tongue gets tired, you will only become more frustrated with yourself.

Try these three fun and easy ways to improve your pronunciation and you won't even realise that you're 'practising'!

1. Watch more television

Yes, I'm really telling you to become a couch potato! The first step to improving your pronunciation is training your ear to hear the difference between different sounds. If you can't hear the difference in length between the vowel sound in 'cap' and the vowel sound in 'cab', you will have a very tough time producing the words correctly on your own.

As you watch TV, be sure that you pay very close attention to how words are pronounced, not only individually, but also when they are strung together in sentences. Try watching shows from different countries and see if you can pick up on some of the pronunciation differences between different varieties of English. If you can read English sub-titles while you watch and listen, it will be even more helpful.

2. Get tongue-tied

Tongue twisters are a fun and challenging way to practise pronunciation and increase the clarity of your speech. It may just seem like play, but many stage actors, speakers and voice-over artists will agree that tongue twisters are powerful tools for warming up the muscles used for speech!

Your Turn

Here are just a few examples you can try. Practise the ones with sounds that are hard for you to pronounce. Start slowly, then gradually speed up and add repetitions when you think you're ready.

I slit the sheet, the sheet I slit, and on the slitted sheet I sit.

Red lorry, yellow lorry, red lorry, yellow lorry.

The very weary wife invited her five friends to make very varied wishes in her lucky wishing well.

Thank the other three brothers on their father's mother's brother's side.

Tim, the thin twin tinsmith.

You can find some great tongue twisters in Craig Staley's Tongue Twister Database:
http://sites.google.com/site/tonguetwisterdatabase/home

3. Practise minimal pairs

Minimal pairs are words that are identical except for the one problem sound you are focused on practising. For example, if you have trouble with the sounds R and L you might practise reading a list of words like read/lead, road/load, fry/fly, fright/flight, crutch/clutch and so on. Slowly say these words out loud, really focusing on the sounds and the way you use your voice. Here are some helpful hints for practising minimal pairs:

Say the words in a mirror. Exaggerate your facial expressions. Watch your tongue, lips and jaw, and note the differences when you make the sounds. Don't worry if you look a little strange at first! As your mouth learns how to make the sounds correctly, you won't have to make such weird faces to produce the correct sound.

Record yourself saying the pairs. Listen to the recording and see if you can hear a difference between how you pronounce the words.

Choose one word from each pair and say them out loud to a friend. Have your friend write down the words he/she hears. See if your friend heard the words you were trying to say. (You can also do this on your own by noting the words you choose as you record yourself saying them. Listen to the recording a few days later and write down the words you hear. Compare your list to the list of words you recorded.)

If you need help coming up with lists of minimal pairs, linguist John Higgins has listed hundreds of pairs in this database: http://myweb. tiscali.co.uk/wordscape/wordlist/.

Hot Tip

Practise your pronunciation in front of a mirror. Watch how your lips, cheeks, tongue and jaw change when you make different sounds.

Taking time to practise your pronunciation is vital if you are to reach your goal of improving the clarity of your speech. Be patient with yourself! This process takes time, but the pay-offs will definitely be worth it.

Hot Tip

If you want help with your pronunciation, join my free international pronunciation program at: www.englishpronunciationcourse.com.

Checklist for getting ahead with global English

1. Remember that every variety of English is equally valid — no one owns the English language.

2. Put just as much effort into understanding others as you do in speaking to others.

3. Don't change your accent, but speak as clearly as you can in international settings.

4. Watch your word stress when you speak with native English speakers.

5. Use common words and simple structures when you speak to people with lower levels of English proficiency.

6. Make sure your consonant sounds are clear.

7. Learn how to stretch out vowel sounds before voiced consonant endings.

8. Group your messages into chunks so they are easier for your audience to understand.

9. Spend time practising your speech with minimal pairs, tongue twisters and by listening more carefully to the TV and radio.

10. Speak up with clarity and confidence!

SECTION 4

Your Communication and Interpersonal Skills

CHAPTER 10

BUILDING GREAT RELATIONSHIPS
How to develop great relationships both in person and in writing

by **Shirley Taylor**
Founder and CEO
ST Training Solutions Pte Ltd

Shirley Taylor has established herself as a leading authority in modern business writing and communication skills. She is author of 12 successful books on communication skills, including the international bestseller, *Model Business Letters, Emails and Other Business Documents*, which has sold half a million copies worldwide and has been translated into numerous languages. The seventh edition of this popular book will be published in May 2012. Shirley also spearheaded the ST Training Solutions Success Skills series of books, which are packed with essential tools and strategies to make you more effective and successful at work. There are currently nine books in this successful series, many of which have been translated into different languages.

Shirley was born in the UK, and has lived and worked in Singapore, Bahrain and Canada. She has almost 30 years' experience in teaching and training. After making Singapore her home in 2002, Shirley established her own company in 2006. ST Training Solutions Pte Ltd has quickly become highly regarded for providing a wide range of quality training programmes specialising in communication skills, conducted by many international trainers.

Shirley is an author, speaker and trainer. She conducts her own successful public workshops and in-house corporate training on business writing, email, communication and secretarial skills.

Shirley is also a popular speaker at international conferences, and is well-known for making all her speaking and training highly engaging, interactive and fun.

Shirley Taylor is current APSS President (2011–12) as well as a member of the Global Speakers Network.

Find out more about Shirley at: **www.shirleytaylortraining.com** and **www.stsuccessskills.com**
Contact Shirley at: **shirley@shirleytaylortraining.com**

HAVE YOU NOTICED that many people seem unable to communicate face to face with colleagues, let alone with employers or clients? They are more comfortable sending text messages or sending a message on Facebook than they are speaking. Some people lack confidence to speak up when communicating, while others are so overconfident that they don't know how to listen.

Successful people don't hide behind their mobile phones or computers. Successful people understand that all outcomes are created by and through interactions with others. They know that if they are to build a foundation for success, both professionally and personally, they need to develop strong relationships. Personal interaction is at the very heart of developing truly effective relationships.

In this section, Shirley Taylor will share some simple yet powerful tools for helping you to build better relationships with bosses, colleagues, clients and friends. You will be able to use these skills immediately to create a more supportive and co-operative working environment, which in turn will increase productivity and bring an improved sense of professional well-being.

Shirley will also help you with your writing skills. You'll learn the golden rules of writing and structuring messages so you get your point across effectively and get the right results. You'll learn how important it is to use email to develop relationships and take them forwards instead of back.

By building strong relationships, you will not only gain the competitive edge in today's workplace, you will reap the rewards and the success that these changes can bring.

⚷ *Secret 37*
COMFORTABLE COMMUNICATION EQUALS BETTER RELATIONSHIPS

After training communication skills for almost 30 years, I am noticing more and more that successful people develop great relationships and use them to build a foundation for success. But how? Before we determine this, let's look at why communication is so crucial.

Communication is at the heart of every organisation. Everything you do in the workplace results from communication. Therefore good reading, writing, speaking and listening skills are essential if tasks are going to be completed and goals achieved. As you develop your career you will find various reasons why successful communication skills are important to you. For example:

- **To secure an interview.** You will need good communication skills to make sure your application letter is read and acted upon.

- **To get a job.** You will need to communicate well during your interview if you are to sell yourself and get the job you want.

- **To do your job well.** You will need to request information, discuss problems, give instructions, work in teams, interact with colleagues and clients.

- **To gain co-operation.** If you are to work well in your team, good human relations skills are essential.

- **To persuade and influence others.** Much of our communication at work will involve persuading others or influencing them in some way.

- **To work well across cultures.** As most workplaces are becoming more global, there are many factors to consider if you are to communicate well in such a diverse environment.

Your effectiveness at work will largely depend on how much people want to interact and connect with you. The route to professional effectiveness is not only paved with knowledge and experience, but also with relationships. If people avoid you, it will be very difficult to do your job. If you are to make successful connections — connections you can count on when you have new ideas and goals — you need to develop great working relationships.

Holy Moly!

It doesn't matter how many qualifications or degrees I get. Unless I can develop great relationships, my success will be severely limited.

Comfortable communication

Have you ever been afraid at work — afraid to ask a question or afraid to make a suggestion? Even if you are a confident person, perhaps you had a feeling more of hesitation or worry. No matter what you call it, chances are your answer is yes. At some time or another, most of us have been fearful or hesitant to offer a suggestion or new idea at work. It can also be difficult to ask for guidance, help, or even time off.

Now consider this: Have you ever been afraid to ask a question or make a suggestion with your family or friends? You probably answered "no," or at least "not as often." The main reason for this is that you almost certainly have better relationships with your family and friends than you do with co-workers and others at the office. You've been around your friends and family longer, and you know their speech patterns, tones, style of joking, and so on. As a result, you are more comfortable and enjoy better relationships with them.

Now think about what it would be like if you could have that same kind of comfortable communication with your office mates. If better communication equals better relationships at home, wouldn't the same hold true for work? Of course it would! Ensuring that you convey your messages clearly and coherently will help make sure you are not misunderstood. This should naturally result in better communication all around. In turn, this will improve relationships significantly.

Remember, though, that the opposite holds true as well. Communication is a two-way street, and good listening skills are half — if not more — of good communication. You don't want to end up misunderstanding someone because you weren't really listening to what they were saying. Better communication results in better relationships because it puts everyone on the same track. Fewer misunderstandings happen when you are clear, when you provide specific details, and when you are all practising effective listening skills.

Reaping the benefits of better relationships

Once you start developing better relationships through better communication, you'll benefit in several ways:

- You'll feel more comfortable at work, more accepted. Most of us want to feel like a valued and valuable part of a group, a member of something.

- With good communication skills, you'll feel like you belong, like you are part of the office community.

- You won't have that fear of stepping forward as much, because as your comfort level increases your professional relationships will strengthen.

- Feeling more comfortable at work will make you feel better about your contributions to the office workload in general. There's nothing like the feeling you get from being a trusted and effective team member.

- You will find you can make suggestions for changing procedures, or even changing a product, without worrying about what others might think.

- Better yet, since you'll feel better about being at work and being around your co-workers and bosses, your morale will improve.

- Improved morale will help you be more productive.

- You won't have that fear of stepping forward as much because you know your co-workers understand you better. You don't need to become friends with everyone; you just need to improve the working relationship you have with them so that working together becomes much more enjoyable for everyone involved.

Improved morale benefits everyone

Good communication is a win/win situation for everyone in the office. Once you improve working relationships with co-workers, you will automatically feel better and work harder. Your co-workers will be happy because there are fewer chances for misunderstandings, and now they know you just a bit better. Your boss will be happy because better communication in the office has resulted in happier workers who are more productive.

So once relationships in the office have improved, do you think you will be as fearful or hesitant next time there is something on your mind? On the contrary, you'll be eager to make that suggestion or ask that question because you'll know that others are willing to listen to you. You'll know they aren't going to laugh at you or roll their eyes, even if you come up with an off-the-cuff comment. They're going to give you the respect you deserve. You'll increase your efficiency and productivity because people won't misunderstand you and you won't misunderstand others.

Now doesn't that sound like a great way to work?

Secret 38
SUCCESSFUL PEOPLE BUILD A FOUNDATION FOR SUCCESS ON GREAT RELATIONSHIPS

Every day we interact with dozens of people, whether it's on the phone, face-to-face, along the corridor, in the lift, in group discussions, meetings, or of course in writing. All outcomes are determined as a result of interactions with others. If people avoid you, it will be impossible to get work done. Your professional effectiveness at work will largely, therefore, depend on how much people are willing to interact with you.

Successful people consider relationships not as a means to an end, ie to get a job done. They understand that strong relationships create loyalty, build trust and instil confidence, and are ultimately the key to success.

Hot Tip

In any job or business, relationship building must be your most important objective. Quite simply, the quality of the relationship will determine the quality of the product or service.

Seven key factors to building great relationships

If you want to build better relationships, both at home and at work, here are seven key factors that I think you need to work on.

1. Be courteous

I see and hear of people who walk into the office each morning with their eyes down, headphones in their ears. They don't even glance at others, let alone offer a simple, "Good morning!" Others can be downright abrupt and disrespectful to colleagues and subordinates. It's no excuse to justify this by complaining of pressures of work. We are all busy! Everyone has a right to work in a cordial environment, and work flows more smoothly when the atmosphere and the people in it are pleasant. Courtesy is the oil that keeps the engine of any relationship running smoothly.

2. Find common interests

How many people in your office do you really know? How many times do you enter the lift with the same person yet never even acknowledge them? Do you walk past co-workers' desks and never nod your head or say "hi"? What a sad way to work. If you make an effort to get to know your colleagues and clients, you can then build on commonalities. For example, comment on a photo or an object on a colleague's desk. You may find you have a story to share, or you may learn something new that you can discuss. Making an effort to gain eye contact, spark up a conversation, smile, even just nod and say "hello" is also a much more enjoyable and rewarding way to spend your day.

3. Build credibility

Very often at work you will have to convince people of your point of view. You need credibility for this. You will gain a certain amount of credibility from your experience. However, if you are to build strong connections, you need to gain respect, create trust, and build rapport. You can do this through being credible. Do you turn up for meetings and share your knowledge? Do you keep others informed? Do you do what you said you would do in a timely manner? Are you honest? Credibility comes with transparency, engagement, and honest hard work.

4. Make others feel important

I'm often surprised that some people have a lot of trouble acknowledging good work, or saying a simple "thank you" for a job well done. Feeling unimportant or unappreciated is extremely de-motivating. If you are a manager, make an effort to talk to your staff about something other than business from time to time. Ask them about their families, their upcoming holiday, their weekend. Listen to them. Show you are approachable. By doing this you will win their respect, and at the same time you'll learn more about your staff and pick up useful information that will help you guide and motivate them. One of the most fundamental rules of developing relationships is to respect other people's feelings. We all like to be recognised and appreciated. If you want to make friends and enhance your reputation as a great communicator, learn how to make others feel important.

5. Show humility

There's nothing worse than someone who brags and boasts about themselves, with their nose in the air and an air of arrogance. These people will have others running away from them rather than wanting to get closer. Humility involves maintaining our pride about who we are and about our achievements, but without arrogance. Humility means having a quiet confidence and being content to let others discover your talents without having to brag about them. Interestingly, very often the higher people rise and the more accomplishments they have, the higher their humility index.

Holy Moly!

If I want to improve my relationships, I must practise humility. It's a strength, not a weakness.

6. Listen actively

Take an interest in other people by listening to them. You may learn some useful information that you can use to create value in the future. Chat to a client about his family. Find out your boss's likes and dislikes. You never know when this information may be useful. When I was a secretary I heard the boss's wife commenting to someone on how she liked a certain perfume, so when it came to her birthday and the boss didn't know what to get her, guess what I suggested? Flatter someone today by getting to know them better through active listening.

7. Be empathic

Empathy is all about getting to know people and understanding how they feel. The need to be understood is one of the highest human needs, but many people don't care or just don't make an effort to find out how we really feel. In my Communication workshops, I find people have a lot of difficulty with empathy or expressing real feelings. I think this is a shame. Just imagine the difference you can make if you really get to know people and understand how they feel. It could really set you apart from the rest, and you would start giving great value that many others don't give.

Your Turn

Think about one of your best relationships at work. Why does it work so well? Why is it successful? Is it because of one (or more) of these seven factors?

Most people would agree that their satisfaction at work is largely derived from the way they, their colleagues and their clients communicate. As with any other endeavour, the more you put into it, the more you'll get back. When you start using these basic success tools for making great connections, you will see the massive rewards they can bring, both personally and professionally.

Secret 39
TO EARN TRUST AND CONFIDENCE, YOU NEED TO WRITE WELL

When you are talking to someone face-to-face, you have lots of visual clues to help you — your tone of voice, gestures, movements and eye contact. It may not be fair, but in the everyday world you are judged and influenced by all these criteria, and more — even your occupation, status, height, dress and the way you look. And like it or not, it's through the way you speak and look that you earn trust and confidence.

So, with none of these visual cues present in written communication, how do you earn trust and confidence when you write letters, reports, email messages, or even social media updates? In written communication you have to find other ways to evaluate the person who is speaking (writing). People do that by looking at 'style'.

How can you improve your 'style'?

Style in written communication does not mean wearing a designer suit to do all your most important writing. Style means several things, including:

- Write appropriately for your audience. You would choose different words when texting your friend than you would in a text to your boss. Abbreviations and acronyms may be fine when instant messaging friends, but they will not give a good impression if prospective employers see a lot of this on your Facebook wall. Writing appropriately for your audience is vital, whether it's a text, an email or a social media post.

- Structure your message logically, with an introduction to set the scene, then all the details in a logical order, then a conclusion and action section telling the reader what you want them to do and how to reply, then finally a close (and I don't mean "Thanks and Regards", but that's a very different issue!)

- Pay attention to proper spelling and punctuation, good sentence construction instead of non-sentences, full spellings instead of abbreviations suitable only for sms. When you've finished your message, read it out loud as though you are speaking. This will help you get all the punctuation in the right place.

- Make your communication look visually-attractive by leaving a line space between paragraphs, using numbered points or bullets, and being consistent.

- Write in a natural style as though you are having a conversation with the reader. Many people think they have to write in a completely different style to how they speak, using age-old clichés and frequently-used jargon. This will not help the reader get to know the real you, and will not set you apart from everyone else. Put your personality into your writing and help to build relationships instead of break them.

Caution

Just because you are emailing a colleague instead of a client, it doesn't mean you can rush out the message quickly without bothering to proofread. Everyone is busy. Show some respect for your colleagues by making internal messages clear and concise, and by proofreading carefully before you hit 'send'.

I recently did a follow-up workshop for a client where I had run my two-day business writing workshop two months earlier. I asked the participants what had changed since we met. They told me proudly:

- We get straight to the point, using everyday language instead of beating about the bush with old-fashioned, useless phrases.

- Our writing process is more focussed from using your four-point plan. That means our messages are structured more logically so the reader can clearly see the action needed.

- We avoid the passive phrases we used to write like 'Please be advised', 'Please be reminded', 'Your co-operation is appreciated'. Now we use the active voice, we get straight to the point, and we still retain courtesy.

- We seem more approachable because our language is less formal and more friendly, as if we are having a conversation. That makes us feel closer to our readers, and vice versa.

What are the benefits of stylish writing?

These participants told me that paying attention to how they write has saved their time and increased efficiency. They felt that being more organised in their writing has helped to enhance understanding, avoid miscommunication, and increase their professional image. In particular they felt relationships had improved, and there was much better rapport with both internal and external customers. How great can that be? It could happen to you too.

What are the consequences?

Now this is the big question. As a result of changing the way you write, what about the upshot, the end result? Here are some of the points that the same participants shared:

- The replies they received were more effective and more positive.

- Requests were confirmed and issues resolved more promptly.

- Productivity and efficiency were enhanced, with both time and cost savings.

- They felt less frustration and more satisfaction.

- External customers had complimented some of them on the change in their writing, commenting that it was more friendly and simple.

- There was less 'ding-dong', or going back and forth to clarify.

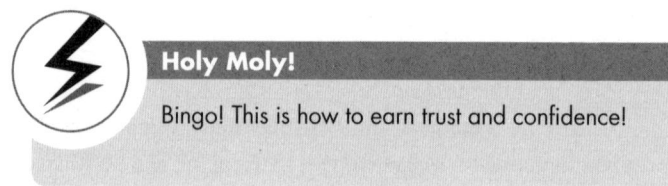

Holy Moly!

Bingo! This is how to earn trust and confidence!

The final point about the 'ding-dong' made me laugh. It's something I hear regularly. How often have you received an email that has been written carelessly, and you have to reply asking questions to clarify? The answer you receive may clarify some issues, but then it raises other queries. Eventually you get the job done, but look at all the wasted time – all the 'ding-dong'.

We all grumble about email overload, but how much of it is self-inflicted? Are we making rods for our own backs because of carelessness and sloppiness in the first place? Surely time spent making sure your message is right in the first place will be time saved cleaning up the mess later.

Effective, stylish writing gives a professional impression of you and your organisation

Effective writing helps to get things done, and it gets the right results. Writing effectively is perhaps the most demanding work we do. If you learn to pay attention to all the various aspects of style in your writing, you will increase the value of what you write, earn the respect of your readers, achieve better results, and you will have a distinct advantage in today's e-world.

Secret 40
IF YOU CAN SAY IT, YOU CAN WRITE IT

Take a look around your workplace. Do the leaders in your organisation write effectively and powerfully? Do good writers tend to get promoted? Do people tend to listen to good writers? Are good writers able to persuade or convince effectively?

More and more of our work today is undertaken through writing rather than in person or on the phone. As we are writing so much more, we depend on our writing skills to influence, persuade, encourage, collaborate, and to lead. However, how often do you notice people talking about the importance of good writing in your day-to-day work? Most people don't really notice the quality of the writing they read — they simply react positively, negatively, or not at all. If you have ever wondered if there's a better way to write your messages so they get better results, there is!

Here are three of the new rules for written communication:

1. If you can say it, you can write it

We connect with the world today largely through email, websites, blogs, texting, and social media. With all these channels we have only bare facts, without tone of voice, facial expressions, body language, or pauses. As we regularly use these means instead of talking, it makes sense to use writing that is as close as possible to spoken language. When you do this, you gain yourself a great advantage — you put your personality and individuality into your message. This will help you to stand out and make a greater connection with your reader.

Dear Sir, As spoken in our telecon, please find attached our latest catalogue for your reference and perusal. Thanking you in advance. Yours sincerely...

You wouldn't say it, so don't write it!

2. Write for today, not yesterday

Yesterday:

Please be advised that a meeting of the Annual Convention Committee will be held on 24 February (Thursday) at 9.30 AM. Approximately two hours will be required for the meeting and you are required to attend to report on progress made since the last meeting. Kindly advise me of your availability at your soonest.

Today:

I'd like to hold another meeting of the Annual Convention Committee on Tuesday 24 February from 9.30 to 11.30 AM. I hope you can attend to report on the great ideas you brought up at the last meeting. Please confirm if you can join us.

Yesterday's writing is passive and wordy, it sounds really dull, and it puts a distance between you and the reader. The way it is written also slows down understanding. Active voice is crisp, clear, transparent, and the personal context makes it more positive and interesting.

Caution

Poor writing damages reputations. Poor writing reflects badly on you and your organisation. As a result, business efficiency is lost, as are opportunities to connect and build relationships with clients, colleagues and collaborators.

3. Aim to build relationships with your writing

In writing, as readers can't see or hear you, people will judge you based on what you write and how you write it. In today's fast-paced, technology-crazy world, it's essential to come across as a human being. If you insist on using old-fashioned or redundant jargon ('Please be reminded', 'Kindly be advised', 'Please find attached herewith', 'above-mentioned', 'reference and perusal', etc) you will obscure the real meaning and will not be adding any personality of your own. Make your writing positive, stimulating and interesting, add some feeling and a personal touch. This will help people get to know the real person behind the message.

Holy Moly!

Using active voice is more conversational. It will bring me closer to my readers and will really help me to develop relationships.

Good writing makes a difference

Good writing is receiving increasing recognition as an essential business skill. It will give you a huge advantage in today's business world. Good writing can help you work more efficiently, build credibility, improve relationships, influence others, win more clients, and achieve your goals.

So take another look around your workplace. Look objectively at the messages you receive, and at the messages you send. Are they full of yesterday's jargon or today's conversational expressions? Will they help to enhance your professional reputation or ruin it? Will they help to build relationships or break them?

Give yourself an edge in this very competitive world by getting to grips with effective writing now, before it's too late!

Checklist for developing great relationships both in person and in writing

1. Have a clear goal in mind before trying to communicate your message to others.

2. Don't weaken your message by using the right words with the wrong tone. Your tone often determines whether listeners are open to you, or closed.

3. Be courteous, even under stress. This can make all the difference.

4. Take time to listen actively. It can make or break any relationship.

5. Use empathy. This will help you to build rapport and be more persuasive.

6. Treat other people in the way they wish to be treated, not necessarily how you wish to be treated. This shows respect and understanding.

7. Remember that improving communication is a work in progress, and you will benefit from continual refreshing and upgrading.

8. Don't let email be a replacement for communication — it is a tool for enhancing communication.

9. Keep your language simple and your sentences short, especially when emailing across cultures.

10. Write for today, instead of yesterday, by using modern language as if you are having a conversation.

CHAPTER 11

COMMUNICATION IN FOUR DIMENSIONS
Building authentic connection and well-being
from the inside out

by **Elisabetta Franzoso**
Director and Principal Trainer
InsideOutYou™ Coaching & Training

Communication expert, Elisabetta Franzoso, is a charismatic speaker, trainer and author. Her infectious and lively energy is matched with a multi-disciplinary background in somatic psychology, image consultancy, Emotional Quotient management, music therapy, Neuro-linguistic Programming (NLP) and creative movement and fitness. Elisabetta holds a Bachelors degree in Education from University of Pavia, Italy, and a Master degree in Psychological Counselling from University of South Australia. She was born in Italy and has lived in Singapore, Indonesia and Spain.

Through her extensive multi-cultural experiences, she has developed a unique way of presenting sensitive topics in a high-energy, thought-provoking in a non–judgmental way. Her interactive style and immediately applicable tips see clients invite her back repeatedly.

Elisabetta is an advocate for personal transformation from the inside out, and the author of the inspirational book *'Stella's Mum Gets Her Groove Back'* – a true story.

Communication in Four Dimensions is the result of her passionate pursuit in seeking an effective and holistic approach to communication.

Her public talks and workshops are testimony of her deep passion to motivate employees and leaders, unleashing their creative and emotional potential, and to empower men and women to achieve emotional well-being and happiness in life through self-responsibility and love.

Find out more about Elisabetta at: www.InsideOutYou.com and www.StellasMum.com

Contact Elisabetta at elisabetta@insideoutyou.com

TODAY WE CAN communicate with anyone, anytime and anywhere we want to. Communicating has never been easier. Ironically though, more communication doesn't mean better communication.

Building awareness about the way you communicate with your inner and outer world is going to be your secret to professional success. It is how you connect with yourself and others that ultimately determines the quality of your life.

When you authentically connect, you will relate to people in ways that increase your influence. As a result, your ability to lead, work as part of a team, and build healthy relationships increases. Your physical dimension connects with your emotional and intellectual dimensions, expressing your inner thoughts and feelings to others through verbal and non-verbal body language, behaviours and actions.

In this section, Elisabetta Franzoso will introduce the secrets for activating the four dimensions of your communication, share practical tools for transforming into a powerful communicator, be able to face difficult conversations, cope with conflicts, and win audiences globally.

Communication in four dimensions isn't a luxury. It's a basic tool for everyone. Used with finesse, it is the key to professional success and lasting well-being.

When you activate your body, you activate your mind.

Mind your intellect! It shapes your health and relationships.

When you manage your emotions, your well-being is assured.

When physical, intellectual and emotional dimensions are active, communication with yourself and others turns honest and effective.

⚷ Secret 41
WHEN YOU ACTIVATE YOUR BODY, YOU ACTIVATE YOUR MIND

Communication starts with your body. You communicate your internal thoughts and feelings to the world through your gestures, movements, eye contact, and physical contact like hand-shaking. The state of your health also has a great impact on the way your body expresses your internal self-talk through your physical behaviour. Your physical health is also a key element in communication: it greatly impacts the way your intrapersonal (internal) communication is expressed through your physical dimension. When you are not well physically, your inner self-talk can give way to confusion and doubt, inability to make decisions, and challenges when you must deliver a speech or a presentation. Your body language can reveal signs of distress, insecurity, and anxiety.

It is, therefore, priority number one that you get to know your body from the inside out and keep your energy in balance. You can do this by assessing your body on a daily, weekly and monthly basis. I'm not suggesting that you need to see the doctor every day. All you need is a simple checklist for building awareness about your physical condition. For example, you could ask yourself questions like these:

- How many hours did I sleep last night?
- Did I take a 15-minute power nap today? If not, why not?
- Did I eat in accordance with my nutrition plan today, eg three pieces of fruit, plenty of vegetables, and a balance of fibre, carbohydrates and proteins?
- Did I exercise, move, or stretch intensively for at least 15 to 20 minutes?
- Did I drink plenty of water (at least 8 glasses)?
- Did I spend at least two to 10 minutes in silence, meditating, praying, or just relaxing and listening to my body?

Your checklist may be longer depending on your personal goals. You may want to create your list with a friend or a well-being coach who can help evaluate it in reference to activation of energy in your body.

Hot Tip

A body that is healthy and vital houses a healthy mind!

If a daily checklist is too much trouble for you, then check on your body at least once a week, perhaps on Sundays. It doesn't take long to do a self-evaluation of your bodily needs and balance, and it can provide great insights. You can create the checklist on your computer and do it even when you are travelling or commuting to and from work. Don't forget to follow up with action steps for consistently activating energy in your body.

Understand when your body speaks your mind

A healthy body is the house of a healthy mind. The mind and body communicate constantly, and you can teach yourself to listen to and understand the messages that come from your internal mind through your body.

How does the body speak the needs and wants of the mind? It does this through physiological shifts and changes, diseases and misalignments, and healing and re-aligning your posture.

Your Turn

If you are to become aware of the internal messages your mind is sending out to you, it's important that you learn to activate what I call your 'body listening skill.' You can easily do this by putting aside just five minutes a day: sit down, start breathing deeply, focus your attention on your body, and scan it from top to toe. You will become aware of what is positive or negative about it, and what needs attention on the inside — your emotions and thoughts or, if you prefer, your mind's attitudes.

Integrate new awareness about you and your body

By the time you have learned how to check your physical needs and habits regularly, and how to listen daily to the signals coming from within and transmitted to your physical dimension through your nervous system, you have awakened to a new awareness – the awareness of your body.

With awareness always comes choice. You can now choose whether you want to keep repeating unhealthy lifestyle patterns, such as forgetting to drink water, eating too much, minimising the importance of peacefully sleeping at least seven hours a night, or not exercising enough.

By targeting your physical habits and making healthy choices concerning your body, you will activate all its functions for a better work, social and family life. Everything will start to improve. Your relationships with yourself and others, your health, and your intrapersonal communication will become more positive. With a little effort, a sense of confidence and well-being will become part of your daily life.

Once you start to really get to know your body from the inside out and keep your energy in balance, you will find that your self-esteem will also improve. As a result, you'll think and feel much differently when you wake up and look in the mirror each morning. You'll find that the motto "I like myself!" will be integrated into your lifestyle easily and naturally. This new positive physical and mental attitude will make you more confident in the way you perceive yourself and the environment. Chances are that you will be able to trust yourself, your communication will become more authentic and, like a magnet, you will attract and build new positive relationships in work and in life.

Secret 42
MINDING YOUR INTELLECT WILL SHAPE YOUR HEALTH AND RELATIONSHIPS

Your intellect is like a muscle, and it needs healthy conditioning. It gives life to thoughts, which trigger emotions and fuel physical and verbal behaviours.

We live in a fast society, moving at a very quick pace. Activating your intellectual dimension (or your logical brain) means targeting the left part of your brain and slowing down its thinking process — so we make fewer opinions, have fewer doubts, preoccupations, judgments, and assumptions. In short, less thoughts, more silence! It's seems a paradox, but it is not: we activate the logical brain by slowing it down and making it quiet.

How? Start by observing your breathing patterns. Then empty your head of all the thoughts that clutter it up. It may seem a challenging process, but it can be started and practised at any age. The best time to slow down your thinking process is early in the morning, but you can do it at any time of the day, even while you are at the office. The benefits of slowing down are immense, but because it takes willpower and determination, this advice is not always easily received and accepted.

Our society is more inclined towards the 'doing' rhythm: producing, being in action, and taking care of personal and business responsibilities. Unfortunately, 'being' (doing less and less) would be criticised. Men and women who are in 'being' rhythm are often judged as not effective in the working world.

Many young people push themselves to do as much as they possibly can. The result is that they think more, judge more, and try to impress more. They often take on more responsibilities than they should or could. As a result of doing too much for others, they over-commit and lose their way.

The path to success and effective living is through leading a balanced life, and balance cannot be attained by 'doing' at the expense of 'being.' To activate your mind is to keep it alive by exercising your intellectual skill (for example questioning your choices and actions when necessary) while allowing for rest and silence too.

Activating your intellectual dimension is about learning to observe your thoughts, visualise your dreams, while challenging yourself through the power of self-questions. You need to de-clutter your logical brain every now and then too as part of the activation, giving it space to rest in contemplation. Activating the logical brain doesn't necessarily mean thinking more!

How do you slow down your mind?

Since body and mind are connected, one powerful way is to breathe more slowly and deeply, inhaling fully from the nose and exhaling completely through the mouth. Your thoughts will become more distinct and you are able to imagine them like sheep floating in a clear blue sky. Each sheep is different from the next. You may be tempted to label them: this one is big, this one is pure white, this one is slow, this one is cute ... or "I like this one," "I don't like that one," and so on. Stop! This is judging or labelling according to your benchmark of values and beliefs. Instead, simply visualise them and count them like we were taught when we were kids and could not fall asleep at night. Numbers do not label, they just help us to count logically.

Count slowly and observe each sheep passing by without adding anything as a description. If you realise you have slipped back into judging or making assumptions, simply be aware of the ability of your mind to lapse into old attitudes and to be hyperactive.

This is the simplest way to start the process of slowing down your intellect and dropping the judgment. To condition your logical brain, you can also start by making use of active, creative visualisation. When the thinking process starts slowing down, you can choose to imagine ideas, goals, and dreams you have, and project them on the invisible screens on the walls of your mind.

Your Turn

When you wake up, visualise yourself at work, or in a meeting you have scheduled for that day, or talking to your boss about a bonus or taking vacation time. This will help you prepare your intellect for focusing on the tasks of the day, and will enable you to activate your intellect and body for being successful, energised and healthy.

By slowing down your logic process and merely visualising your goals and certainly not stopping the mind from being active, you don't become a spectator. You simply provide your logical brain with time to rest and enjoy and observe in silence. By slowing down the logical process, you nurture the functional activation of your rational ability and skills.

Hot Tip

Slow down to let go of the unnecessary self-talk that builds up a state of emotional imbalance. Then you can visualise the goals and dreams you want to achieve and build a foundation for synergies and synchronicities to take place out in your world.

Integrating the power of focus

Now that you have slowed down your thinking process and activated a process of observing your thoughts and visualising your ideas and dreams, it is time to understand the meaning of nurturing the ability to be intellectually in 'focus'.

Focus is the ability to be still and concentrate all your attention on a particular activity or person. It is the capacity to be present to yourself, in the moment — NOW.

Eckhart Tolle wrote a wonderful book that I recommend to everyone: *The Power of Now*. When you read it, you will be guided to a deep understanding about why being more present to yourself leads to being more effective in work and communication, for it leads to a real connection with yourself and others.

When you are present in your own actions and able to slow down the rational brain, you can respond to situations and people instead of just reacting to them. You can choose deliberately to question your choices instead of jumping into assumptions or verbal and physical behaviours that you might deeply regret later. And you can keep your intent in mind much easily.

Some clients ask me, "How can I become more effective and stop speaking before I think carefully and evaluate what I want to say?" This behaviour is typical of someone who has a fast, sharp temperament: he thinks and acts out at a fast pace rather than slowing down and focusing on and contemplating the issue first.

When you are present, you can recognise when you are thinking too much and acting too little, or when you are stuck in a negative thinking process that causes a negative mood and prevents you from seeing opportunities and turning stagnant situations into brilliant gifts for your life.

Focus always brings you back to the moment. It takes you away from a worrisome future or a past filled with negative experiences that turn your present into a prison for you and your relationships.

To activate your intellect completely, practise focusing, and every time you observe your logical mind slipping forward or backward, bring it back to the present moment with your willpower. It is a deliberate choice.

Activating your focus is part of the process of activating your intellectual dimension. This choice, together with the decision to slow down your thinking process, observe and visualise your goals, will lead you to re-condition your logical brain. Revitalised with new positive energy, your logical brain will fuel a state of total well-being in your physical dimension and relationships in every area of your life.

Secret 43
WHEN YOU MANAGE YOUR EMOTIONS, YOUR WELL-BEING IS ASSURED

Your emotions are energy in motion. They are irrational, genuine, bubbling, stubborn and playful like a child. Your emotions move and follow your thoughts. You generate a positive idea, and voilà — a positive emotional response surfaces immediately from your heart or your stomach. It's the same for negative emotions. Often you don't even realise it, since you are not always present in the moment; you may be disconnected because you have the ability to split from your moods, especially when they are identified as dangerous and painful. When you get up after an awful nightmare, your emotional mood can be affected by it in a negative way that can disrupt the beginning of your day and affect your actions. You can then allow yourself permission to 'feel' or detach and choose with your logical brain to repress or let go.

In Transpersonal Analysis, the four basic emotions are examined: fear, anger, sadness and joy. You can spend hours studying the myriad emotions that colour your life. Perhaps you are familiar with Emotional Intelligence (EQ) and why you need to develop the right side of your brain.

Emotions can spice up your life or make it miserable if you deal with them the same way you did as a child. They can be powerful tools or they can destroy your dreams of success and keep you small and powerless for the rest of your life.

If you don't get to know your emotions, you miss a very important part of your life and you may be unable to choose not to succumb to them. Emotions are irrational and unpredictable, but when you understand how to manage them, you can master them for your own good instead of letting them control your behaviour. The first step is to identify your full range of emotions and recognise that they are there inside of you and that they affect your body language, actions, results, relationships, and well-being.

Holy Moly!

When I gain power over my emotions and use them in a healthy way, I can be fully human and a fully alive communicator!

It is time to discover the kid in you

In each of us there is a kid. Many call this kid the 'Inner Child', and I agree that it is a sort of lost child dwelling inside of you of whom you are not conscious. Kids are wonderful and inspiring, and they know how to live in the moment. They are open, adventurous and curious, and they take risks. That is why it is easy to teach them. Their minds and spirits are soft, and, like a sponge, they absorb any information or message coming from their environment or another person.

They can also be stubborn, rebellious, undisciplined, unstable, and moody. The 'kid in you' is the same. It responds like a little child in situations of peril or pain. It chooses to protect itself, and can suddenly become angry or grumpy, or flee away in shame and isolation if caught doing something wrong. If you don't discover the 'kid in you', you can find yourself at risk when facing adult situations; you react as you used to in childhood. When you were young, such reactions served to protect you against being scolded verbally or physically and emotionally attacked or manipulated.

When you communicate, it is important to understand and unleash the kid in you. When you communicate at work, with yourself, or with others, you can choose to allow the positive emotions of your Inner Child to come alive, spicing up your presentations and conversations. That emotional aliveness, if well managed, adds value to you as a human being and helps you build connections with your audience. People in every country and from every culture understand and are generally attracted by the emotional power stored within others. Make use of yours!

Caution

The more you act as adult only and repress the 'kid' in you, the more you live a lopsided life. It is important to reconnect with the child in you: be childlike, not childish.

Shaking your emotions shifts your intellectual and emotional state

Feelings are energy; repressed feelings block energy. You don't work at your best level when your energy is blocked. You become stagnant, not only in your brain activity but also in your physical actions.

Shaking your emotions is something you knew how to do well when you were a child. You were jumping, bouncing, and climbing; you were moving and using a great range of physical motions that enabled you to shake the stuck emotions stored in your body. Therefore, it was easy to shift quickly from a state of joy to one of anger, or a moment of passion to a time of sadness. As children, we were emotionally fit.

As you got older, you may have lost that capacity, influenced more by your logical brain judging your emotions and labelling them as good or bad, making you identify more with some than with others, basing your choices on what you had learnt in your environment and culture as a child.

202 88 ESSENTIAL SECRETS

Emotions are accepted and expressed in different ways in different cultures, but many people find it hard to talk about their feelings, either because they do not know how to identify or manage them, or because they believe that it is inappropriate to share them.

Emotions affect your body language when you communicate, and the more they are blocked or repressed, the more your body remains stuck, creating a lack of flexibility and a limited range of motion. One way to enjoy your emotions like a child again — able to shift emotions quickly and unblock them, liberating their powerful energy throughout your full being — is to play with your body and set your emotions in motion.

How? By dancing, shaking, jumping, running, rolling, stretching, exercising, walking, biking, climbing: in short by practising any physical activity that sets your body in motion from top to toe. This helps you to be flexible and physically energised, activates your emotions, and supports the shifting of energy. It revitalises and invigorates brain activity, and your brain becomes a propelling power for whatever project you face.

Secret 44
WHEN PHYSICAL, INTELLECTUAL AND EMOTIONAL DIMENSIONS ARE ACTIVE, COMMUNICATION WITH YOURSELF AND OTHERS IS EFFECTIVE

You reach out to others and convey messages through and with your body

To activate your relational dimension means to recognise how thoughts and emotions are connected to your body and how they convey a message to your team, colleagues, boss, friends, relatives, and children. Often this happens as a first impression.

The most natural way to convey your emotions, thoughts and beliefs is to learn to communicate them through your body movements. It is your personal responsibility to check your body language and the physical messages you are consciously or unconsciously sending out. This involves more than your body shape, the way you dress, or the way you make yourself up or groom yourself.

I suggest that you:

- **Check your facial expression and gestures.** Did you know that the part of the body that is used most in communicating assumptions, beliefs, and values and in expressing emotions is the face? It is remarkable that across cultures there is universal agreement about which facial expressions indicate positive and negative emotions and thoughts. You normally do not have any problem identifying someone who is angry, worried, impatient, anxious, happy or joyful. Videotape yourself, take pictures, and do some self-evaluation.

- **Ask a professional to assess the flexibility of your body and spine.** Your body sends out strong messages that come from within and remain stored in your cellular system. The more rigid your body is, the more challenging it is to connect with others. A body that is open, fluid and smiling creates attraction and works as a magnet in your relationships.

- **Consider engaging in movement activity at least twice a week.** Start slowly, and, if you can, have someone create a plan and follow up with you.

When you relate to others you must engage with your intellect

Many of us are very intellectual when it comes to communication. Many also have repressed emotions they cannot identify or express; they communicate only through logical expression.

You must keep this in mind during your conversations. Body language and a charming smile that invite people to engage with you are not enough for effective communication if the person receiving your message has a strong logical side that dominates their conversation.

Here's what I suggest you do:

- Organise your thoughts and ideas well before engaging with your audience, keeping in mind that what you say should match your body language.

- Observe the receiver of your message. Let go of assumptions and opinions. You might be surprised what you can discover by simply observing your audience and being open and curious with your intellect.

- Enrich your sharing with data and information that will help the audience make sense of what you speak about. Use the power of questions to get deeper into the conversation or to get to know your audience better. Add to your sharing personal stories that are logical and make sense in regard to the topic being discussed. Your thoughts and ideas can be supported by slides, props and handouts if you are delivering a presentation — they can reinforce visually what you say intellectually.

- Use a benchmark of values and beliefs to decide which people you want to have deeper relationships with. Relationships can be superficial or deeply meaningful. According to what you want, you can engage with people in a way that best suits your communication style, preferences, and hobbies.

- Listen carefully with your logical brain in focus so you can avoid misunderstandings and pose appropriate questions when you need clarification.

Communication also means sharing your emotions with others. Communication is about understanding if and when emotions are blocked inside your physical system that prevents your genuine connection.

Dr. Lim Yun Chin, Dr. Ko Soon Meng, and Robert M. Solomon, in their book *The Hurting Heart: Overcoming Emotional Distress*, affirm that "When we communicate we must learn to share not only what we think or have done, but also how we feel. This will create a positive environment which will minimise unhealthy responses to painful human feelings."

Emotions are contagious and they are there to communicate to you and help you communicate with others. Each of them, no matter how much you love or reject them, has a specific purpose.

In order to connect with your audience, be it one person or 200 people, you need to develop communication skills that enhance the depth with which you share with each person. You need to share not only your ideas and opinions, but also your feelings. This serves to connect and defuse negative emotional and intellectual energy too. In fact, a thought or a feeling shared with others is a thought or a feeling whose negative effect on you is reduced. Sharing begins with using your body language and verbal power.

Holy Moly!

True connection happens when my head (intellectual dimension) connects to my heart (emotional dimension).

When you are able to connect in this way, you move to a different stage in your relationships. Denying your feelings or driving them out of your life will not help you transcend the thick wall that first impressions create; rather this prevents relationships and communication from being genuine and real. By learning to recognise and identify your emotions, you can use them to their greatest benefit. And by learning to share your innermost emotions, you can break down the wall and build true rapport with those who live and work with you.

Understanding, activating, and managing your emotions in a new way brings you the gift of sensing and managing others people's emotions, too. The connection then is assured. You understand when you should 'listen' to another's emotions, showing your empathy, and when you should remain on the surface. In relationships, this approach is crucial for wielding influence; it is difficult to have a positive influence on someone else without first sensing how they feel and understanding their position.

No matter how intellectually brilliant you may be, that brilliance will fail to shine if you are not persuasive. And being persuasive means seeing things through the power not only of your mind, but of your heart, too. It means connecting and building a life of authentic relationships and well-being from the inside out.

Caution

Failing to connect emotionally with your audience, despite your best intentions, causes you to fall to the bottom of the influence competence hierarchy. You may mean well but you lack the emotional ability to get your message across.

Checklist for activating your Communication in Four Dimensions

1. Prepare a daily/weekly checklist for your physical dimension (your body habits checklist).

2. Find a 'buddy' who can motivate you and check on your physical habits at least once a week.

3. Start making time every day to close your eyes and be in silence for two minutes, giving attention to what is happening inside and what messages your body conveys.

4. Visualise for a few minutes every day a clear blue sky, and imagine your thoughts floating. Practise this activity by sitting (not lying) in bed.

5. Take time every day to go in a quiet space where for two to three minutes you use the power of your imagination. See yourself achieving the goal you have in mind. Focus with your thoughts and feelings, and make it as real as you can.

6. Expand your emotional vocabulary by searching on the Internet for a variety of emotions, and start integrating them when you speak with colleagues and friends

7. Take time with a friend once a week to explain a situation expressing your thoughts and emotions with clarity.

8. Integrate some form of exercise, movement or dance in your weekly routine.

9. Shake your body once a day for about one to five minutes. Do it to unblock emotions that are stuck.

10. Remind yourself on a daily basis: "When I am able to activate my Four Dimensions regularly, I will be able to manage my communication effectively with myself and others."

CHAPTER 12

INFLUENTIAL NETWORKING
How to charm the room and expand your connections

by **Karen Leong**
Director
Influence Solutions Pte Ltd

Karen Leong is an influential communication expert. Highly regarded for her transformational programmes, Karen has helped thousands of executives, senior managers and sales professionals achieve results professionally and personally. A highly sought-after speaker and facilitator, Karen's most requested seminars include *Influence 247*, *Influential Networking*, *Influential Presentations* and *Influential Leadership*.

Karen is the director of Influence Solutions Pte Ltd, dedicated to unleashing performance potential in organisations. She is a master trainer for American Society of Training and Development's Improving Human Performance certification programme. A Certified Public Accountant, Karen has a decade-long corporate career spanning audit, consulting and a corporate education with KPMG and KPMG Consulting. Karen is also a successful entrepreneur and was profiled as an innovative talent in a television feature. Well regarded as an influential communication expert, she is often interviewed in the media to share her insights on the art of influence.

Karen believes that, with influence, anything can be achieved. Her personal mission is to help people become naturally influential, and therefore catalysts for positive change.

Find out more about Karen at: **www.karenleong.com**
Contact Karen at: **karen@karenleong.com**

NETWORKING IS ONE of the most effort-efficient and leveraged ways to expand your sphere of influence. The right relationships can open new doors and enhance your ability to make things happen.

However, most of us either dread networking, or don't do it well enough for it to be effective.

Entering a room full of strangers at a business or social event can be intimidating. Yet networking events are great places to develop professional and personal contacts. If you are uncomfortable with or ineffective at networking, you will miss opportunities to build connections, gain referrals, nurture relationships and achieve greater success at work.

Expanding your area of influence is more than just following traditional networking advice, making small talk or turning on the charm. Influential networking is about creating memorable first connections and nurturing rewarding relationships that lead to new opportunities and experiences for everyone.

Karen Leong shares simple, practical and powerful techniques on how to maximise your return on investment in networking and be an effortless influence. Her easy-to-implement action plan will not only unleash your natural confidence, it will also fast track you to the top.

🔑 *Secret 45*
PLAYING THE HOST AT ANY EVENT EXPANDS YOUR INFLUENCE

How do you feel when you walk into a room full of strangers? Intimidated? Uncertain what to do next? Unsure how to blend in and feel at ease? Welcome to the club! You are not alone. If you are like most people, networking feels like work, especially if you believe you are not a natural extrovert. The good news is that you do not have to be a social butterfly to be an influential networker.

Do you know people who seem to effortlessly charm the room? Do you wonder how easily or why people gravitate towards them? Have you ever wondered how do they do it? Let me share the secret with you:

They play host. Even when it's not their event.

Let us briefly examine the difference between the mindsets of a host and a guest.

- **Hosts**. What do hosts do? They are in charge of organising the event, ensuring things run smoothly, and, most importantly, making sure their guests are comfortable. The host will be at the door greeting people, making introductions, offering drinks to guests, and ensuring everyone has a great time.

- **Guests**. When we are invited to networking events, many of us reach there with a guest mentality. After all, we are invited guests. Therefore, when we turn up at an event, we immediately look for the host to make us comfortable. If there is no such host to be found, that's when we start feeling uncomfortable in the presence of so many other strangers, all of whom appear to know each other.

Act like the host

The key to reducing your fear of networking is to change your attitude: stop being a guest, become the host. The most influential networkers have a host mentality even if they are guests. They put other people's feelings ahead of their own. And in doing so, they forget their fears.

Here are four ways to play host:

1. Save the wallflowers

The most popular spot for people who are alone at a networking function is the wall. It is far from the action in the central zone, since the loners do not wish to be conspicuous. Many of us have been in this situation where we are wallflowers — standing alone, but not really flowering, but rather withering by the wall.

What is the security blanket for wallflowers? Yes, you guessed it. The weapon of choice is their mobile phone! Wallflowers will be looking at their phones, or tapping on them as a form of distraction, to make it look as though they are busy – anything that does not make them look lonely and desperate.

You can spot a wallflower easily; she/he is generally alternating between staring at or playing with their phone, and surveying the room. Wallflowers hope to spot someone they know, or better still, that someone will come by and rescue them from the misery of their lonesome existence.

Here's the good news. Wallflowers are the best people to approach at networking events. One way to forget your nervousness when attending an event alone is to focus on saving people who are wallflowers. They will be most eager and grateful to speak to you when you approach them. So don't give it a second thought – spot a wallflower and introduce yourself – see how eagerly they befriend you.

2. Make introductions and connect people

Many people attending networking events are takers rather than givers. It is natural to want to benefit from greater connections, which can help you in your career or business. Of course, this is important, but it is ultimately very limiting if you make this your sole focus.

Instead of being a taker, be a rain-maker. Hosts add value to their guests by introducing people who they think will enjoy each other's company or can benefit from knowing each other.

You start playing host at any event when you help connect people to one another. But what if you do not know anyone to begin with? Remember the wallflowers we just discussed? After getting to know a wallflower, you have gained one new friend. It is psychologically easier to approach another person (who may also be another wallflower) as a duo. This will help both of you to expand your connections.

Holy Moly!

When I save a wallflower, I'm not only saving the other person. I'm saving myself too. Plus we may make more friends together!

What is the best way to introduce people to each other? Start with what's outstanding or interesting about the person. Such an introduction not only earns you tremendous goodwill from both parties, it also helps to pique people's interest, and is a great way to get the conversation going.

When you start connecting people, they will remember you as someone who has a quality network of contacts and is generous enough to share them with others. They will tend to return this favour sooner than later. And thus your network grows exponentially.

3. Approach the people you want to meet with the feel of familiarity

What is one of the most effective ways to connect directly with business leaders or corporate executives? Emailing or calling them involves getting past gatekeepers and being relegated to the queue. The obvious answer — a face-to-face connection. Many top executives now leverage on speaking at conferences to enhance their visibility, or as a marketing initiative for their companies. When you attend such events, approach these speakers, preferably before they speak — there is much less competition from other people, and you become more memorable when you introduce yourself. If you approach them after the conference, introduce yourself and share what you liked about their presentation.

Use this approach when you chance upon someone whom you want to meet at a networking event, or even on the street. Speak to them as a peer. What is your interest in contacting them? Introduce yourself, share where you came to know them, and suggest a follow-up. It is usually easier to get a 'yes' from a person face-to-face, than go through the faceless communication of an email or call.

This personal approach builds a sense of familiarity, and opens the door to a future connection.

4. Form a tag-team

Hosts usually enlist a core group of helpers or friends, especially when organising large events, to ensure that the party flows smoothly and everyone is taken care of.

By forming a tag-team with another friend (or newly befriended wallflower) who is attending the same networking session, you can help each other. Your partner should ideally be someone who shares the same networking principles as you. That is, he or she is also interested in meeting other people and making the most out of an event.

Both of you start out together, and approach people as a team. You can mutually edify each other when making introductions — this means communicating what's great about each other. It's so much easier to build credibility when someone else affirms your qualities, rather than blowing your own trumpet.

When you are both comfortable, move on separately, circulate and mingle with different people. This is a leveraged way of meeting more people. When you find yourself alone again, you can always look for your partner and join her in conversation with whomever she is talking to. Or find another wallflower to save.

After the networking event, you can also share the beneficial contacts you have made with your tag partner.

When you start using a host mentality, you will find it is easy to expand your sphere of influence at networking events. This builds on the principle of generosity, that is, by putting other people first. You will create tremendous goodwill with everyone you meet. Most of all, you will find it's much more enjoyable when you put your insecurities aside and just focus on making friends. People will be attracted to you when you are having fun, and you will naturally become an influential networker.

Secret 46
BEING APPROACHABLE CAN INCREASE YOUR RESULTS

Networking is not just about working the room on your own. Imagine having other people gravitate towards you instead. There are simple actions you can take to dramatically increase your results. Here are four ways to make it both easy and attractive for people to approach you.

1. Position yourself in the hot spots

Hot spots are areas of high activity and human traffic. People usually gravitate towards food and beverage areas — that means the buffet spread and the bar. One easy way to make friends is to join the buffet queue, and pass on an empty plate and cutlery to the person behind you. Such a simple act creates an opportunity for both of you to carry on the conversation after the "Thank you!"

The most common table arrangements in networking events are high cocktail tables without chairs for people to rest their food and drink. This informal arrangement means we can walk around and mingle. These tables offer great areas to network from, they offer others a natural reason to approach the table (to rest their food and drinks) and present you with an opportunity to make more friends. All people need is a simple "Can I join you?" to enter into a conversation with you.

2. Wear a 'wow'

Many people in the corporate world dress in neutrals and dark formal colours – black, blue, and white. While these are safe professional colours, they tend to make you blend in with the majority rather than stand out. Why not inject a splash of colour that brings out your personality, and catches the attention of people around you? This may be something as simple as a red scarf for women, or a scarlet shirt (under a jacket) for men.

Accessorising is another great way to add pizzazz to your look. Wear a piece that has personality and can become an obvious talking point. This can be an outstanding brooch for women, or perhaps a stylish hat for men. Flip through business fashion magazines for ideas on add-ons that can make people go "Wow". This gives them the natural inclination to approach you, often with a comment, "I can't help but notice that lovely scarf you are wearing" or "where did you get this from?"

Likewise, when you see another person wearing a "Wow", go up to the person and give an earnest compliment, like "That's such a lovely..."

Remember, everyone likes to be appreciated; that's why this will always bring a smile to the other person's face, and it is possibly the best and fastest way to break the ice.

3. Make eye contact and personalise your smile

People like people who like them. If you seem friendly and interested, people are more inclined to approach you and return the friendliness. This appears to be such a simple concept, but many people who are not confident in a room of strangers tend to look straight ahead instead of at people, trying to appear purposeful and not desperate.

The magic lies first in your eye contact and then your smile. When you see someone walking by, look into their eyes. This acknowledges their presence. Follow this up with a smile.

I do not recommend having a perpetual smile. Not only is this tiring but it will come across as fake. Smiling a second after you have made the initial eye contact with the person shows that the smile is just for them. This is a way of acknowledging that they are sharing an experience with you by being at the same event, and communicating that they are acquaintances and friends whom you haven't met till now. Almost always they will naturally reciprocate with a smile of their own, then all it takes is a simple "Hi" to get the conversation going.

Caution

Acting busy or uninterested is a recipe for being left alone at any networking event. Don't make it difficult for people to approach you.

4. Share the limelight with a question

If you are the keynote speaker at a conference or networking event, that naturally gives you maximum visibility, and people will usually approach you after your session.

However, if you are not the speaker, one way to share the limelight is to ask a question during the Q&A segment. This gives you the opportunity to introduce yourself and your organisation. Keep your question concise and relevant. Speak clearly and confidently. This will instantly build your credibility and recognition at the event. Whenever you do this, do not be surprised when people approach you afterwards with the comment "Great question!" That is the opening you need to make another friend.

Secret 47
BEING INTERESTED IN OTHERS WILL MAKE YOU MORE INTERESTING

Networking is a great way to meet people outside your social and professional circle. It often leads to job opportunities and open doors to new customers. Many people see the value in networking and go to events with the agenda of selling themselves. However, it takes less effort and is potentially more rewarding when you shift the focus from being interesting to becoming interested in others. The result? You gain the opportunity of connecting with the other person in the way that matters most to him or her.

1. Compliment the person

People love compliments. When you see someone wearing something unique or displaying a standout quality, approach the person and compliment him or her. If you see a lady wearing an eye-catching accessory or a man with an interesting tie, approach them and share how it caught your eye. The conversation can easily lead to where they bought the item, and go deeper into their interests and likes, and this becomes a great platform for mutual appreciation and connection.

2. Have a conversation before exchanging name cards

It is considered part of business etiquette to exchange name cards at a networking event. Too many people let their name cards do the talking for them, and suggest a name card exchange before even having a conversation or connection with the other person. This can imply that you are only interested in what you see on the name card, and not the person.

Successful networking is not based on the number of name cards you collect at an event. A name card collected does not imply a connection made. If you pass your name card to someone and leave before establishing a connection, it will usually find its way to the bin.

The key to making a connection lies in personalising your conversations, preferably before exchanging cards. That is what will make people remember you. This makes it easy to establish a quality connection in just a few minutes if you connect with something personal about them.

Hot Tip

People value name cards more if they ask for them. How do you get people to ask for your name card? Start a conversation first, and when there is a connection, ask the person for his name card and he will naturally ask you for yours!

3. Make the approach by highlighting a connection

We intuitively make first impressions about everyone we meet. This happens in a matter of seconds, based on how they look, their body language and often who they remind us of. Learn the art of sizing people up at a networking event.

It is generally easier to open a conversation by asking a closed-ended question, one that requires a short answer, rather than an open-ended question. No matter what the answer, it will give you a sense of whether and how to continue.

Based on what they are wearing, try and guess their most likely link with the event. Phrase it in a positive way. You will then appear to have a commonality with the other person, and are achieving this by simply asking a confirmation question.

For example, you can ask, "Are you part of the organising committee?" If the answer is no, then you can follow up with "Which organisation are you with?" or Where are you from?" or "You looked so at ease here that I assumed you were." (And smile!)

4. Engage people by discovering their WTF: Work, Thoughts, Family

Many people attend networking events with the sole aim of making contacts to achieve greater sales, open doors to job opportunities, enhance personal experiences. In short, it is all about *them*. These conversations start with the other person highlighting their achievements, or pushing their products and services. This overly sales-oriented approach relegates the other person to being a prospect rather than a potential relationship. What do you think happens next? Normally this approach will trigger a fight or flight response.

The solution? Ask questions. Listen more than you talk. People love to talk about their work, express their thoughts, and share about their families. Discovering people's WTF allows you to learn more about what is most important to the person.

Work

The favourite question asked during a networking situation is "What do you do?" The response from most people is for them to state their profession or job title; that is they are speaking from a professional rather than a personal capacity. To engage them on a personal level, make your questions about them. It can be as simple a question like, "How long have you been in this company / industry / job?" or "How did you get started in this business / career?" or "What motivated you to join this profession?" or "What is the best thing you like about your profession?"

Thoughts

An effective conversation opener is to mention current trends or hot topics making the news today. Asking people what they think about the current political or economic climate can lead to an exchange of views and even common thoughts, which allows you to build initial rapport. You can then build a deeper connection when you ask questions to uncover people's inner motivations and aspirations. Questions like, "What inspires you?" or "What do you want to achieve in your profession?" show that you are genuinely interested in what is important to the other person. With this understanding, you know how best to add value and contribute to the other person.

Family

People are more than their jobs and professions. One great way to take the conversation to a more personal level, especially if the other person is of a different nationality, is by asking them where they are from. This is a great lead in to sharing information about each other's backgrounds, schools, children and spouses. You may discover you have a lot in common, and this helps build a sense of kinship.

Being interested in people is about making it more about them than yourself. By taking the focus off selling yourself, and on connecting with people, networking becomes a more fulfilling and rewarding activity. You will have greater clarity on how best to follow up with people, and engage them effectively by customising what you offer with what best meets their needs and interests.

Secret 48
YOU MUST NURTURE YOUR NETWORK BEFORE YOU NEED IT

If your keep-in-touch strategy is self-serving, people will soon regard mail from you as spam. That is why it's important to be a giver, not just a taker. Developing rewarding relationships is about following up with people in a way that adds value to them. Be generous, and your network will do the same for you.

1. Connect on social media such as Facebook or LinkedIn

Instead of playing with or staring at your mobile, use it to take a photo. Offer to email the photograph to your new contacts, and this provides an opportunity to ask them for their email addresses. Invite people into your social network by uploading the photos and tagging them. Presto! A memorable start to a new friendship! Social media offers you a simple and effective way to keep track of important events in people's lives – birthdays, anniversaries and special accomplishments. Being in touch on special moments are the building blocks of any sustainable relationship.

2. Arrange for coffee or lunch

The objective at a networking event is to develop initial rapport with people you meet. You then agree to follow up with a meeting to uncover potential collaboration or synergies. Meeting in a relaxed setting is best to develop a personal relationship. It is easy to arrange lunch on a workday, if both persons are working in the same area. Everybody needs to have lunch, and most people are open to new lunch companions. For a shorter catch-up, meeting for coffee is effective. To create a truly memorable experience, simply follow these guidelines:

Select a place that you can call your own. Do you have a venue in mind where the staff takes extra care of your needs? This will add to the overall experience of the guest, and they will be impressed that you attract such personal attention and care. If you haven't cultivated such a venue, fret not. Decide on a few venues that you enjoy going to, and make it a point to get to know the manager and staff there. Service staff are often under-appreciated, and when you care enough to know their names and compliment them on good service, they will make the effort to serve you and your guests better. Leave a tip for exceptional service.

Suggest a venue that provides a unique experience that your guest will appreciate. It can be a newly-opened themed restaurant for guests who love to try out new concepts, or has a signature dishes that will whet any appetite. If you know your guest's favourite cuisine, she will also be heartened that you have taken the extra effort to recommend a restaurant that suits her taste.

3. Be a connector

People are continually looking for contacts to help them with a variety of things — finding a job, finance for their business, engaging an accountant, lawyer, or even a potential mate! A powerful way to build up a quality network is to be a connector. If you come across contacts that will be useful to your network, offer to link them up. However, it is important that you treat your current network with respect and only link people up when there are obvious synergies.

4. Be an information broker

One of the most powerful commodities today is information. Many people are starved for time, and your ability to provide relevant information to them would be appreciated. I discovered that people are most grateful for information that can help in their wealth, health and children. A timely stock market analysis report, an article listing proven solutions to alleviate Repetitive Strain Injury, or information to help a child secure a place in school of choice can earn you grateful brownie points.

5. Host an event

This does not have to be as daunting as it sounds. Start with hosting small things like an office lunch gathering, or organising coffee for a new employee to meet the rest (this will not only hasten the new entrant's integration into the company, it will also gain you a new ally). You can also organise a networking lunch or drinks and invite your contacts who share certain synergies. A good host creates an experience for his and her guests, introduces people to each other, and ensures that everyone has a fulfilling time.

Your Turn

Think about three people you would like to keep in touch with. How can you re-connect with them memorably?

People love new experiences, and they will be grateful that you are a catalyst and made it happen.

Checklist for how to be an influential networker

1. Have a host mentality, not a guest mentality, even if it's not your event.

2. Save the wallflowers. Be proactive in approaching people who are alone.

3. Make introductions and connect people.

4. Approach people with a compliment.

5. Form a tag-team.

6. Make it easy for people to approach you. Position yourself in hot spots where there is a flow of people.

7. Wear a 'wow'. Put on an accessory that is eye-catching.

8. Make eye contact and smile when you meet a stranger.

9. Make your conversations about the other person. Uncover people's WTF (Work, Thoughts, Family).

10. Nurture your network before you need it.

PART 3

Influence
and Sales

> " *You may fool all the people some of the time, you can even fool some of the people all of the time, but you cannot fool all of the people all of the time.*"
>
> — Abraham Lincoln

SECTION 5

Speaking to Influence, Persuade and Win

CHAPTER 13

SPEAKING TO INFLUENCE AND WIN

How to influence people to your way of thinking

by **Eric Feng**
Training Director
Point Communications Asia

Eric Feng is public speaking coach who has personally helped more than 3000 business leaders and CEOs to influence and inspire their audiences through their presentations.

Apart from teaching them how to deliver memorable business and technical presentations, Eric also guides corporate leaders and senior management to effectively convey their messages through business narrative (better known as storytelling).

Eric has written three books on business communication. His second book *Get To The Point* has sold more than 10,000 copies, and is now widely recognised as a resource for business presenters in Asia.

Eric's success and achievements in the speaking industry have been featured on both local and regional media, like *The Straits Times*, *The Business Times*, Prime Time Morning, 938LIVE and Channel 8.

Find out more about Eric at: **www.ericfeng.com**

Contact Eric at: **eric@ericfeng.com**

YOUR SUCCESS AT work has a lot to do with your ability to influence people to your way of thinking. If you want a promotion, you will need to convince your boss to choose you over your more experienced colleagues. If you want help with a project, you will need to persuade your colleagues who are themselves living out a packed schedule. If you want your plans to be implemented, you will need the buy-in of your stakeholders. If you want to get your team to put in more effort in their work, you will need to motivate them. Whether you are an executive, a manager or a director of your organisation, you need to know how to influence. When you master this highly-coveted skill, you will avoid frustration, save time, and you will make the most of every opportunity that comes your way. Here's the good news — influence is a skill that you can learn. In this section, Eric Feng will share with you four time-tested influence tactics that have helped politicians, celebrities and world leaders win the hearts and minds of that people. When you start applying these tactics at work, you'll have to start getting used to having people agree with you all the time!

⚷ *Secret 49*
PEOPLE BUY PEOPLE FIRST

Let's face it. Life is a popularity game. The person who is more well-liked tends to get more favours, clients and opportunities. You may not like that, especially if you are not on the receiving end of it. But it does happen and it happens all the time. Call it prejudice if you want but the fact remains: people buy people first, even before your ideas, your products or your organisation.

When you learn how to make people like you, they will treat you better, buy more from you and say yes to your requests more often. If you do it right, they will even go the extra mile to personally help you to achieve your goals.

During my workshops, I often write this on the whiteboard:

>   I   LIKE   YOU

We all want to be liked, especially since we know that people buy people first. But here's what most people don't realise. For you to be liked by another person, you first need to establish something.

I will then proceed to write this additional word on the board.

      I   (AM)   LIKE   YOU

So there lies the secret: For people to like me, I must first show them that I am like them, because people like people who are like them. That is also why "birds of the same feather flock together"!

People like people who are like them.

Next time you have a conversation with a new person, focus on creating as much common ground as you can. It can be via their passions, their pains or their values.

Hot Tip

The deepest way to establish commonality is through values, that is, what is important to the person. Not only will this help you gain likeability; sometimes it may even help you land the biggest deal of your life.

I'll never forget when I met the HR director of one of the largest financial companies in Asia. It had the potential of being a deal of a lifetime and, as you can imagine, my team was extremely nervous but excited. Unfortunately, the HR director (let's call her Jamie) was not exactly excited. I got the impression that she was not at all impressed the moment she saw me. I could tell from her disengaged body gestures — no smile, folded arms, stiff posture. She was even leaning backwards with her chin high up.

"So you are Eric?" she asked with a tinge of disappointment.

"Yes I am. It's a pleasure meeting you Jamie!" I attempted a big warm smile, only to be met with her icy cold stare. I tried making small talk with her, but that went badly, like eggs on a stone wall. I tried 'shooting' electricity at her — my weak attempt at charming her — and it also failed like a silly joke. It was as if she was an insulator or something! That moment, I felt like Superman without my powers. Heck, Jamie was my Kryptonite!

"Well Eric, since you are here to *help* me, let me start by telling you the problem." said Jamie. Ouch! Lots of sarcasm there. She then went on and on for at least 30 minutes telling me about the problem in detail. She might as well have thrown in her personal problems too. I suspect she was trying to intimidate me, and she was doing a very good job of this.

To be honest with you, I was absolutely clueless. I had no idea how to even start solving the problem for her, as it was a deep-rooted organisational problem. But since she wanted my opinion on how to solve it, I started with, "Jamie, this is like eating an elephant. You have to eat it piece-by-piece."

"What did you say?" said Jamie. That was when I started panicking. In my head, I was thinking, "Oh no! She is either a vegetarian or an elephant lover! I should not have used that elephant analogy." But I repeated myself anyway.

"You know something, Eric, that was exactly what my boss said to me too!" and then she gave me a weak smile.

We did not become best of friends in that conversation, but at least we got onto more equal grounds. How? By sharing a common value — a value that even her boss had shared. And because I said the exact same thing as her boss, she could not help but have some respect for me, because I was thinking like her boss, who she obviously respected a lot.

I later did my homework and discovered that she loved Japanese food. In our next meeting, I started comparing myself to a sushi chef. Not only did it help me communicate what I could offer in a more memorable fashion, it also won me some more points as I demonstrated that I knew something about what she loved. We eventually won her over and had the opportunity of working with her organisation.

So remember this principle well: people buy people first, and for people to like you, show them that you are like them!

Secret 50
PEOPLE ONLY TAKE ACTION WHEN YOU MAKE THEM CARE ENOUGH

In 2006, researcher Paul Slovic at the University of Oregon, and colleagues Deborah Small of the Wharton School and George Lowenstein of Carnegie Mellon University, performed an interesting behavioural experiment: A test group of people was divided into three sub-groups. The first group of people were asked to read a set of statistics, highlighting the massive challenges faced by Africans. After reading the statistics, they were asked to donate their money to *Save the Children*, an internationally active charity that helps support children in developing countries.

The second group of people were given a story and photo of a poor, starving seven-year-old girl named Rokia.

The people in the first group, who saw the statistics, donated an average of $1.14. The people in the second group donated an average of $2.34 — more than twice the amount of the first group.

The experiment got even more interesting with the third group. This group were given both the statistics and the story to read. Surprisingly, the average donation was significantly less than the second group, who only saw Rokia's picture and read her story. On an average, the third group only donated $1.43, compared to the $2.34 donated by the second group. Somehow the statistics — which were supposed to demonstrate massive human suffering in Africa — actually made people less charitable.

The researchers attribute this nearly 40 per cent fall-off to what they call the 'drop in the bucket' effect. When people read about Rokia, their emotions were engaged and they were inclined to give. However, when people read about the millions who were in distress, "the data sent a bad feeling that counteracts the warm glow from helping Rokia," said Slovic. People would still give, but they gave less.

Holy Moly!

The minute I get the person to think, I make the person less able to feel, which reduces their impetus to action. If I want the person to take action, I must engage their heart, not their head

Now that you know the key to getting a person to act is by engaging their heart and making them care, how exactly do you get them into that emotional state? These are three hot buttons to press:

1. Pleasure

Many influencers are quick to take advantage of this emotional hot button by appealing to their listeners' self-interests. When you demonstrate how the person can achieve their needs, wants and desires through your products, services or ideas, they will be more inclined to listen, because ultimately people are moved to act in self-interest.

Your Turn

The next time you try to persuade your listeners, be sure to answer these three critical questions that they are silently asking: (1) So what? (2) Who cares? (3) What's in it for me?

2. Pain

Pain is another powerful stimulant to action. As human beings, we are conditioned to avoid pain, and we will do everything in our ability to avoid or remove it. To successfully influence a person, you must take advantage of this phenomenon by helping them to identify and re-experience their pain. Here are some qualifying questions to help people uncover their pain points.

- "What are some of the key challenges that you are facing at work?"
- "What are your most pressing problems relating to XYZ?"
- "What are the consequences if you were to fail?"

The more a person talks about their pain, the more real it becomes for them. To deepen the pain, ask "why?" For example, "Why is this a challenge for you?" A powerful follow-up question you can also ask is, "How do you feel about this?" Avoid asking 'thinking' questions, as it will dilute the emotions you were trying to generate.

3. Direct experience

Jon Stegner was a senior purchasing executive of a manufacturing company. When he first took up the position, he discovered that his factories were purchasing 424 different kinds of gloves. Every factory had its own supplier and its own negotiated price. The same glove could cost $5 at one factory and $17 at another. Stegner tried telling the management team many times about the problem, but nothing changed until he came up with this brilliant idea.

236 88 ESSENTIAL SECRETS

He collected a sample of every one of the 424 gloves, and tagged the various prices on them all, together with the names of the factories using them. Stegner then gathered all the gloves and put them in the boardroom for the division presidents to view. Not surprisingly, they were taken aback when they saw the towering stack of gloves.

Everyone was shocked to see identical pairs of gloves at vastly differing prices. One was marked $3.22 while another similar one was marked at $10.55. Many were dumbfounded, and at the end of the 'tour', they understood the gravity of the problem.

Would spreadsheets and statistics of their bad purchasing habits have done the trick? It's most unlikely. But when the division presidents *saw* the result of their bad purchasing habits for themselves, they were fully convinced of the situation.

As a tool of influence, personal experience is a hundred times more powerful than words. It gets people emotionally involved very quickly and leads them to the conclusion you want them to make, without you having to say a word.

So there you have it, three powerful ways to get a person emotionally engaged: pain, pleasure and through a direct experience. Ultimately, people will not care about what you have to say until you show them how much you care about them. So an important quality all influencers need to possess is empathy — the ability to see and feel from the person's point of view — because only then will you be able to speak their language and successfully influence them to your way of thinking.

♀ *Secret 51*
THE KEY TO INFLUENCE IS NOT TO TALK, BUT LISTEN

A critical mistake that people make when they attempt to influence is by talking too much. There are three reasons why I would encourage you to talk less and listen more.

People don't buy because they understand your product or your service. People buy because they feel you understand them. The only way they can feel understood is if you give them a chance to express their concerns, their grievances and their expectations.

No one likes to be told what to do. Sales guru, David H. Sandler, asserted that, "As a rule, prospects are programmed to resist salespeople who try – directly or indirectly – to tell them what to do." No matter how 'right' you are about your prospect's predicament, no matter how many advantages your prospect can gain if they buy from you, and no matter how good a deal is that you are offering your prospect, they won't appreciate it if you tell them. They won't even believe it, because they are conditioned to resist anyone who challenges their status quo.

An influencer's job is not to give information, but to get information. During your initial meeting with someone, your main objective is to uncover the reasons why and under what circumstances they will say yes to you. For that to happen, you must ask the right questions and let them do the talking.

Caution

If you find yourself talking too much in an attempt to persuade, you are on the wrong track. Finish up and get back into the game with a question. The more you know about the person, the easier it will be to influence them.

There are two powerful types of questions you can ask.

1. Qualifying questions

These are open-ended questions that will get the person talking about their pains, pleasures, values and expectations. This type of question usually starts with *who, what, when, where, how and so*. For example:

- If you are selling an online payment software, you could ask, "What are some of the challenges that you or your customers are facing right now with your online payment gateway?" (PAIN)

- If you are an agency manager trying to recruit an executive to join you in the insurance business, you could ask, *"What kind of your career will get you excited?"* (PLEASURE)

- If you are a training provider pitching to a Training Director, you could ask, *"What are the three most essential qualities you are looking for in a training provider?"* (VALUE)

By asking all these qualifying questions, you will notice all the valuable information they are sharing with you. Now you must use them to your advantage. Demonstrate how your idea, product or service can help relieve their pain and bring them pleasure. Show them that your values are aligned to theirs. Ensure that their expectations are met with the things you are selling or proposing.

2. Clarifying questions

Never assume anything! So for example, if your prospect says, "Cost savings are important to me", a salesperson would usually jump the gun and focus his entire sales pitch on just cost savings. What would be better is for him to clarify. What does the prospect mean by 'cost savings'? What are those costs? Is anything else important to him apart from cost savings? By clarifying, you can avoid being misled by the prospect (cost saving may not be the real reason) and you may end up helping your prospect discover more reasons why he needs and wants your product.

Clarifying questions are also powerful against objections. For example, if your prospect says, "Your price is too high," don't go into defensive mode just yet. Instead, ask your prospect what he means by this. Let's consider how the conversation could go if you clarify:

Prospect: Your price is too high.

You: You must be telling me this for a reason.

Prospect: Well, we are under a tight budget.

You: What do you mean by a tight budget?

Prospect: We have to justify to our boss if we are going to need more budget.

You: Ok, I see, anything else?

Prospect: We also need a good reason to switch to your product.

You: For example...?

You: Hmm... perhaps the service recovery process can be more efficient. We have been receiving some complaints lately from our customers.

Notice how a window of opportunity opens up for you when you clarify. Now you have a hook you can use to create the sale.

Your Turn

Next time you attempt to influence, prepare a set of questions to ask. For each of the category (pain, pleasure, value, expectation) list down at least five qualifying questions relating to your product or service.

The more you know the person, the easier it is to persuade him or her to your way of thinking. Unless you can read minds, the next best way to get into the head of the person is to ask questions. If you listen hard enough, he might just reveal to you the way into his heart.

Secret 52
FACTS TELL, BUT STORIES SELL

When Subway was first opened in United States, it was quickly categorised as fast food. As a result, they were slapped with all the negative associations that came along with food served at similar fast food restaurants — oily, unhealthy, high cholesterol.

Subway's marketing team tried to change the perspectives of consumers by highlighting the healthiness of their sandwiches with facts and figures. But they failed. That is, until Jared came into the picture.

Jared Fogle was a 16-year old college kid who suffered from obesity. He weighed 425 pounds and wore size XXXXXXL shirts, the largest size shirt in big-and-tall clothing stores.

One December afternoon, Jared was struck down with edema, an abnormal accumulation of fluid in the body. Untreated, his condition would lead to diabetes, heart problems and even early heart attacks. Then came his doctor's stern warning: "Unless Jared loses weight and changes his lifestyle, he might not make it past the age of 35." This shocked Jared into deciding to lose as much weight as he could — and fast! Motivated by one of Subway's ad campaigns, he decided to give their sandwiches a try. He devised a Subway diet that comprised a foot long veggie sub for lunch and a six-inch turkey sub for dinner. After staying on his diet for three months, Jared lost 100 pounds (45 kg).

Happy with the results, Jared continued with his diet and kept losing weight. Eventually he dropped from 425 pounds to a far trimmer 180 pounds. Oprah heard about Jared's story and invited him to appear on her show, where Jared's story was told to millions of Americans.

In 1999, Subway's sales were flat. However, Jared's story helped change the minds of millions of skeptical consumers, many of whom later became big fans.

Fast forward to the company's sales results for the next two years: in 2000, sales jumped 18 per cent, and in 2001, they jumped another 16 per cent. This was in stark comparison to the smaller sandwich chains such as Scholtzsky's and Quiznos who were growing at about seven per cent every year.

Here's an important lesson to learn from Jared's story: facts tell but stories sell. But how does one tell an effective story? Here are five pointers to take note of.

1. The change idea behind the story must be crystal clear

If the story is going to work, you must be clear about what you want to change. In Jared's example, the change was in consumers' opinions of Subway sandwich, from 'unhealthy' to 'healthy'.

2. The story must be based on an actual example

Once the change idea has been identified, think of a specific example where the change was implemented with positive results. Make sure the story is real and easily verified.

Hot Tip

Remember to give the name, date and place where your story happened. These details may seem trivial but they signify that your story is true.

3. The story must be told from the point of view of a single protagonist who must be someone the audience can relate to

No one will care about your story unless they can see themselves in the protagonist's shoes. Therefore, it is extremely important to tell the story from your listener's point of view.

If you are trying to influence a client who is a CEO, you need to tell a story about another CEO, preferably someone of similar age and background as him. If you are trying to influence your sales force, you need to tell a story about a salesperson who faced similar challenges as they are facing.

4. The story must be told with little detail

Going back to Jared's story, does it matter to you what subject he is studying? Or what other food he loves to eat? Or even the dreams he has? No, no, and no.

In Jared's story, the story focuses solely on how Subway sandwiches helped him to lose a lot of weight. At the end of the day, it boils back down to the change idea you are trying to implement. Keep that in mind and your story will be sharp and precise.

Caution

Don't fill your story with too many unimportant details, or clutter will be its main message.

5. The story must be linked to the purpose of telling it

A story is simply a recount of the past, but what makes it powerful is its ability to move people into the future. If you don't link the story to the change you want them to make, you will leave them wondering, "Erm... so what?" or "What has this story got to do with me?"

Many people can tell stories, but only few can tell them effectively. With these five pointers, you can be assured that your story will be persuasive and memorable. More importantly, the next time you need to influence someone, resist telling, ordering or threatening. Instead, tell a story. You will be surprised how much more effective and effortless it will be to influence that person.

Checklist for influencing people to your way of thinking

1. Get the person to like you first by demonstrating that you are like the person, because people buy people first.

2. Establish common ground as soon as you can via their passions, their pains and most importantly, their values.

3. Answer the following three questions that the person is silently asking: "So what? Who cares? What's in it for me?"

4. Appeal to the person's self-interests by showing how he or she can achieve their needs, wants and desires through your products, services or ideas.

5. Help them to identify and re-experience their pain because the more uncomfortable they are in their current situation, the more open they are to accepting your solution.

6. Create a direct experience that will get them emotionally involved very quickly and lead them to the conclusion you want them to make.

7. Prepare a set of questions that will help you to identify the person's desires, challenges, values and expectations.

8. Ask clarifying questions to help you discover more reasons why the person would want to buy your idea, product or service.

9. Tell an effective story, one in which the change idea is clear and based on an actual example.

10. Ensure that your story is told from the point of view of a single protagonist who is someone the person can relate to. Remember, facts tell but stories sell.

CHAPTER 14

PERSUADING WITH POWER
How to get your message across to any audience

by **David Goldwich**

CEO
David Goldwich International

David Goldwich, the Persuasion Doctor, is committed to helping people get what they want. A 'reformed' lawyer, David teaches people how to play the negotiation game and become more assertive, compelling and persuasive.

David has MBA and JD degrees and has practised law in the United States for more than ten years, arguing before judges and political, government and community bodies. An engaging and award-winning speaker, David uses humour and stories culled from his own experience as a lawyer, businessman and father to help people reach breakthrough changes in their personal and professional lives. In his work on persuasion, David draws from fields as diverse as psychology, law, social science and advertising. He is author of several books and numerous articles in his field of expertise – persuasive communication.

An American citizen, David enjoys art, music, the beach, red wine, chocolate, and anything Italian. He gives talks and conducts public workshops and in-house training programmes in persuasive business presentations, negotiation, organisational storytelling, and other areas of influence and persuasion.

Find out more about David at: **www.davidgoldwich.com** and
http://thepersuasiondoctor.wordpress.com
Contact David at: **david@davidgoldwich.com**

BEING ABLE TO stand up and address an audience with confidence, poise and polish is nice, but it isn't enough. Today's business audiences are becoming more sophisticated and discerning. They hear a multitude of messages from many different sources. Why should they pay attention to you, and why should they accept your message?

In this chapter, David Goldwich will share some powerful techniques for crafting and delivering persuasive messages for even the most demanding audiences. How can you use framing to influence your audience and gain their buy-in? How can you make your message memorable and have a lasting impact long after you leave the room?

David will also look at two very different types of content: quantitative data and stories. Numbers, statistics and graphs may look like they are carved in stone, but you can shape the way you present them. And while numbers are not always interesting, they are often necessary. However, for the sheer ability to move people, nothing is as compelling as a story.

⚷ *Secret 53*
WHOEVER FRAMES THE QUESTION WINS

You may know the story of Tom Sawyer whitewashing his Aunt Polly's fence. One fine sunny morning, Aunt Polly assigned Tom this unpleasant task. As Tom toiled away, other kids interrupted their play to tease him. Tom pretended not to be bothered, and told the others it wasn't *work*, it was *fun*. After all, it's not every day you get the chance to whitewash a fence.

It wasn't long before the other boys were begging for a turn with the brush. Tom expressed doubt as to whether to let others share in his fun, which made them even more eager to do it. Soon all the boys in the neighbourhood were lining up for a turn, and trading their prized possessions for the privilege! Tom relaxed in the shade enjoying his windfall while the others completed his chore.

Tom Sawyer was able to persuade others to do an unpleasant task by framing it in a positive way. The other boys adopted his frame and agreed to his proposal.

A frame is a mental filter that influences the way a person views a situation. We develop frames based on our own experiences, stereotypes and cultural influences. Most people will adopt a frame without giving it much thought. They see the world in a way that just seems normal to them. However, they can often be swayed to adopt another frame depending on word choice and situational context. *This ability to shape another's perceptions is too powerful to ignore!*

Two people can look at the same situation and interpret it differently. One sees the glass as half empty, the other as half full. One sees a risk, the other an opportunity to gain. How you see it depends on the lens through which you view the issue, or your frame.

Holy Moly!

I can influence the way a person interprets a situation, depending on how I present it to him.

How can you use framing to become more persuasive? There are two ways to create a frame: with words and context. Choose your words carefully. Words are often loaded and can have a strong impact on an audience. Tom Sawyer refused to define painting a fence as 'work'. Referring to it as work would have doomed his efforts to recruit helpers. Instead, he framed it as 'fun'.

You can also look at ways to reshape the situational context. Tom Sawyer did this by suggesting that painting a fence was a rare opportunity to be relished rather than a chore to be avoided.

Consider the following ways to frame issues:

1. Problem/opportunity

We rarely hear of 'problems' in business — it sounds negative. A 'problem' is more likely to be framed as a challenge to be met or an opportunity to be exploited. By changing a word, you have not changed the situation, but you have changed the way people see the situation.

Caution

A frame needs to be credible to be persuasive. In the movie 'Apollo 13' the line was "Houston, we have a problem." Reframing it as "Houston, we have an opportunity" would not have been believable!

2. Gain maximising/loss minimising

People behave differently depending on whether they see a proposal as an opportunity to gain something or a potential loss. Expert negotiators know this, and they will frame a proposal in terms of what their counterpart stands to gain. Looking at it from that perspective, your counterpart will be more likely to make generous concessions than he would if he were thinking in terms of what he would be giving up. In other situations you might choose to play upon your audience's fear of losing.

3. Traditional/cutting edge

A fine chocolatier might emphasise its traditional approach to making chocolate, even though it is housed in a fully-automated, state of the art factory. A printer might play up its cutting edge technology. Both are using their ability to choose words to influence the way others perceive them.

4. Classic/outdated

In 1985, Coca-Cola made the mistake of changing their amazingly successful formula in favour of 'New Coke.' They quickly had to bring back the original formula to avoid making a disastrous situation even worse. They didn't call the original formula 'Old Coke' or even 'Original Coke' — they called it 'Coca-Cola Classic.' Classic sounds better than old.

A master persuader thinks about how best to frame issues. The next time you find yourself asking for support from others, think of a way to make your request irresistible. How might you influence your listeners by choosing one word rather than another? How can you frame a situation to make it more appealing to your audience?

Secret 54
USING A PHRASE THAT PAYS WILL MAKE YOUR MESSAGE STICK

Your audience sees and hears several thousand messages every day. These messages come from all directions: email, conversations, meetings, newspapers, TV, and other sources. All these messages add up to a lot of noise, making it hard for any message to stand out. And after your audience is bombarded by thousands of messages, you expect them to remember *yours*?

This is a tough challenge, but you can do it. You just need a 'money phrase' — a memorable phrase or tagline that captures the essence of your message and stays with your audience. It is a catchy, concise way to summarise your message. It helps your message stand out from the noise. You must aim for your money phrase to be repeated by members of your audience well after your presentation has ended, so that your message sticks.

Caution

Do not assume your audience is interested in your message. They have a lot on their minds already. You need to earn their attention by standing out with a memorable and compelling message.

Imagine the CEO of ABC Corporation is addressing his employees. He says, among other things, "We need to be more innovative if we are to stay ahead of the competition." Will his employees act on his message? No. They probably won't even remember it once they get back to work.

Now imagine the CEO of XYZ Corporation addressing his troops. He says, "We've been boxed in by stagnation, routine, tradition. We need to start thinking out of the box!" Back in the office, people start parroting his phrase. "Okay, let's think out of the box." "Now you're thinking out of the box." "That's the kind of out of the box thinking we need around here." The CEO's message survives the meeting, sticks to people, and becomes part of the culture.

Marketing maven Seth Godin wrote a book called *Purple Cow*. His idea is that you need to be remarkable to stand out from the crowd. Plenty of people had already written about the need to stand out from the crowd, to differentiate themselves. But Godin's money phrase – 'purple cow' – makes *him* stand out.

Similarly, the concept of 'critical mass' was around long before Malcolm Gladwell wrote his bestseller *The Tipping Point*. Critical mass and tipping point mean the same thing. Gladwell did not even coin the term 'tipping point', but he owns it now.

So how can you create a money phrase to help sell your own ideas? By thinking like a poet! These techniques can help make your money phrase pay off:

- **Alliteration.** Use the same sound at the beginning of two or more words in close proximity to make your message more memorable.

    Examples: Sell the sizzle, not the steak; more bang for your buck; compassionate conservative.

- **Rhyme.** Use the same sound at the end of two or more words, like a poem or song.

    Examples: Walk the talk; prime time; nitty gritty.

- **Meter.** A catchy cadence, rhythm or inflection can make a message stick. This technique is more about the *way* you say it rather than the words themselves.

    Examples:

    "You're fired!" (Donald Trump)

    "I'll be back" (Arnold Schwarzenegger)

    "It keeps on going ... and going ... and going ..." (the Energiser Bunny).

- **Imagery.** Use descriptive language (especially adjectives and verbs) and metaphors to paint mental pictures that stay with your audience.

  Examples: Think out of the box; purple cow; sharpen the saw.

- **Play on words.** Hitch a ride on someone else's money phrase by making it your own.

  Examples: Since Watergate, scandals are often described as _____-gate; Got _____? (after the "Got milk?" ads); I ♥ NY and subsequent variants.

Hot Tip

You can use poetic techniques such as alliteration, rhyme, imagery and word play to craft a memorable money phrase.

You may have noticed that some of these money phrases sound a lot like clichés. True, but they were fresh and memorable when they were new. When the CEO of XYZ Corp. first said "think out of the box" it was a revelation. It has since lost much of its power, but only after serving his purpose. The message is clear: you need to coin your own money phrase rather than just use someone else's cliché.

There is one other point you need to know about a money phrase. You can offer it, but only your audience can decide whether to accept it. To increase the odds that they will take away a money phrase, consider using more than one potential winner. And get in the habit of using alliteration, rhyme, metaphor and descriptive language that paints mental pictures to make your message memorable.

Secret 55
YOU CAN USE NUMBERS, STATISTICS AND GRAPHS TO PERSUADE

Business is often described as a numbers game. We look at costs, profit margins, sales volumes, interest rates and other numbers to make sense of where we are. Numbers are a great way to keep score.

We can use figures, graphs and statistics to persuade. Quantitative data can be measured. Numbers either add up or they don't. Charts and graphs look official and irrefutable. Numbers, data and trend lines give us something to compare.

Where do numbers and statistics come from? They are often just a guess, educated or otherwise. Statistics look official, but they are not the same as facts. While they are intended to help us understand numbers and make sense of the world, they are often biased and manipulative. They can make a weak argument sound persuasive. Mark Twain said, "There are three kinds of lies: lies, damned lies, and statistics." Thus, you need to be on your guard when evaluating quantitative data. You can also choose your numbers, graphs, and statistics wisely to put your own proposals in a favourable light.

Several agents in a real estate office claim to be the top producer. How can that be? One agent has the greatest number of sales, another has sold the greatest total dollar value of property, yet another boasts the highest average selling price, and a fourth earned the highest commission. There is more than one way to be number one. Look for the way of expressing numbers that best supports your interests.

For example, suppose we want to express the average selling price of homes in a neighbourhood. We can choose from several kinds of averages, the most popular being the mean (the sum of selling prices divided by the number of homes sold) and the median (the midpoint of all the selling prices). The mean could be greatly affected by a small number of very expensive (or very cheap) homes. The median price would give a more realistic figure in this example.

When using charts or graphs, be aware of how you depict the data. How far back do the data go? A short- or medium-term trend may not tell the same story as a long-term trend. By using a break in one axis you can create a truncated graph that emphasises differences in the data. On the other hand, a stretched out axis minimises differences.

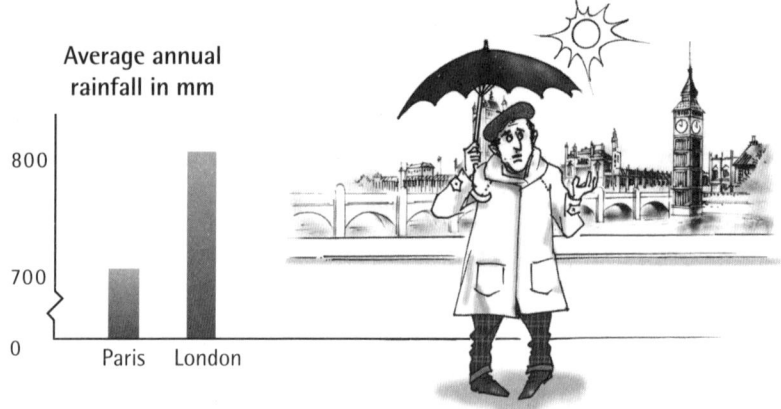

This graph compares average annual rainfall in London and Paris. It looks like it is far more likely to rain in London than in Paris. However, if you eliminate the break on the vertical axis and extend the numbering to zero you would have a more accurate picture. In fact, Paris gets nearly as much rain as London.

Your Turn

The next time you need to include quantitative data as part of a proposal, try to express it several different ways, using different types of charts and graphs, statistics, percentages, etc. Ask a few trusted colleagues or friends which method puts your proposal in the most favourable light. Just remember that if you are too extreme in massaging your numbers, your credibility will suffer.

We can also emphasise the difference between two numbers by using the contrast principle. Figures expressed in proximity to other figures look different from figures viewed in isolation.

For example, an appliance salesman will show you a very expensive model before enticing you to buy a mid-range model, rather than a cheaper one. Compared with the expensive model, the mid-priced model looks like a bargain. Similarly, you might not ordinarily wish to pay a large sum for a car audio system, but when you compare it with the price of your new car it doesn't seem so expensive.

You can use analogies and metaphors to put numbers in perspective. Our friend Malcolm Gladwell, mentioned earlier, claims that it takes 10,000 hours of study to become truly accomplished in a given field. It is hard to appreciate the impact of a number — especially a large number — unless it is put into a context that we can understand. Ten thousand hours sounds like a lot, but is it? An hour on the dance floor with a new love seems to fly by, while an hour in the doctor's waiting room seems interminable. So what does 10,000 hours mean?

Well, if you work 40 hours a week and take only two weeks' vacation, you put in 2,000 hours a year. So 10,000 hours is the equivalent of working full-time for five years. Having put our 10,000 hours into this context, we begin to appreciate the magnitude of the number.

Hot Tip

If you wish to persuade, don't just throw numbers or statistics at your audience. Think about the numbers, the various ways you can express them, and the effect you are seeking. Then choose the way of expressing the number that has the greatest impact from your perspective. Put the number into a context that is meaningful to your audience.

⚷ *Secret 56*
STORIES ARE MORE PERSUASIVE THAN LOGIC

Telling stories is more than a folksy way to relate to others. It is a powerful and persuasive medium that you can use to get your message across with maximum impact and minimum resistance.

Most business people use memos, email and bullet points to convey their message. They gather facts, devise arguments and construct chains of reasoning to persuade their audience. However, logic, reason, and data lead to analysis and debate; stories tap emotions and lead to action. *Stories move people.*

Bosses, sales prospects, and others we encounter in business tend to be skeptical. When confronted with facts or logic, business people adopt a critical thinking mode. They look for flaws in your arguments and try to shoot you down. They perceive your facts to be biased and self-serving.

When listening to your story, your audience goes into 'acceptance' mode. They do not try to poke holes in your story. Your story carries your message through. The emotional content of your story can trigger hot buttons and prompt your audience to act.

You can use stories to effect many purposes in business. Today's most effective leaders tell stories to win buy-in for their ideas, transmit values, and inspire their people.

You can also use stories to:

- Introduce yourself and position yourself in the way you wish to be perceived
- Break the ice, connect and build rapport with your audience
- Build trust and establish credibility
- Introduce your company, product or service
- Promote your brand

- Transmit knowledge, values, and organisational culture
- Communicate a vision and drive change
- Motivate and inspire people

Perhaps the most common use for a story is to illustrate a point. We learn to do this from an early age. You can tell a child, "Don't tell lies," and he will resent the moralising tone of your lecture. If you tell him the story of the boy who cried 'wolf' he will get the message.

We meet new people all the time in business — new customers and prospects, colleagues, contacts at networking events, and many others. You can use a story to introduce yourself while positioning yourself the way you want to be perceived. Here's an example.

Let's say you are a salesman. How would you like to be perceived by your customers and prospects? As professional, competent and trustworthy? You could tell them "I'm professional, competent and trustworthy." That would sound self-serving, so it would not be very believable.

Now suppose you tell them a story that *portrays* you as professional, competent and trustworthy. They would probably accept your story on its face value, and your message would get through.

Another common purpose for stories is to communicate values. Nearly every company has a cluster of core values listed as a series of bullet points in their brochures and on their website. One of these core values is invariably 'customer focused.' As customers, we know this is often not an accurate depiction of how we are treated, so we tend to be wary whenever we see the words 'customer focused.' Imagine using a story that demonstrates your company's commitment to its customers. People who hear such a story are more likely to believe you care about them.

Stories are compelling. Stories are memorable. Stories are powerful! So why don't we tell more stories in business settings?

Perhaps we are afraid we might appear undignified or unprofessional. Most top executives issue decrees and give orders. They are direct and to the point.

Not many business people are known for telling stories. However, some very influential leaders were known for their stories. Lincoln, Jesus, and Gandhi come to mind. They were effective in large part because they frequently told stories.

Holy Moly!

I can tell a story about myself that positions me the way I want my audience to perceive me.

What makes for a good story? A good story is

- Relevant – the message should be clear and applicable to your situation.
- Personal – tell your own stories that will resonate with your audience.
- Vivid – involve all the senses, paint a picture that is easy to remember and *feel*.

The important thing is to be sincere, authentic, to connect with the audience. If you are telling your own story and are genuine, your audience will accept both you and your story. They are also likely to accept your message.

Finally, avoid stories that involve sex, religion, politics, racial or cultural sensitivities, and ridicule. Even if you do not offend anyone directly, someone might form a negative opinion of you because of your insensitivity or poor judgment.

Your Turn

Use a story that highlights a personal quality that your audience will value. It could be about a challenge you overcame or a turning point in your life. Refine and polish it until it is concise, and practise until you can tell it smoothly. You will use it a lot, so make it shine!

Checklist for getting your message across to any audience

1. Choose your words carefully to create the impact you want.

2. Frame issues in the way most likely to persuade your audience.

3. Craft a money phrase that captures the essence of your message and sticks with your audience.

4. Use rhyme, alliteration, meter, imagery and word play to create a memorable money phrase.

5. Present numbers, statistics and graphs in the form most favourable to your proposal.

6. Beware of quantitative data that have been manipulated to mislead.

7. Put numbers into a context that is meaningful to your audience using analogies and metaphors.

8. Tell stories to get your message across with maximum impact and minimum resistance.

9. Introduce yourself with a story that positions you the way you want to be perceived.

10. Move your audience to action with relevant, personal and vivid stories that tap into emotions.

SECTION 6

Selling and Winning Business

CHAPTER 15

PITCHING PERFECTLY TO WIN BUSINESS

How to prepare and deliver a pitch that persuades,
conveys credibility and packs a punch

by **Tina Altieri**
Managing Principal
Media Australasia Xchange (MAX)

Tina Altieri is a dedicated trainer and presentation specialist who has earned respect through her 23 years in the Australian broadcast news business. As a TV presenter, professional speaker and master of ceremonies, Tina has been the public face of thousands of conferences, forums and public presentation events. She has been seen on Western Australian television for over two decades as a news presenter and lifestyle programme host.

Tina has developed many exclusive results-oriented training programmes for professionals seeking the skills, strategies and confidence for powerful public presentations and media Interviews.

Tina was born in the port city of Fremantle, Western Australia, and commenced her career as a radio reporter. She soon moved into the realm of television news and became the youngest TV newsreader in Australia at 19 years of age. Between 1996 and 2005 Tina was Australian correspondent for Channel News Asia, and also trained on-camera news presenters for Channel News Asia in Singapore.

Tina has spent the past five years as a specialist presentation skills and media trainer based in Singapore. With an impressive coaching list of leaders from over 30 Southeast Asian organisations, Tina is passionate about the possibilities that stem from communicating powerfully. A sought-after speaker/trainer in Australia and the region, Tina always makes it her business to ensure everyone walks away from her workshops re-energised and ready to pitch at their peak — powerfully and convincingly!

Find out more about Tina at: **www.maxcommunicate.com**
Contact Tina at: **tina@maxcommunicate.com**

EVEN FOR THE most confident person, it can be a daunting experience to present your company, your product or service by way of making a pitch to a group of people.

In today's economic climate, there has never been such an emphasis on value for money. Companies are now placing potential candidates on a shortlist. These lucky few have to sell themselves in a 'live' presentation. There is so much riding on those few minutes when all eyes are on you.

We know an audience forms an impression in the first few seconds when watching a presentation. Is the presenter nervous? How well-prepared is the content? Does the pitch ooze strength and professionalism? If confidence is the key to winning over our audience and winning the business, then why do the majority of presenters pitch poorly?

Tina Altieri will reveal what it takes to develop and present with impact by following the vital presentation techniques that distinguish you from the rest. She will give you the confidence to deliver powerfully every time.

Tina will also help empower you to write using your best voice. You'll discover the perfect pitch buttons to press when it comes to the spoken language and what an audience remembers about you and your pitch.

Secret 57
IF YOU PITCH WITH PRECISION, YOUR AIM WILL BE SUCCESSFUL

Imagine what you might be able to achieve in business and in life if you could 'win the pitch' every time? Imagine being able to deliver your presentation and always have people comment on how powerfully you come across? If you want your customers, clients, stakeholders, colleagues and bosses to see you in a position of strength, there's just one thing you need to do — aim your pitch with precision.

Despite the onslaught of new communication technology, the need to communicate powerfully and pitch successfully in front of audiences, large or small, seems to be more important than ever. Why then do most people spend so little time in precision planning and preparing their presentation for maximum, positive impact?

Learning to pitch and present confidently is a powerful way to sell yourself and your message. In my experience, the most perplexing question when it comes to delivering the perfect pitch is, "How do you know if you're presenting well or hitting the mark with your audience?"

To answer that question, let's take a look at how a great pitch looks and feels like from the stage using my 'WOW' Factor.

W   Wide open faces

O   Open for business

W   Wake up vocally

W: Wide open faces

Think back to when you made your last presentation. What do you remember about the people looking at you? Were they attentive and facing you front on, or were they side-seated so they could effectively hide their phone as they spent your entire presentation sending text messages and checking their email?

Did they nod in acknowledgement of your key information, or were they gazing into space completely unaware of the brilliant idea you just told them?

Are your presentations full of impactful language dotted with colourful phrases and vivid descriptions? Or do they sound more like an instruction manual that effectively sends your audience to a far more interesting place – daydream island? If you have failed to attract that wide open sea of faces, then it's time for you to address your attention-grabbing techniques.

Accomplished professionals often know what it feels like to have an audience in the palm of their hands. This doesn't mean that to be a great pitcher your audience must agree with everything you say. Rather, it's about building that immediate connection from what you say and do. Some people call it building a likeability factor or building rapport with your audience. I like to think of it as making a connection with those who've come to hear you. By being in front of you, your audience has given you perhaps one of the greatest personal gifts of all – their time. This is a rare opportunity to build trust and goodwill, be sincere, be entertaining, be in control, and be there to take care of your audience for the amount of time they've given you.

Caution

Even if your business pitch is aimed at a small audience and will not make or break your company's fortune, you must still treat each presentation as an important one. Too often I hear businesspeople dismiss a small pitch as insignificant, so they prepare very little for it. As a result, they develop a reputation for delivering inconsistently. Remember: every pitch is important. People are constantly judging you on your ability to persuade, inform and influence them. Besides, you never know who's in your audience!

O: Open for business

Whatever type of presentation you are giving, whether pitching for new business or presenting to your board, it's vital that you give your audience a compelling reason to want to listen to you, believe you, and to march to the beat of your drum for the length of your presentation. Think about this – if you were an office, would it say 'open for business' during your important pitch? Or do you have a tendency to show that you're unsure, hate the idea of public speaking, and wish you didn't have to do this? Your body language speaks volumes about you. When you openly demonstrate to your audience that you're delighted to be there for them, it will make a huge difference to the way you come across.

W: Wake up vocally

I can't begin to tell you the number of times I've seen some high-ranking, highly paid professionals deliver a pitch with zero 'care factor' in their voice. By suggesting that you 'wake up your voice', I'm suggesting that you inject a level of energy that helps you sound passionate and committed. Not only should you make sure you 'look alive', you should also 'sound alive', as if having an enthusiastic or high energy conversation with the audience. When you deliver with animation and energy in your voice, it's a sure-fire way of fast tracking your progress from technical expert to persuader.

Holy Moly!

It doesn't matter how skilled I am or how knowledgeable I am on a particular subject. If I can't demonstrate it with conviction in my body language, my voice and my words, then I'm not pitching to win.

As you can see from these concepts, using my WOW factor reminds us that pitching for business involves shutting yourself out from your own head and entering the heads of your audience. When you make the decision to be there for your audience more than for yourself, you will experience that elusive WOW factor and know you are in your business peak performance zone.

Secret 58
WITH CAREFUL PREPARATION, YOU CAN HAVE YOUR AUDIENCE IN THE PALM OF YOUR HAND

When you have a new presentation coming up, do you sometimes wonder where to start? If so, you're not alone. Most people find this very frustrating. Do you want to persuade and influence your audience in the first couple of minutes of your presentation? Do you wonder where to begin in creating a watertight, persuasive argument that will win over your audience? Let's look at this important stage in more detail.

Even before you begin to write a word of your presentation, it might help if you consider a simple, one-line objective. Having completed research on your audience, you need to be crystal clear about what it is that you want your audience to learn or feel or understand by the end of your pitch. I suggest you create an emotive or motivating phrase to help you achieve this aim. For example, do you want to *persuade* your audience to agree on a new way of doing business? Or do you intend to *stimulate debate* on a particular topic? Perhaps you want to *generate enthusiasm* or *inspire* them to think more creatively on a certain issue?

This objective is for your eyes only and you don't need to tell your audience. Quite simply, this is an exercise for you to set your sights on your destination and get your motor running.

The more specific you make the objective, the easier it will be for you to decide what information to include or omit in your presentation. If you consider including any key points in your pitch that do not help you achieve your one line objective then those points should be removed.

If you keep your objective highly optimistic, chances are you will approach the pitch with a great deal of enthusiasm and drive. Someone who is pitching with the aim of generating excitement, stimulating debate or converting thoughts will automatically present with far more conviction than a person who simply wants to give their audience information, "share some ideas" or "say a few words" about their product or service.

Here are some examples of one-line objectives:

- To excite and inspire my team to adopt a new workplace policy that will save time and make them more efficient.

- To stimulate discussion on the pros and cons of job-sharing, and encourage them to vote on the issue at an upcoming meeting.

Your one line objective will simply help you to keep your audience at the forefront of your mind. There's little doubt the more optimistic you are in your approach, the more likely you will succeed in persuading and influencing your audience.

Your Turn

Think back to your last presentation and pitch. What would have been your objective? Create a one-line objective that would have given you the ammunition to further inspire or convince your audience. Would you have presented differently if you'd had that aim firmly at the front of your mind? Would you have 'won' the pitch?

Here are two other preparation techniques that need your attention. I like to remember them by way of *Fits and Starts* – beneFITS and STARTing techniques

BeneFITS

It's human nature for audiences to seek reassurance that your presentation will be meaningful and relevant to them. Unfortunately, too many presenters stop way short of giving the audience the benefits because they are so caught up on explaining the features. It will really help if you describe the specific benefits to the audience for adopting the course of action you are advocating.

What's the difference, you might ask? A feature is a fact or quality about you or your company. By contrast a benefit is how that feature will directly help your audience.

Here are some benefit triggers that you could include in your next pitch.

- The reason I've unveiled these latest statistics is so that you can ...

- It's important for you to know this because when you ...

- What this means to you is that next time you ...

When you know the answers to these questions, you can then focus on your audience's needs rather than on yourself. This is reassurance if you are someone who constantly worries about "will the audience like me?" or "will they think I know what I'm talking about?" These benefit triggers remind us that we should focus on what the audience needs to hear from us, in other words what they should know and what they would find interesting.

Hot Tip

If you develop a habit of translating your key pieces of red hot information into benefits for your audience, there's little chance that listeners will drift off with that common thought about presentations, "So what?"

STARTS

So you've got yourself a list of fascinating key points, and some enthralling facts and figures to reveal. Now for the bad news – unless you've written the perfect pitch, no one will remember everything you say because of short attention spans. Communication experts will tell you that less than 10 per cent of your information is retained by audiences after they have witnessed an uninteresting and dull presentation.

Here are some of the sinful starts that I've heard. Always avoid openers like these as they will set you back in your presentations.

- "When I was asked to make this presentation, I wondered what I was going to talk about." (Usually these kind of speakers never do find out!)
- "I really don't know too much about this specific subject but I'll give it my best shot."
- "My topic today is to address you on the subject of..."
- "I learnt only yesterday that I had to give this pitch so I want to apologise in advance."

Here is something that is guaranteed to improve that dismal 10 per cent recollection statistic – an engaging introduction.

A great presenter will always grab the audience's attention at the beginning of the pitch, even if they are presenting a technical or dry subject. Opening with impact is important because it is your first opportunity to convince your audience that you have something of value for them and that you're not wasting their time. A solid introduction will win over your audience's attention because it will involve your listeners.

Here are some ideas to make your opening memorable:

- An interesting or thought-provoking question aimed at the audience.
- A 'factoid' – a striking statistic or a little known fact.
- A short anecdote relevant to the topic.

Holy Moly!

I really need to work on a powerful, engaging opening so that I capture the audience's attention. Then I can launch into the subject swiftly.

Make or reinforce a connection with your audience by getting a positive response in your opener. Perhaps get a show of hands to get them thinking quickly. The sooner you can get a positive response from your audience, the quicker you'll have them exactly where you want them. Seeing your audience take the bait and become engaged in your presentation will also work wonders on your anxiety levels.

Secret 59
TO MAKE THE GREATEST IMPACT, YOU MUST CHOOSE YOUR WORDS CAREFULLY

In my years of experience as a speaker and professional MC, here are what I consider to be the two most perplexing questions on a speaker's mind:

1. How can we make ourselves memorable to an audience (for all the right reasons)?

2. How can we turn resistant listeners into true believers?

One thing that will definitely help to make or break your pitch is your language. Imagine a presenter who uses formal, highly technical language, almost as if they are a walking, talking document. Now compare that to a presenter who uses colourful, vivid phrases and explanations that are thought-provoking yet clearly understood by everyone. There's little doubt that language is king in the preparatory stages of your important pitch.

Words can really pack a punch when you step into the boxing ring of live presentations. Let me share with you this formula of FREE speech that I hope you will use to liven up your language. Gloves up. Game on!

F   Fit, flab-free phrases

R   Repeat what's important

E   End with power

E   Emotionally charge your work

Let's look at each of these in detail now:

F: Fit, flab-free phrases

The way we communicate in this high-tech age has changed dramatically thanks to social networking sites and blogging. We speak more economically now, so in your presentation you must also follow this rule rather than delivering in long-winded, complicated sentences. It will help your audience follow your thoughts if you develop your main points by way of short, sharp headlines or statements to help you sell your ideas more persuasively. If you use analogies or similes that relate to the point you're making, this will evoke striking images or pictures in the minds of audience members.

I've long remembered the senior financial planner pitching for business to a large organisation by way of using metaphors to explain how his service can partner with the organisation. He explained how his planning service moulded itself on a role similar to a navigator in an international car rally. His financial planning helped his clients (ic: the rally car driver) to successfully navigate the tight twists and curves in the road ahead. He spoke of journeying with them for the entire race with constant commitment and loyalty.

During his pitch, he used phrases like 'navigator precision' and 'rewards for high performance in tough economic times.' He won the pitch by a mile. The feedback linked back to his success with the colourful phrases that were more memorable than his competitors who were heavily technical in their language.

Colourful terminology will always be remembered over concepts that are convoluted. This is not to say that you can use slang or 'dumb down' a technical presentation. Instead, look at ways of translating the material in a style that carefully explains the message. Once the audience has grasped some difficult information and has been able to digest it (thanks to your translation), your audience is most likely to join you down that persuasion pathway.

Holy Moly!

It doesn't matter how good my material is. If I can't find the words to capture people's imagination, not just their intellect, then I've not pitched as powerfully as I could.

R: Repeat what is important

We have already examined how short an audience's attention span can be, and for many good speakers this repetition rule ensures that a particular theme or idea sticks. Your audience will recall sections of information that you repeat often. But beware, this is not a license for you to rattle off four major points many times over. Instead it's an opportunity to repeat your main theme often enough so it leaves no doubt in people's minds about what they should remember.

Imagine a reader who has not grasped a concept or hasn't appreciated the significance of some information. They can easily go back to the paragraph and read it again. A listener doesn't have that luxury, and often key messages will be missed.

It's always a good idea to re-package the key points you're making in simple terms. In other words, dress them up in different ways (using vivid language as discussed in the earlier section) and always try to link those points back to your main theme. In that way you will find yourself repeating that big picture theme a few times.

E: End with power

When it comes to the grand finalé, what many speakers don't realise is that the conclusion often determines the success or failure of a pitch. Just as it's important to begin strongly, the end must also leave the audience with a confident and assertive lasting impression because we know audiences are likely to absorb the final thing you say. Generally speaking, the ending should be rammed home in an unforgettable and brief climax. It should include a call to action or food for thought. It's your opportunity to package the presentation neatly, giving the audience a feeling of having come 'full circle'. It's your last chance to fully persuade, stimulate or inspire – whatever your objective. Audiences appreciate and enjoy this level of closure to a presentation.

I am often disappointed for a speaker who has obviously spent many hours carefully compiling their introduction and main body of the presentation only to drop the ball at the conclusion and end abruptly with a lame statement such as, "Well ladies and gentleman that's it, I think. Does anyone have any questions?"

Perhaps that speaker was counting on a dynamic conclusion to magically flow from his mouth at the precise moment. The reality is, they rarely do. A solid ending requires careful planning in advance.

Caution

A conclusion is not your cue to offload a series of points that you didn't have time to include in the main body. Now is not the time for new facts, just a call to action that creates an impact in three to four sentences.

E: Emotionally charge your work

I can just see all the technical presenters now rolling their eyes at the call to inject emotion into their very straight-down-the-line business presentations.

Believe me, so many business people, when required to give presentations, struggle with this final rule of perfect pitching. Many professionals, such as solicitors, accountants or engineers, believe that appealing to an audience's emotions will make their presentation 'too soft' and therefore compromise their credibility. However, there is no escaping the fact that the majority of listeners will remember ideas and information that appeal to their emotions.

Without a doubt, it is emotions, not reasons, that stir the heart and compel an audience to think, act or feel in a certain way. When it comes to public speaking, the word *emotion* sometimes conjures images of an audience being reduced to tears by an evangelical-style preacher. Could this be the reason why so many presenters distrust emotion for fear of 'having to come out of their shell' or being perceived as 'over the top?' But remember this communication rule is about personalising the presentation and finding commonality with your audience. When you include a human angle or a real life story to illustrate your point, this will help you press the emotional 'hot buttons' of your audience.

Never underestimate your personal experiences and anecdotes that have had a profound effect on the way you think or act. Audiences love them, provided you explain them in an interesting, engaging way, and make it obvious what you learnt from those personal experiences, and what they too can learn. This is a wonderful opportunity for you to fully engage your listeners.

⚷ *Secret 60*
THERE IS NO ULTIMATE SECRET TO A WINNING PRESENTATION! SIMPLY AIM FOR CONNECTION, NOT PERFECTION

Imagine you have been dropped suddenly into the centre of city that you have never visited before. You are told that you must find the office at 3730 Main Street. You have no map, no directions, and what's worse – there are no street signs or numbers on the buildings. Chances are you'll have a difficult time ahead of you. You're likely to take wrong turns, hit dead ends, and wind up totally confused and lost.

The same thing can happen to your audience if you don't have a solid structure and signposts in your presentation or pitch. In a written paper or a book, you can use chapter titles or sub-headings, numbered lists, bullets, transitions – all sorts of signposts that will explain to your audience where they have been and how that relates to what is coming up. Similarly, in order to maintain a connection with your audience, you must provide a basic structure that makes it easy for listeners to understand and follow the flow of your presentation.

Maintaining connections

In my first three secrets, we've discussed how to create a powerful connection right from the beginning of your presentation. Once you get into the body – or the meat – of the presentation, you need to maintain that connection and strengthen it. We've also discussed how word choice, anecdotes and emotions can help maintain your connection with your audience. You can also strengthen it through the presentation's basic structure.

When considering the structure of your presentation, your introduction should, as a general rule, be followed by the main body. Just as the introduction can send your audience into dreamland if it doesn't grab them right from the start, the main section can lose them, even if you took hold of their attention at the beginning.

The main section of your presentation should include only three or four main points. To flesh out these sections, use my PREP guide:

P   State the main *point* of the section.

R   Give a *reason* for the point and provide any supporting facts necessary for your audience to understand the point.

E   Personalise your point by sharing an *example* that reinforces the point.

P   Restate your *point* to wrap up.

So you have the entire presentation put together? Now it's time to practise it
out loud. You might even try recording it and then playing it back. You want
the flow to sound like natural speech, like the spoken word instead of the
written. Don't hesitate to change any areas where you feel uncomfortable or
you sound tedious. If you feel that way when you practise, imagine how your
audience will feel when they hear it!

It's OK to use notes

Most successful speakers agree that trying to memorise everything can be
a recipe for disaster. Have your notes, whether bullet points, or written out
word-for-word, at the ready. You might want to highlight key words or phrases
so that when you take a quick look at your notes you can pick them up at a
glance. Put your notes on a table so that you can keep walking back to check
on them. Whatever you do, you must not be seen to be reading from them.
Make it look and sound natural.

Expecting the unexpected

You must plan ahead for the unexpected. Regardless of your best efforts, you might end up with one of those nightmare scenarios – your projector fails, your computer crashes, you drop your notes, or you have to deal with difficult and sensitive questions. Think of all the possible things that could go wrong and plan for them – just in case.

Holy Moly!

All the best preparation in the world can't prevent hiccups that may arise. I must anticipate the hurdles and be flexible enough to deliver my pitch, no matter what the circumstances.

If your projector fails, simply continue your presentation without the visual aids. Remember, what's on your slides are only aids. Plan ahead for dropped notes: number each page front and back so you can easily put them back in order. What would you do if you were told you had just 10 minutes to present your pitch instead of the 30 minutes you'd planned for? Can you extract the essence of your presentation in a shortened version without losing the power of your pitch or losing your cool?

Prepare for questions

Instead of fearing an interrogation, use your question and answer session as an opportunity to build rapport with your audience. Anticipate questions from the audience and prepare answers ahead of time. Here are my top ten tips for answering potentially difficult questions:

1. Ask for clarity if you're unsure what the question is.

2. Watch out for negative or loaded questions. Never endorse the negative – try to reply in the positive.

3. Answer a rambling question — by picking one part of it and responding only to that part.

4. Never try to fool the audience with an answer if you're unsure. Try something like, "There is no right or wrong answer to that question, but my years of experience in this industry tells me..."

5. If you don't know the facts, it's best to admit this straight away rather than hedging around the issue.

6. Learn how to give non-answers for questions you're not prepared to answer. Try something like, "That's a very good question and that's exactly what we're looking into. It would be premature for me to comment before our studies are completed but let me point out..." Then go onto make your positive comment.

7. Never give a hostile audience member the impression that you don't want to answer his or her question. Remain respectful and polite. If appropriate, redirect challenging questions back to the audience.

8. Don't over answer. Steer away from long-winded responses. Instead keep answers brief and to the point. If necessary, arrange to continue the discussion with that person afterwards.

9. Watch out for non-question questions. If someone makes a statement and waits for you to respond to it, then politely ask, "What is your question?"

10. Watch out for hypothetical questions. If they are not part of your game plan then be ready to respond with answers like, "Let's leave that up for the forecasters but what we know to be the case right now is..."

By carefully structuring and signposting your presentation, you will maintain the connection with your audience. This means never allowing them to get 'lost' in your detail or drift from your important messages.

Your role is to take your audience — no matter how large or small — on a journey with you, your journey of persuasion. Making your structure easy to follow will help you to deliver more successfully every time.

Checklist of items to remember when you're presenting to win:

1. Create a one-line objective, so you're clear on your aim.

2. Provide facts and benefits, but don't make your pitch a data dump.

3. Choose words and phrases carefully — vivid yet thought-provoking, intelligent yet concise.

4. Connect with your audience, grab their attention, right away — remember to involve their emotions.

5. Repeat key points to make your message stick.

6. Develop a powerful conclusion.

7. Present an 'open for business' attitude and look alive; be optimistic!

8. Follow a structure that involves no more than three or four key points.

9. Practise your presentation out loud.

10. Be ready in case technology fails you.

CHAPTER 16

PERFORM BETTER, SELL MORE, EARN MORE

Secrets to boosting your effectiveness in sales and earnings

by **Rob Salisbury**
Managing Director
Strategic Resources International P/L

Rob Salisbury, B. Com., CSP, is a Managing Director and Director with several companies in Australia and Southeast Asia. As a speaker, trainer and MC, he's been hired and re-engaged over 2,000 times by more than 500 US, Australian, Southeast Asian and European organisations.

Rob's early achievements included national sales achiever status with a US Inc. 1000 MNC, a multi-sport triathlete and senior team leader/VP for two international training organisations. He was an Executive Director of the National Speakers Association of Australia from 1999 to 2003 and a two-term, award winning President of the NSAA in Sydney.

Consistently rated among top speakers by Business SWAP International (1994 to present), Rob has been an advisor to Asia Professional Speakers Association in Singapore (2004 to present), a Singapore *Straits Times* feature writer and speaker (2007 to present) and a mentor to managers and leaders within non-profit and profit organisations.

Find out more about Rob at: **www.strategicresources.com.au**
Contact Rob at **rob@strategicresources.com.au**

"You can have everything you want in life; if you help enough other people get what they want"

— Zig Ziglar

THE FOUNDATION TO achieving a high income in sales and business is in mastering key performance areas that deliver results to your clients, business contacts and those in your relationship circles or networks.

Stop and think for a moment about this question – how important is it, on a scale of 1 as low and 10 as high, that you have a fulfilling career or earn a high income?

By understanding the true needs, wants and desires of your customers, colleagues and contacts, you can generate an endless opportunity of business as a sales, service and information provider.

However, there are several areas that can hinder or prevent average producers from becoming highly paid professionals. If you want to be among the top in any field of expertise, it's important to master issues that are rarely addressed, such as low self-esteem, standards of conduct and skills or the competencies of your trade.

Yes, you can achieve much more, and yes, you can do it much easier by adopting strategies that high achievers use to boost their performance in sales or service to super star status.

In this section, Rob Salisbury will share insights learnt from his involvement with hundreds of achievers. You will learn key tips and techniques that, when applied, can build your effectiveness and results so you can enjoy one of the best earning years in your career.

The key will be in finding the tips that apply to your personal situation and then integrating them into your plans and activities as soon as possible.

Secret 61
YOUR PERSONAL EFFECTIVENESS IS THE KEY TO HIGHER EARNINGS

When I ask top sales professionals in management and leadership roles what their core drivers are, they often say it's their own high expectations that they will succeed in their company role or career.

Upon further research, these achievers have learnt the pitfalls and challenges that keep average people average. Top people do the opposite of low performers. They focus on 'dollar productive activities' to leverage their personal effectiveness and generate massive results in business, so therefore, they earn a higher income.

I refer to these top individuals as 'Performance Champions'. They possess an internal DNA or code of habits as human 'performance' beings that is often missed when first meeting them.

Learn well and you will earn well

There is no shortage of distractions that could come your way in the next 24 hours that could hinder your sales activities or servicing clients or existing customers.

A friend could call you to have a chat, a car horn might blare as you sit in a coffee shop making calls, a person standing near you may ask for directions, or while you are paying for something a song playing in the store may remind you of a fond memory.

One of my earliest mentors shared a 'focus' tip with me from his record-setting performance days in becoming the number one producer in US real estate five years in a row. Broke at the age of 20, he achieved superstar sales status and became a self-made millionaire by 27.

He said, "We often know what to do in sales, yet we do not do what we know. Focusing on the tasks at hand is often more stressful than just doing them. Don't think too long — DO."

Within hours, I had the Nike slogan 'Just Do It' in a plaque on my work desk, on my car visor, in the front of my time planner and on the back of my shower at home. I found his words and motivational tips helped me make quick decisions about the tasks before me.

My minimum weekly goal was to see 20 qualified decision makers. Figuring out who had the potential to say yes to our company data processing and computer technology products was the most important use of my time. I referred to it as the 'golden hours'.

I understood the benefits of what we could do, and I highlighted the value of it to out-think, out-perform and out-produce our local and regional competitors.

That year, I was the only rookie to go over the company's set sales targets in our US west coast office. My reward for working smart and putting in the extra efforts was in being invited to a 120 per cent Sales Achievers Club held at the Marco Island Florida Marriott Hotel.

With all flights and expenses paid, it was great to network with company leaders and dozens of other US, Canada, Mexico, Europe and Asia quota-busting sales achievers.

Holy Moly!
People don't change until they realise the benefits and then the pain of change is forgotten.

How can you become part of the three per cent group?
Next time you are travelling through your neighbourhood or city, take a good look at the new houses or buildings along the journey. Each of these structures required a solid foundation to last the test of time and to create an asset of value for the owner.

Similarly, you need a solid foundation to achieve a high income in sales. By mastering key sales performance strategies and understanding the needs or desires of your customers and contacts, you can generate an endless revenue stream as a sales and personal services provider.

What sales success habits do you need to integrate to become one of the three per cent and then the top one per cent in your company or industry?

What drives you?

While the potential of high earnings in sales is a motivator and incentive for many, it is not the core driver for everyone.

Some identified drivers and rewards of high performance leaders and sales people are:

- Personal or professional fulfillment
- A sense of security
- Winning and achievement
- Recognition or acceptance by others
- Earning a great income
- Love of family or from community

Identifiable de-motivators or disincentives are:

- Loss of security or credit
- The fear of failing or loosing
- Non-acceptance by peers or community
- Not earning an income
- Inability to change or make progress

What is it that fires you up about a job or career in sales? Equally, what areas are de-motivational or could prevent you from gaining the type of top results you desire?

Hot Tip

Success in sales is understanding what you can do for the customer, not what they can do for you.

Secret 62
TO WIN MORE BUSINESS, YOU MUST ADOPT HIGH PERFORMANCE SELLING HABITS

The quick way to improve in sales or service roles is to grasp the knowledge and competency of those who are already in the top positions or jobs that you desire.

You can create exponential results by modelling the behaviour, activities and habits of those who have achieved the results you are seeking. Many of the greatest business, political and sporting successes were, at first, super failures. They turned their failures into successes and learned their competitors' secrets and weaknesses to help them achieve better results. They sought answers to their questions and then went to work to apply them to their trade.

> 'I hear and I forget — I see and I remember — I do and I understand'
>
> — Confucius (551 BC – 479 BC)

Which one of these four types of sales people are you?

1. **Performance Champions:** They do whatever it takes (ethically) to get the job done. This is why they are among the top three per cent, if not the top person.

   They arrive early for appointments with clients or colleagues. If for any reason they are behind, they call to advise others in respect of their time.

   The sales performance of one champion producer will often produce more than the bottom 40 per cent of any organisation.

2. **Steady:** This person is fundamental to the operations and profits of companies. They are among the most loyal team players and stable employees.

   They arrive at work on time, rarely leave until work is completed, are easy to work with and are dedicated to the mission or purpose of the organisation.

   The performance level of a steady sales or service person is what keeps companies in profit and in leader positions. They are not noted to be top producers like a champion. However, they are very productive, have a good attitude and an excellent work ethic.

3. **Borderline:** This type of sales person frustrates sales management. Simply said, they are not good enough to keep, yet not bad enough to terminate.

   They are the opposite of steady sales people in nearly every way. They are late for work or appointments, their paperwork is messy, they often blame others for their misfortune and can create dissention among others.

   This type of sales person can be 'saved' with good training, a strong manager and discipline to company standards. This person can also de-motivate others with caustic or cynical behaviour.

4. **Learner (or Apprentice):** New to sales, this type of person is very curious, a bit scared, yet well mannered and teachable. With the right training, they can become steady producers very quickly and in the right circumstances, a performance champion.

   Experience has shown the best place for a learner is under the direction of a steady type or in direct support with a champion. These strategies in modelling and behaviour adaptation can help ensure the success of the learner or apprentice nearly every time.

The traps and pitfalls of most adult day care centres (the office)

One of the most popular TV shows on American and British television is a show simply called, 'The Office'. Excusing the Hollywood comedy side of this drama for the moment, the culture depicted in this regional paper supply company is fairly close to the reality of some firms.

When mixing up the personalities such as champions, steadies, borderlines and learners, it is possible to see the amount of jockeying for a better position that goes on with this television show. With each episode, someone is trying to either save their job, upgrade their status or maintain the status quo in the company.

In today's office environment, it is imperative to have a personal code of ethics, work habits and protocols in place. Avoiding jealousy, negative thinking, gossip and playing favourites can help to develop leadership qualities that shine with other colleagues in the form of respect and trust. By doing this, many people can survive and thrive amidst today's Gen X, Y and Boomer office workers.

Caution

One per cent of your 24 hour day is equal to 14 minutes and 40 seconds. Invest this time wisely into high payoff areas. Keep idle chit-chat, email or social media to a minimum.

The mindset of super sales achievers and service providers

Research has shown that academic, scientific and business experts often differ on universal truths, principles and philosophical areas regarding success. However, they do agree that it is difficult to measure the desire level of some people to survive or succeed.

The 1976 Academy Award for best picture was 'Rocky'. This was a good example of what can happen when a person considered 'borderline' is given a shot at fame and respectability.

Psychology, personal determination and small achievements are on full display as Rocky goes the full distance to find respect and redemption from his past failures in life and boxing.

Who are the role models and people that really motivate you? What can you do to learn from them as quickly as possible? How can you adopt their mindset and skills as yours? Have they written a book, produced a DVD or CD learning programme or a television program like Donald Trump or Lord Alan Sugar of the Apprentice show in the USA or UK?

Save time and increase your earning potential by learning from those who have already achieved much of what you want to get out of your future and career.

Hot Tip

The road to success is littered with good intentions. To achieve a worthwhile result or goal, take action today.

♀ Secret 63
IF YOU WANT TO EARN MORE, YOU MUST LEARN WELL

When I started university, it became apparent that I needed to upgrade my high school study habits if I hoped to pass the assignments and exams set by my professors. Armed with new study skills, I disciplined myself to go to the university library and study halls to ensure I gave myself the highest possible chance of passing each assignment.

Invariably, I completed my business degree courses with extra time as a graduating senior to hone my interviewing skills. I booked in as many opportunities as possible to meet with on-campus company recruiters who might be hiring just to obtain more interviewing experience.

With a similar focus and discipline, I researched the companies I was qualified to be interviewed by. Two weeks prior to graduation, several job offers came forth and I was soon employed by an Inc. 1000 firm with training in the San Francisco, Colorado and Boston regional offices.

Within weeks of joining the firm, I learnt that going beyond the company induction training I could ensure a significant edge over other sales people.

I found that applying the secrets that helped me to do well at university would also give me the edge over my peers. As a sales executive and account manager, I started by investing five per cent of my net income back into sales courses, business networking events and books written by experts.

I was reading a book a month, and one that helped me immensely was written by Mark McCormick. He ranked among the 400 wealthiest people in the United States, and almost single-handedly reshaped the professional golf and tennis industries over a 40 year career.

His book, *What They Don't Teach You at Harvard Business School: Notes from a Street Smart Executive* was the number one title on the *New York Times* bestsellers list for 21 weeks.

When reading his book, I felt McCormick was talking directly to me. I found that the more I applied his ideas to my own situation, the luckier I was each month in my corporate sales and major account manager roles.

At the time of his unexpected passing in 2003, Mark McCormick had amassed a personal fortune of over US$750 million. He is one of the very few people unanimously inducted by peers into two Sporting Hall of Fames — Golf in 2006, and Tennis in 2008.

Mastering selling basics and become a service professional

Taking it to another level, I knew that if I was to fully understand the advantages and benefits customers could gain from my company's products and services, I needed to research my top competitors' products and services.

Along the way, I was writing dozens of thank you and appreciation notes to clients and contacts to remind them of my visit days earlier. This was an extremely valuable sales and income generating tip I learnt from my mentor and America's number one sales authority, Tom Hopkins. This small discipline helped me to develop better relationships with my customers and contacts, and expressed in words how much I valued their time when at their office or work premises.

New business flowed in from minor and major account contacts. I received referrals from my contacts, and key decision makers made faster and bigger buying decisions.

Your Turn

What are you doing to master your trade or craft? What are you doing to shape who you are as a competitive force or identity in your community or industry? What books, seminars or role models should you study to separate yourself from others as a sales or service leader? Do you thank customers for the business they give you?

Hot Tip

"Invest the coins in your pocket into your mind and your mind will fill your pocket with coins."

Benjamin Franklin, America's first self-made millionaire. His image adorns the $100 bill, and he is the only citizen to be on US currency who was not a President.

To win big business, put strategic selling ideas and servicing methods into action

One of the companies I have been doing business with for many years has over 467,000 employees worldwide and services a client base across 220 countries. Recently one of their Asia senior sales divisions won new business with an existing account in the amount of 9 million Euros (US$12 million). This was a multiple team member sales effort with dozens of factors involved, and competition from many other international vendors. My client's senior sales team put in a significant effort over several months to be the vendor of choice in this competitive bid.

What stands out for me isn't that they won this business, but the unexpected windfall of more business within weeks of this contract being awarded.

How did they do it? My client's sales and service teams applied the fundamentals of their company values and principles as a business team rather than as individuals.

The service, quality and pricing on offer to the client were all promises they could deliver. They combined this with the team's strengths and service track record, and that's what won them this fantastic new contract.

The windfall was in being awarded an additional 31 million Euro (US$42 million) because of a complete team and service approach as demonstrated weeks earlier.

Ask and don't be surprised when you receive

In business, if you don't ask people to buy from you, chances are they won't. Like a professional golfer on tour, the key to winning tournaments is not in the shots that produce a hole in one, but being within striking distance of the cup. This is what will create the best chance of sinking the ball and how consistent victories occur.

One thing for certain is that it pays to invest time in studying your wins. If you are part of a team, how did everyone play their part to gain more business? If you are a solo operator or small to medium enterprise, how can you operate quicker, more effectively and keep your service at a high level?

Hot Tip

To get more business, ask people to buy from you sooner and more often.

Secret 64
IT TAKES DISCIPLINE AND COMMITMENT IF YOU WANT TO DO WELL

The top professionals in every sporting field understand the concept of spring training and going back to basics each year in their particular field of expertise. If we look at the winners who get to the top of their sport or career, it's most unlikely to find they were born lucky. For example, mega sports stars like six-time world National Basketball Association (NBA) champion Michael Jordan of the Chicago Bulls, or MVP and five-time NBA world champion Kobe Bryant of the Los Angeles Lakers. These guys are known by millions of fans for the discipline, work ethic and skill they bring to their craft.

Michael, Kobe and other top sport figures have been paid millions each year to do what others might view as easy. However, it has taken years for these superstars to make it look so simple to the rest of us. The fact is, they paid an early price to develop their skills by seeking help and guidance from top trainers and coaches during their professional development. It's this dedication and commitment that has led them to being at their best.

The willingness to learn, change and adapt during difficult times

It is easy to be blasé when performing well or employed in a comfortable or safe role. Being an achiever can lead to laziness in reinforcing the fundamentals.

It is an error in judgment to think that what brought a person to a winning career or life will simply keep them there.

People with extraordinary achievements are often ordinary people who applied the 'extra' to complete a task or get the job done. If you want to be in the top three per cent of any field and an expert it is critical to keep enhancing your skills and go far beyond what is expected.

This is even more important when there are economic, company or market fluctuations. For these and other reasons, a person must be willing to go back to the basics of their trade or profession each year to gain a fresh perspective and keep up to date with the latest trends.

Ant philsophy

As a young boy, I was fascinated by the paths ants would take. They would go up, over or around any twig, rock, sand or dirt I put in their way. Ants intrigued me because they didn't let things get in their way of reaching their goals. They simply redirected their energy until they found a new direction towards their nest.

Ants have always been among the most focused and results-oriented insects on the planet. They understand they must contribute with effort and work while the sun is up. They know that sooner or later a rainy day will come along that may prevent them from going outside to gather food or resources to support the ant colony.

Ants have innate daily, weekly and monthly performance measures because the life cycle of an ant is about 60 to 90 days. They have a performance strategy that works wonders and it is simply this: work until they have achieved their desired outcome or die trying.

Like ants, to achieve certain objectives, we need to know what our performance levels need to be and how long it will take for us to achieve them.

Handle fear and rejection to excel in relationships and business

Recently, Singapore Prime Minister Lee Hsien Loong gave the opening keynote at the World Chinese Entrepreneurs Convention in Singapore. His speech to some 4,000 delegates called upon Chinese entrepreneurs worldwide to modernise their companies and ways of doing business in order to be more competitive. In his speech, he suggested that to be successful in the new global economic environment, the Chinese cannot rely solely on their connections and long-standing networks commonly known in Asia as *guanxi*. He said that they "... have to upgrade themselves and raise their game to remain useful and to keep their market positions." He further said, "Sometimes the (Chinese) founders are reluctant to do so as they fear 'losing control' over their business, but this is a necessary step for the company to compete internationally and be truly world-class".

When I was in my early 20s and new to professional sales, my sales career mentor Tom Hopkins advised me to "Do what you fear most and you will control fear." One of my fears as a young University graduate going into my first job in government account sales and servicing was in meeting high level military personnel. My job was to service and sell our Inc. 1000 company technologies that were used in data processing centres.

In facing my fear as a civilian and sales person, I learnt military rankings and language that was commonly used by the US Air Force, Army, Navy, Special Forces and supporting branch personnel. As a rookie, I learnt to embrace my fear of the unknown while meeting my government customers and the high ranking female and male decision makers within the military.

I have met with Lieutenants, Captains, Colonels and even 1, 2 and 3-star Generals in my career including 4-star General Norman Schwarzkopf, the top Army commander at Ft Lewis located about 75 kilometres from my company's head office in Seattle, Washington.

Win more business by increasing your energy, enthusiasm and concentration levels

In my early years of sales and then into management, I was shocked at the gap between rookies and the veteran sales professionals in relation to attitude, personal energy and concentration levels. I found that new sales recruits were not under the same stress or time pressures to solve customer and client issues in the beginning of their careers, while veterans and older sales people had been doing this for many years.

After a few years, it seemed that the excitement and enthusiasm of a new sales person would give way to the mental fatigue and stress of the veteran who had been solving the client's challenges or issues. I realised this downward cycle might be a high price to pay for becoming successful if I didn't adjust this to my own situation.

I found a key was in learning what I needed to do as a competent professional while retaining my youthful perspective and vibrant enthusiasm. It came down to a balance of work and play. I learnt to drink ample amounts of water each day instead of coffee, tea, fizzy drinks, beer or alcohol.

I ate more vegetables and fruit instead of fries, burgers or quick sandwiches that were so easy to find. I turned off the television to get adequate sleep, and added at least 30 minutes of walking, swimming or gym work to keep my body and mind alert.

What I lacked in sales and account experience was made up with renewed energy and enthusiasm to serve the client. This increase in competence and confidence led to more business, responsibility, promotions and income.

Hot Tip

What you do or don't do to increase your income is a choice. You are in a position to reinvent and recalibrate your future much like Madonna has been doing ever since her first album was released in 1982.

The 'Material Girl' has consistently been among the highest earning female entertainers, and keeps reinventing herself to stay current. As recently reported in 2011, the Queen of Pop earned over $110 million in 2010 and was once again, the highest earning artist in the music industry with Celine Dion second and Beyonce Knowles third.

Checklist to perform better, sell more and earn more

1. Study the top sales and service professionals in your city, country or industry, because successful people leave clues.

2. Research the top ways you can meet and gain profitable and loyal clients or customers.

3. Delegate anything and everything to others in order to focus on sales and servicing activities that generate high sales and cash flow to your business or company.

4. Ensure your key clients and customer details are consistently up to date in your database, and stay in touch often.

5. Upgrade your sales standards and service skills by learning from those you like, trust and respect who are already leaders in your field.

6. Learn to thank and appreciate people regularly for the little things they do to help you.

7. Present yourself in the best manner possible at any given moment — you never know where you will meet your next new client or customer.

8. Invest 30 minutes a week to review your best sales or servicing success. Relive the moment and consider how to improve it for next time.

9. Use your top motivators to help you focus on the key areas and activities to bring you results and opportunity.

10. Go back to the basics of your trade each year to reinforce the skills and strategies that peak performance champions use in their businesses or companies.

PART 4

Productivity and Leadership

> *The productivity of work
> is not the responsibility
> of the worker but of the manager.*
>
> — Peter Drucker

SECTION 7

Your Productivity, Decision-making and Creativity

CHAPTER 17

INCREASING PROFITABLE PRODUCTIVITY
Four secrets to increase individual and team productivity

by **Tim Wade**
Motivational Business Growth
Speaker and Consultant

Tim Wade is a motivational business growth speaker who specialises in developing and motivating people to produce positive results. Corporate and government clients across Asia engage him for performance improvement conference keynotes and workshop facilitation sessions. His content incorporates Productivity, Change Management, Leadership and Performance Psychology elements to drive performance improvement. His style is always inspiring and motivational, and he delivers with energy, engagement and quality content. His audiences love laughing while they learn, and being inspired to make positive shifts through the insights gained in his sessions.

Tim Wade developed and incorporates the V9 Profile in his programmes to help individuals and teams raise their accountability and awareness of their mindset and behavioural responses to challenges. He combines his university degree in psychology with over 18 years of corporate leadership and award-winning consulting roles to deliver powerful presentations founded upon solid research, corporate experience and his engagingly entertaining and motivating style. Tim Wade is a Past President of APSS (2010–11) and a member of the Global Speakers Federation.

Find out more about Tim at: **www.TimWade.com**
Contact Tim at: **tim@timwade.com**

INCREASING PRODUCTIVITY IS fundamental to profitable business improvement and personal effectiveness. We become more valuable when we can do more with less resources or in less time. This creates a surplus in resources, time or capacity, and when we use that to be more profitable, we win. When we waste the surplus or spend it on unprofitable activities, we have wasted our efforts. There are actions we can take in our personal life, business life and in the way we think and approach challenges that will have a positive impact on our results.

In this section, Tim Wade will share some of these actions you can immediately implement. You'll learn how sleep can impact your productivity by 25 per cent, and what you can immediately do about it. You'll discover how to immediately increase accountability so that your completion rate increases by 77 per cent. You'll learn specific techniques to increase and sustain team productivity improvements of over 10 per cent. And you'll understand how to help yourself and others shift mindsets to the kind of positive possibility thinking that not only empowers and motivates, but also delivers up to 400 per cent improvement in results.

Really? Can we do that? Tim Wade says, "Yes we can!"

Secret 65
YOU CAN IMPROVE PRODUCTIVITY BY 25% IF YOU GO TO SLEEP

"I declare I'm going to increase my productivity, and the first thing I am going to do is go to sleep." This certainly seems like a peculiar way to start a section on productivity. How can going to sleep improve your productivity? Essentially, productivity is the quantity of work performed per unit of time. Sleeping suggests I'm doing nothing, and therefore I am unproductive. Well, that's why this is a secret.

Let me first ask you a few questions. You might want to jot down your answers next to them:

- How many hours of sleep do you get every night?

- Does it vary between weeknights and weekends?

- Do you find yourself in a deep sleep or quite a shallow sleep, waking up frequently?

- Are you often tired or drowsy during the day, and especially after a meal?

When I speak at conventions and workshops about productivity and performance improvement, I always include a section on sleep. I ask audience members to tell me how much sleep they think they should get each night. Most people shout out eight hours. When we do a show of hands as to how much sleep they actually get, the majority of people get between six and seven hours of sleep a night, some as low as four or five hours. Very few people are getting 8 hours of sleep. If you're tired or drowsy during the day, or even after a large meal or during a lecture or training session, it means you're sleep deprived (even if the trainer really is boring).

Here are four pieces of sleep research that you will find interesting:

- When a person is told that they are to sleep for as long as they like and get up when they feel rested, they will sleep for about eight hours and thirty minutes.

- When we don't make suitable deposits into our sleep account, we carry a sleep debt that we can only repay with sleep.

- When someone has one hour of sleep less than is optimum for them, they will be 20 per cent less alert the next day.

- The brain organises only 50 per cent of the growth experiences and information learned from the previous day in the first six hours of sleep. The other 50 per cent occurs in the two hours after that.

Holy Moly!

Being sleep deprived by one hour a night can reduce alertness by up to 20 per cent during the day! That increases errors, reworks and costs, and can result in missed opportunities and lost sales.

This has important ramifications in our search for productivity improvements. We are less alert by 20 per cent if we have seven hours sleep when we actually need eight. This means that we can improve our alertness by 25 per cent if we are well-rested, because from 100 per cent to 80 per cent is a 20 per cent drop, but from 80 to 100 is a 25 per cent increase (since the increase is from the starting point of 80).

Faster retrieval, faster recovery

Increasing our alertness improves our awareness and reduces our mistakes. Plus for those of you who have been known to be disorganised, this will reduce the confusion and increase the organisation. Why is this so? Well, with optimum sleep our brain finally has the extra time to organise all the things it learned and experienced, so when you need to access this information quickly while awake, it will be archived and indexed for you to retrieve quickly.

That quick retrieval and ability to resume work after distractions sees us dramatically improve productivity. Also, the reduction in mistakes and work that needs to be corrected enables us to utilise that time on more productive and profitable activities.

Your Turn

Establish a sleep routine that will ensure you wake up at the same time each day and that you get eight hours of sleep. Keep a sleep journal that records the time you went to sleep and the time you woke up, as well as how you felt during the day. Apps like *Optimism* and *Sleep Cycle* might be useful to help you keep track, but you can just as easily note the times in your calendar program.

Caution

Don't sleep in to try to catch up on sleep. It will disrupt your sleeping patterns. Instead, it's better to take a short nap (under 30 minutes) around lunch time and go to bed earlier to make up for lost sleep.

Hot Tip

Make sure your bedroom is as dark as possible. Consider having a timer on your bedside lamp so that it switches on about ten minutes before your alarm. Showering before bed means the body experiences a temperature drop from being in the shower to being out of the shower. As this simulates the drop in body temperature when we go to sleep, it can aid us in being ready for sleep as well as being a useful routine to create a neural association between the shower and the sleep routine.

Secret 66
YOU CAN IMPROVE PRODUCTIVITY BY 77% IF YOU INCREASE YOUR ACCOUNTABILITY TO OTHERS

Some speakers like to talk about a study that was done in 1953 at Harvard or Yale or Stanford in the USA. The study essentially found that only 3 per cent of final year students had written down their goals, while the remainder either knew what their goals were but hadn't written them down, or they had no goals at all. Then, 20 years later, a group of researchers followed up on the Class of '53 and found that those 3 per cent were earning more than the other 97 per cent combined. Moral: write down your goals.

Hooray for writing down our goals! The only problem is that this study never happened. However, with such an urban myth floating about, a study was eventually conducted at the Dominican University of California in 2007. While writing down your goals did see an increase in likelihood that your goals would be achieved, there were actually four steps that dramatically and significantly increased the chance of accomplishment.

The four steps are:

- Write down your goals.
- Write down your action commitments to achieve those goals.
- Share your goals and action commitments with a friend.
- Send a weekly progress report to the friend.

The study recorded the success of the group who not only wrote down their goals, but also wrote down action commitments, shared them with a friend, and sent weekly progress reports to the friend. This group accomplished 77.6 per cent more of their listed goals than those who had goals, but who had not written them down.

Holy Moly!

Clarity, commitment, external accountability and disciplined follow-through really works!

What does this mean in business?

In business this comes down to goal clarity, task clarity, commitment to action, leveraging accountability and, importantly, reporting on progress. The action of frequently reporting on progress keeps the goals and actions top-of-mind, and no one likes to deliver a report that has no progress on it.

Be careful you don't procrastinate through over-reporting. We can spend so much time reporting (whether on paper or in meetings) that we don't get any actual work done. Make the report simple. If steps and deadlines are clearly articulated in the beginning, then reporting should be transparent and relatively easy. Good project managers do this particularly well. They might simplify reports with traffic lights or a selection of icons to indicate whether tasks are progressing or stuck. Occasionally, when we are relying on other people for part of the work, this can slow you down. It's a good idea to create new tasks along the way to ensure that these are also on track.

Hot Tip

Proactively create a performance report of your progress towards achieving certain goals. This will support your progress and be a useful record at bonus time too!

If people in your team resist the added reporting measure, simply let them know that you want to help those who are struggling and reward those who are doing well. Also, be aware that this is a warning sign that they may wish to conceal a lack of productivity. It might be valid, however, because of the volume of their workload. In this case, help them create a simple, workable report that is goal-focused and highlights exceptions rather than normal, unchanging activity.

Your Turn

1. Set a timer, and give yourself two minutes to write down a list your goals.

2. In six minutes, write out action commitments for each goal.

3. Then take ten minutes and share your action commitments with a friend, colleague or manager.

4. Send a weekly progress report to this person.

Just do it!

It's important to note that while you are doing this, you must actually do the work. That's where self-discipline comes in. In the course of developing models for improving productivity and personal performance, individuals and leaders must also focus on character development. This is influenced by the culture of the organisation and the character of the leader.

Your character is developed by exercising your self-discipline through trials and challenges, and in how you respond to victories. You can endure challenges by activating your strength of perseverance and self-leadership, by leveraging external accountabilities that emotionally influence your behaviour, and by putting yourself in an empowering and motivating environment as often as you can! You can further develop your character by responding to your victories with grace, gratitude and humility, rather than by taking all the credit or reacting with arrogant self-assurance and selfish pride. Wouldn't the world be a happier and more positively productive place if we all did this?

Character development is a life journey. It's important that leaders learn to recognise the various areas in which individuals need more attention than others. Leaders must recognise that staff development involves more than process training and the accumulation of skills. Leaders must sometimes create the challenge.

Secret 67
YOU CAN IMPROVE PRODUCTIVITY BY 10% IF YOU TELL EVERYONE TO IMPROVE BY 10%

Now this sounds as churlish as 'The Secret' method of sitting in a corner and wishing for a Ferrari to appear, but the difference here is the sequence of actions.

For a number of my consulting clients in Asia and Australia, I was responsible for helping them deliver an increase in performance levels. The measure was based on customer satisfaction, and one key factor was the productivity level of individuals. No matter what their existing productivity level was (some were very fast, some were very slow and everyone else was average), it can be improved by 10 per cent.

It is essentially the same logic as saving for investment: what you can buy with $100 is essentially the same as what you can buy with $90, so save 10 per cent of your income and invest it. Here we want to save 10 per cent of the time it takes to do something and we will invest it in a number of ways. So if we can reduce the time it takes 100 people to complete a series of tasks by 10 per cent, then we really only need 90 people to complete those tasks. This means we can invest the surplus 10 people in any number of ways:

1. We can save the cost of 10 staff. If these staff have salaries of, say, $30,000 a year, and then we add on another 30 per cent or so of 'on-costs' per person (costs such as various insurances, compulsory government savings plans and operational and equipment overheads) that would mean a saving of $400,000 per year for these 10 people.

2. If we have 10 extra people, we can reallocate them to more revenue-generating functions (and now you know that they would need to bring in an extra $400,000 of annual profit to account for themselves).

3. If we have 10 extra people, we can take on more work without having to hire more people or replace departing staff.

4. If we have 10 extra people, we can finally conduct the training that was postponed and further increase our productivity, quality and service delivery.

5. If we have 10 extra people, we can engage them in process improvement activities.

This last one is important. Some people might think that to get a 10 per cent improvement you might need to tell people that you want a 15 per cent or a 20 per cent improvement, then even if they miss the target and only deliver 10 per cent, you'll be secretly happy. You might think others need to be told to deliver a 100 per cent improvement for you to get 10 per cent more out of them! Well this last group might need to find another job, but for the rest, I still believe you can tell them the truth and they will deliver it. That's partly because there will also be a team working on process improvements, and their job is to increase process efficiency by 10 per cent as well.

This is how I helped some of my major clients achieve sustainable productivity improvements of between 18 to 21 per cent with their departments of between 180 and 300 staff. We focused on reducing unnecessary workloads, like the rework caused by errors mentioned in the first secret about sleep, as well as reducing unnecessary tasks or steps in the process of getting things completed. When you remove the speed bumps, it's much faster to get from A to Z.

Sometimes we needed to rearrange the order of some processes to make things much faster. For example, how many call centres have your most frequently used features right at the end of the long list of menu options?

Holy Moly!

If you often need to get from A to Z without having to go through the whole alphabet, you could simply rearrange the letters like they are on a QWERTY keyboard and you'll be there in no time! What other areas of your life or work need optimising?

Know your workload triggers

The other key piece of work to focus on is your understanding of those things that act as key triggers for additional workload. Workload volumes can change dramatically because of internal triggers, such as the marketing team releasing an effective campaign, or sales offering incentives for a limited time, or an IT issue that causes customer interaction difficulties. It might be as simple as your manager coming back from a meeting, or an unpredictable phone call. Some things are more predictable than others. The trend, coupled with understanding and experience, will help predictability.

Workload volume variations can also be the result or external triggers, such as the Government announcing a policy or fiscal shift that generates a flood of enquiries. Similarly, if a product is found to be faulty, or a celebrity suddenly endorses your product, these could also trigger increases in your workload.

Any number of gifts or crises can cause more work. The point is to understand what those triggers are so that you have a response strategy and a greater deal of certainty around your ability to respond. Confidence in your response ability, and clarity of actions in such circumstances, reduces fear and the ineffective panic that sometimes follows uncertainty.

Uncertainty reduces positive productivity for many people. This is because these people focus on doing what they know rather than what may need to be done. For this reason, four elements are critical in understanding your workload, its triggers and your responses.

1. Understand your workload triggers and what to do in case of (workload) emergency.

2. Communicate the strategy effectively.

3. Train the response ability effectively.

4. Cultivate a positive mindset in yourself and your staff... effectively.

This last point refers to a person's conditioned evaluation processes when receiving information. They will filter the information based on internal rules and values, which will determine what they focus on, the emotion that they associate to the information, and their willingness to perform the tasks required. If they are unwilling to do this, productivity suffers, no matter how much you communicate or train them. We'll get to that in Secret 68.

⚲ *Secret 68*
YOU CAN IMPROVE PRODUCTIVITY BY 400% IF YOU DEVELOP A MINDSET OF VICTORY

Can we improve productivity by 20 per cent across the entire organisation? For some people the answer will be, "Never in a million years". Then they will go on to explain all the reasons why it won't work and why it can't be done. For others, they might agree with you in the meeting but sabotage in silence with claims of, "This will never happen. Let's just wait until they give up". A third group might evaluate their opportunity and ask, "What's in it for me?" While a fourth group will declare with belief and positive possibility, "Yes we can!"

What makes these four groups different, and who do you want on your team? While there is a place for risk evaluation and understanding the challenges ahead, I'm sure you want people who will get on board and positively work towards achieving the result. But what happens if you have a group of naysayers, or a pack of saboteurs, or an army of mercenaries instead of a team of positive action-takers?

These four groups are biologically similar but psychological different. They are displaying one of four default mindsets that have been conditioned over years of often unconscious reinforcement from experiences, successes and failures, as well as from parents, teachers, peers and leaders.

Are you a Victor, a Victim, a Mercenary or a Martyr?

When I present my V9 profile to seminar audiences and workplace teams, I explain the four mindsets of the Victor, the Victim, the Mercenary and the Martyr, and how each impacts productivity and output. 80 per cent of most organisations would be populated with Victims, Mercenaries and Martyrs. In short, Victims blame everyone else but themselves, Martyrs complain that they work hard for little reward or recognition (but that's usually because they rarely complete anything and because they are so busy being disorganised and unresourceful), and Mercenaries will do anything for money (and nothing without it) making any change costly and unpleasant.

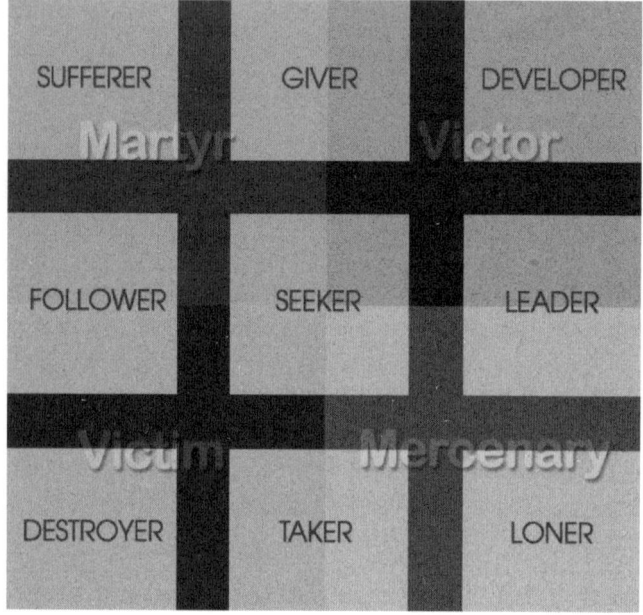

The V9 Profile — © Tim Wade.

People with the Victor mindset are action-takers who frequently display four key characteristics. They oscillate between the characters of the Leader, the Developer, the Giver and the Seeker:

The Leader has a clear vision and mission as well the ability and confidence to influence others to help them get there.

The Developer helps others to improve themselves, their business, their teams and their results.

The Giver offers time, energy, enthusiasm, skills, talents and resources as well as money so that others can make use of these for a greater good.

The Seeker asks more empowering and encouraging questions in an effort to find better ways of doing things, and to gain insights and knowledge from themselves and others.

It is the combination of these four characters, not just dominating with one or two, that cultivates and sustains the Mindset of Victory.

So how do we get a 400 per cent productivity increase? Well, if someone is disorganised, angry, blaming others, or not trying until they are paid more, they will be performing at a level that might see them barely get by. They are doing just enough to be better than the worst performers, or hovering around mediocre. What's worse is that they are often unaware that they have settled for this standard.

Hot Tip

Seek teachers who not only impart skills and tools, but who also raise self-awareness and personal accountability. This is because your results will come from behaviourial shifts and transformations in attitude rather than just an increase in knowledge. Cultivate a Mindset of Victory and follow through with positive action!

20% Pareto 80% Principle

If we look at the Pareto principle when applied to work — that 80 per cent of your results will come from 20 per cent of your effort — then surely our goal is to discover what that 20 per cent of productive effort actually is, and then spend the remaining 80 per cent of our effort also doing that. If we do that, our productive effort would shift from being 20 per cent to 100 per cent, increasing by a factor of five. If we did that, our productive results would increase from 80 per cent, by a factor of five, to 400 per cent.

So what do we do with the 80 per cent of activities that we were doing that weren't producing any results? We can eliminate them, delegate them, ignore them or outsource them. At worst we can significantly reduce them once we increase our awareness of them.

Typically this 80 per cent is made up of activities that people do because of uncertainty. They might be uncertain or fearful about performing the more productive activities. They might also be unclear about their goals and tasks. Without clear goals we tend to lack the inspiration of purpose. Without a clear purpose we fail to adequately prioritise. Without prioritisation, we can find ourselves doing anything else but actually performing and accomplishing those tasks that we need to complete. When that happens we are left to our most fundamental motivators to guide us; pleasure and pain. One we are attracted to, the other we avoid. In this case, the pleasure of procrastination numbs the perceived pain of performing at a higher standard. This results in the longer-term pain of dissatisfaction and regret, which can only be overcome by performance to improve self-respect.

Caution

When you find yourself procrastinating, spend a moment evaluating your feelings towards the challenge that is ahead of you. This is a critical moment; the moment where you are really choosing between perseverance and avoidance. Positive perseverance breeds success. Inappropriate avoidance results in failure. Focus on the victory that lies beyond the effort. Sense the peace beyond the discomfort. Then choose to do what is necessary.

The good news is that the decision to shift to a Mindset of Victory can be made immediately, and the process of reconditioning can begin just as quickly. It begins by adopting the positive curiosity of the *Seeker*. Ask questions that lead you to the outcome in an empowering and positive way. For example, rather than look at yourself in a mirror and ask, "Why am I so fat?" (which will deliver several possible answers that are unpleasant to hear and painful to face), instead the *Seeker* who has a Victor mindset would ask, "What can I do now to become even fitter?" (which encourages, emboldens, and empowers positive action).

Caution

When you beat yourself up for having failed or having made a mistake, your brain releases the numbing hormone cortisol which, when constantly released due to lots of negative conditioning, eventually numbs us into apathy. Forgive yourself quickly, learn, establish a strategy correction, and move forward again. Ensure you frequently celebrate your victories and the successes of others!

As your *Seeker* character asks better questions, your *Leader* character will begin to form clearer goals and tasks. From here the *Leader* can set sail for their goals and influence others to join them to help achieve their mission. The *Leader* will also continue to recondition with positive encouragement, motivating yourself and your team to keep taking action, to move forward through any resistance and truly believe, "Yes We Can!"

Hot Tip

When you celebrate your victories, your brain releases the pleasure hormone dopamine, which strengthens and grows the neuro-pathways associated with producing the celebration. This enables easier access to repeat the activity with greater skill for more frequent success. Celebrate every victory with positive self-talk, encouragement with others, and for the big milestones: a party!

To cultivate and sustain your Mindset of Victory, be aware of your own behaviour and how you are responding to tasks and situations. Self-awareness is critical, and if we are sleep-deprived, we are less alert remember? That's why so many people are on reaction-autopilot rather than conscious care. And to take control in uncertainty, they get angry. Fuelled then by a lack of sleep and empathy, arguments ensue and we are mightily unproductive.

Take care of yourself. Think well of yourself and others. Ask better questions. Evaluate the triggers for your workload and think of ways to do things even better. Be more clear about your goals and your purpose for achieving them. Share these with others to raise your own level of accountability. Persevere and apply yourself. Celebrate your victories with great gratitude and humility. And have a good night's sleep!

In order to 'have' the outcome you desire, you need to first 'be' the sort of person who achieves them. So: Be aware. Be clear. Be positive. Be curious. Be productive. Be grateful. Be rested.

Here's a helpful formula: Be + Have = Behave

And there you have it. How we behave shows who we have chosen to be and what standards we have chosen to have. Now go and be someone who not only harnesses the power of their *Seeker*, but who also inspires their *Leader* to implement actions that create positive change. Yes we can!

Checklist for boosting productivity and increasing positive results

1. List your top five goals or operational deliverables. Make sure you include a 10 per cent productivity improvement target, and dates by which you commit to achieving these goals.

2. As a *Seeker*, ask "what can I do now to … {insert the word 'perform', 'produce', 'do', 'achieve', 'complete', 'become', or something similar}… even more … {insert the goal, result or task here}". Do this for each goal.

3. Write down your various answers and any measures and deadlines that each might have.

4. Write down a list of the top five things that might hinder you from achieving each goal.

5. Seek further: ask what you can now do to remove or reduce this hindrance in a positive and effective way. Write down your answers.

6. Organise your lists, your goals and your thoughts. Share some of your key decisions and commitments with a friend, peer, manager or mentor who can approve or refine the list with you. They may help to remove or reduce some of the obstacles. Ask them to hold you accountable to delivering against this list, and commit to report to them regularly.

7. Condition yourself to believe that you can do it, that it is possible, that with the people around you also holding you accountable, your mantra becomes, "Yes we can!" At any sign of quitting or procrastinating, reaffirm and persevere… "Yes we can!"

8. Go for it! Take action despite distraction, and keep persisting when you feel like resisting. It is no coincidence that the slogan for Nike is "Just do it!" In ancient times, Nike was the fabled Greek goddess of Victory. Only in positive action do we taste authentic victory. Yes we can! And if you really feel like you can't, remember "Yes we can!" has the word 'we' in it for a reason. Seek.

9. Measure your performance and journal the results. Keep a note of what you did right, and what went wrong, keeping an eye on maintaining (or even increasing) quality levels while speeding up output. For those things that are more quality related, rate them from 0 to 10, where 0 is abysmal and 10 is outstanding. For everything else, use the actual numbers.

10. Celebrate when you hit your target! Then focus on maintaining that standard for the next 28 days so that the pace is conditioned and habituated. Reward yourself along the way for each and every success! Persist. Celebrate with each progressive step and milestone reached along the way! Yes we can!

CHAPTER 18

DYNAMIC DECISION-MAKING

Upgrade your thinking skills to make better decisions, solve problems faster and be more creative

by **Tremaine du Preez**
Head of Organizational Learning
The Leadership Consultancy

Tremaine is an author, leadership coach and keynote speaker for The Leadership Consultancy, a boutique coaching and training consultancy based in Singapore.

Originally from Cape Town, South Africa, she has developed an approach to leadership and human capital development that fuses the best of Eastern, Western and African ideas. Having lived in Asia since 2003, she works throughout the region helping senior executives, government officials and MBA students develop their leadership, problem-solving and decision-making skills. She firmly believes that everyone should benefit from the research and advances in mankind's understanding of how to use our minds to their full potential.

Tremaine has an MSc in Financial Economics from the University of London, holds the International Capital Markets Qualification from the Securities Institute of London, and is certified in Neuro-Semantics.

Find out more about Tremaine at: **www.LeadershipConsultancy.org**

Contact Tremaine at: **info@leadershipconsultancy.org**.

THE DECISIONS YOU made yesterday have created your life today. The decisions that you make today will determine your future success. Do you have a reliable decision-making strategy that allows you to tackle tough challenges with ease and get the results you expect? If you don't, you are not alone. Throughout our lives most of us are constantly taught *what* to think, yet we are given few clues on *how* to think. Or perhaps complexity, short time-frames, information overload and past failures leave you uncertain of how to tackle tough challenges or make you wilt when faced with complex decisions?

In this chapter, author and coach Tremaine du Preez will share practical tools and reliable techniques to help you understand and upgrade your thinking and problem-solving skills. You will learn how to avoid costly mistakes and boost your decision-making confidence. Tremaine shares the latest in neuroscience, decision science and critical thinking to take you on a concise and fascinating journey towards using your thinking tools better to think smarter and work smarter.

Secret 69
THERE IS SUCH A THING AS TOO MUCH INFORMATION

Information is power, right? So if a little information is good then a lot has to be better. How much information do you receive every day from the media, email, text messages, blogs, newsletters, other people, books, ebooks, advertisements and other sources? Does all this information leave you feeling empowered or a little jaded at the end of the day?

Technology is rapidly changing our relationship with information. We used to have to *go to* information during office hours. Now it comes to us – 24 hours a day, 7 days a week. Yet we continue to crave more and more bits and bytes of data in the hope that we will be better informed, make ever better decisions and have better ideas. This first secret reveals how too much information impedes our decision-making ability.

What is your information diet?

Our love of information can be likened to our love of food. We need a certain amount and variety to stay healthy and informed. If we have just enough, we feel well and in control of our diet and health. Too much information, like too much sticky toffee pudding, will leave us feeling bloated and unable to digest it all.

Are you fully aware of the role that information plays in your life? Are you always connected to an information source? Let's audit your information diet to get a handle on your relationship with information. We'll see if your diet is healthy and well controlled, spinning out of control, or somewhere in between.

Over one week, take note of how much information you receive or interact with, or *consume*. This can include receiving and responding to email and text messages, web surfing, Facebooking, tweeting, reading printed media (including junk mail and flyers), watching the news on TV, your computer, iPad or reader or any other electronic information source specific to your company or job. Gossip and water cooler chat doesn't count, fortunately. This could be a time consuming exercise so jotting down an approximation at noon and at the end of the day should be fine. Now, when you have an idea of your information diet, ask yourself the one million dollar question — how much of this information truly adds value to your decision-making ability and productivity during your workday? Be absolutely honest with yourself!

Information overload can affect our reasoning, judgment and physical health. Many clients tell me they are either overworked, stressed, tired, have a demanding boss, spouse or family, or haven't had a holiday in ages. Very few consider that they could be suffering from information overload, until they examine their information diet and realise just how much of the information they are exposed to doesn't actually add value to their thinking or their lives.

Make information work *for* you, not *against* you

We love information because it increases our confidence in our decision-making abilities. Handicappers at horse races rely on information to make accurate predictions about which horse is going to win the race. You would think that having more information than other handicappers would certainly lead to better decision making, right? But hold on, not so fast! Research[1] shows that handicappers with 40 pieces of information made no better predictions than those with five. What did change, however, was their confidence in their decisions, like the sugar rush that comes from eating too much candy.

Caution

Be careful of assuming that more information will lead to better decision making. There is a point at which information confuses and derails our thinking, leaving our decision-making ability worse off.

Take control of information to maximise your productivity

Information has to be constantly disciplined. It is important that we set our own information boundaries and only accept information that truly adds value to us. Much like choosing wholegrain crackers to snack on instead of candy!

Here is a suggestion that may seem rather radical at first. Feel free to dismiss it. However, if you truly want to get back control of your information diet, read on. Set specific and limited times for various information sources and repetitive work. For example, checking email only once every hour at 10 minutes to the hour will leave you to work and concentrate for 50 minutes totally uninterrupted. Of course, it's even better if you can check mail a maximum of two or three times a day. This suggestion tends to cause disbelief from my students. The truth is that it can be done, but we are so terrified of missing out on something super important, something that could change the

[1] Slovik, Paul. y. 1973, *Behavioral problems of adhering to a decision policy.*
Available at ww.decisionresearch.org/people/slovic

course of history, that we stay slaves to the ping or the pop-up of our mailbox. We are often not in a position to send an immediate reply or to action a message but we still allow ourselves to be disrupted just to read it.

Your Turn

Go on, pick a day where you check your mail at regular intervals. It's liberating, although perhaps a bit nerve-racking at first. It puts you straight back in control of your daily agenda. Information is no longer power. Controlling it is.

Secret 70
EMOTIONS ACTUALLY HELP US MAKE BETTER DECISIONS

I have a host of books on my bookshelf that cover the topic of decision making, usually describing various analytical models and processes. The purpose of many of these is to remove the influence of emotions from our decision making. Decision Science is now proving that the missing ingredient in these models is the fact that they *don't* take account of emotions. So how can we use emotion as a decision-making tool without letting it derail our thinking?

Emotions affect everyone's decision making

We are all faced with hundreds of decisions every single day. To hit our alarm's snooze button or not, what to wear and eat for breakfast, whether to exercise or not — these are some of the decisions we face before we even arrive at the office. How come we are able to sail through these daily decisions relatively easily? You already know the answer to this. How do *you* decide what to order from a menu or which dress or tie to pull from the closet? Yup, you ask yourself: "What do I *feel* like eating or wearing?" We use feelings every day in making all sorts of decisions, for good reason.

The emotional centre of our brain can comprehend much more, much quicker, than our logical brain. Often, when we are overwhelmed by facts, a lot of information is compacted into an intuition, or a 'gut feel'. This inexplicable emotion, or hunch, that you feel is a messenger with a very important message.

Holy Moly!

I wouldn't be able to make a single decision if my emotions were not available. If my emotional brain were damaged I would struggle to decide between simple alternatives.

Managing your emotional red flags

So emotions play a positive and important role in every decision that we make, but I bet you can think of a time when an emotion wreaked havoc on a decision or hijacked your response to a situation?

Emotions are very fast. If you blink your eyes once you will know how fast a quarter of a second is. This is how long it takes for your emotional brain to receive information and generate a response, an emotion. It takes the thinking side of our brain quite a bit longer to catch up. Think of the last time you cried in a movie or got so mad at a driver that cut you off, that you shouted at them. Perhaps you have said something during a heated argument or debate that you regretted later? Was it logical to do these things? No. Did you do them anyway? Yes.

Emotions that have the potential of hijacking our ability to reason through a decision, or rogue emotions, belong to our flight or fight response. They serve us well when our lives are threatened and we need to make split second decisions, but sometimes they can get confused about what exactly a life-threatening situation is.

Caution

We may think that responding with an emotional outburst will let people know that we are angry and they will take us seriously.

But think about this; if somebody responds to you by getting angry and shouting, do you really listen to what they are saying?

An emotional outburst triggers the fight or flight response in the listener. He or she cannot hear your argument or message because they are too busy deciding how they will defend themselves against your outburst. Plus, they will have *less* respect for you because you can't control your emotions.

A rogue emotion is like a bull. If left alone in a meadow, it will mind its own business. If provoked, it gets nasty, single minded and very destructive. What can tick a bull off faster than one can say "olè"? A red flag!

Do you know exactly what ticks you off? If we know what our red flags are, it is easier to anticipate when our decisions are in danger of being hijacked by an emotion. Anticipating very strong emotions will allow you to manage conversations far better, prevent outbursts and remain clear-headed when it counts the most.

To determine your red flags, spend some time reflecting on those conversations in which you responded with an outburst or said something you later regretted. Do you see a pattern in your responses? These will be your red flags. Most of us have only two or three but that's enough to do serious damage.

Use emotions to improve your judgment

When faced with an important decision, get up close to your emotions and experience them fully. After all, they are going to happen with or without permission. But once you have rubbed shoulders with them, take a big step back and ask yourself exactly which emotion you are experiencing and why. When it is time to finalise your decision, ask how your thinking would change if you removed the emotion from the equation. Not easy to do, but it will save you potential heartache later, for sure.

Secret 71
A GOOD CREATIVE STRATEGY CAN HELP ANYONE HAVE GREAT IDEAS

It is tempting to believe that great ideas just arrive, out of nowhere, when least expected. Or that, "I just wasn't born creative," is an excuse for not having great ideas. In reality, people who are considered 'creative' such as artists and entrepreneurs usually follow a fairly rigorous creativity process that allows them to incubate and grow ideas into masterpieces or innovations. Anyone can generate great ideas and creative solutions when we use such a process over time.

Setting the scene for creativity

The creativity process is like a roaring campfire. Unless you are Harry Potter, you can't just throw down a pile of logs and command them to burn. Dry logs must be positioned in a certain way, to allow for ventilation. A spark is needed to ignite a flame and, hopefully, set fire to the perfectly positioned pile of wood. A fire also needs some kind of fuel, twigs or paper to allow the spark to turn into a flame. In the same way we need something to fuel our creative fire. Here are some tips on how to create an environment to foster creative thought.

- Know your subject well. Immerse yourself or team in the details of the project, data, history and other known information and latest best practice.

- Check out someone else's backyard. Have other industries or groups had similar problems? How did they solve or approach them?

- Create a creative space. A boardroom or office cubicle is seldom an effective place to stimulate original thought. Try a 'teamthink' session in a coffee shop, park or a pier — anywhere out of the norm.

Allow incubation time for your creative seeds to germinate. Whether you need to grow a big or small creative solution, your efforts will be given a considerable boost if you take a break from the project.

Hot Tip

According to research[2] at Harvard University, if a break from a problem includes sleep, you are 33 per cent more likely to come up with a more creative solution than before.

Questions to produce creativity on demand

It's not always easy to know exactly where to start when the pressure is on and creative ideas are expected from you. Here are some questions to help kick start the process:

- How do I/we feel about this?

- What do I/we believe but cannot prove?

- What conventional wisdom is attached to this, and will it still be valid in ten years time?

- What is the current status quo and what would shatter it?

[2] Leslie Berlin, The New York Times, 28 September 2008.

- What if our success was guaranteed?

- What is the real issue that needs addressing, and where did it come from?

Better brainstorming to produce results, not compromises

According to the originator of traditional brainstorming, Alex Osborn, there are four basic steps:

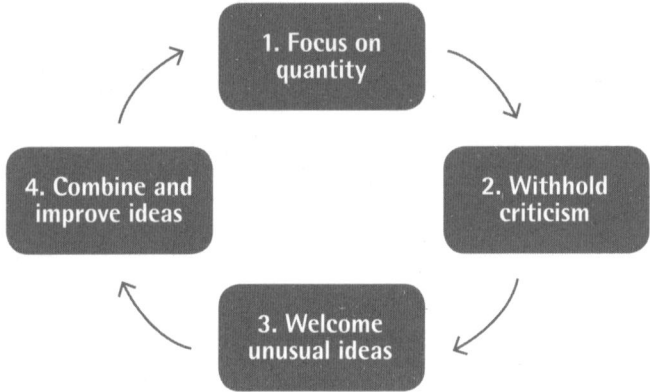

We all know how it goes: a problem is presented and everyone offers ideas on how to fix it. No one is allowed to judge or pass comment. Ideas are then combined and blended together.

The trouble with traditional brainstorming

In its traditional form, brainstorming converges different ideas into possible solutions. Breakthroughs aren't always guaranteed. Free-riding is often present and individual buy-in to the process can be low as rewards go to the group. Research has not found evidence that traditional brainstorming effectively increases the quantity or quality of ideas generated.

To get the best out of a brainstorming session and yourself, first invite participants into a creative frame of mind by setting the scene as described above. Here are some ideas on how to improve on traditional brainstorming for breakthrough results.

1. Prepare for the storm

Asking each participant to think of or investigate their own best suggestion before coming to the session will vastly improve the quality of ideas presented. It will also mean that nobody can eat the free pizza without offering a good idea in return. Each participant should share their own idea *before* the free flow of ideas begins, so no idea or person is drowned out.

2. Think up a storm

Here are some tips to extract maximum value and creativity from the group.

- Keep the group as small as possible.

- Assume nothing. Ask for ideas about what caused the problem or led to the need to brainstorm. This will set the scene and make sure that everybody knows exactly what he or she is there to do.

- Provoke. Look for loose associations that can contribute lateral thoughts. Naming a new trendy shoe? How about exploring the names of hip or upcoming neighbourhoods in your target market. An energy drink? How about popular trends in action movies?

- Challenge conventional wisdom and comfort zone thinking.

- Ask for ideas and solutions, which would ordinarily be spoken, to be written on cards instead, anonymously.

Now, remember that brainstorming is a process to generate ideas that lead to solutions. It's not meant to generate the final solution. For that you need a more structured and analytical process.

Secret 72
GETTING OUT OF YOUR COMFORT ZONE CAN HELP YOU MAKE GREAT DECISIONS

'Thinking outside the box' is an enormously overused cliché. Someone, somewhere must have known exactly what and where our box is, but forgot to tell the rest of us. In my experience, the *box* is nothing more than a metaphor for uncreative thinking and narrow decision making. The good news is that there are very real reasons why we struggle to come up with ground-breaking solutions, make the same mistakes over and again, or find it hard to go against the status quo. This is not because we have our head in our box, but rather because we are creatures of comfort and habit. Our comfort zone plays an enormous role in the alternatives that we come up with and the decisions that we make.

Holy Moly!

Comfort and habit are far greater influences on my ability to think creatively than my legendary box!

Here are the options we usually have when faced with decisions. Can you see how they could be the sides of our mythical box?

- Do nothing
- Procrastinate
- Do what's always been done
- Ask someone else to do it for you
- Do something different

Our comfort zone is carefully constructed over time through our trials and errors. In it, we can work and live with no discomfort or risk. We only need to do enough to keep things the way they are. We stay in it as much as possible because stepping out is challenging, risky, and frightening.

Caution

Staying in our decision-making comfort zone is fine when it comes to picking a holiday spot. Not wanting to step out of it when making tough decisions can lure us into accepting the default option of doing nothing and accepting the way things currently are. Better options might exist that aren't ever explored.

The dangers of comfort zone thinking

Here are some of the consequences of letting our comfort zone lull us into regularly accepting the status quo.

- Supporting a failing project for longer than we should.

- Searching for fewer alternatives than we should.

- Keeping leaders, governments or employees in their positions for much longer than they should be.

- Accepting poor service because we don't want to complain or make a fuss.

- Accepting the default option, even when it isn't the best option, because investigating other options is too expensive or time consuming.

- Staying in relationships, jobs or living environments that may not be ideal for us.

Hot Tip

Highly successful people regularly step out of their comfort zone. They know there can be no breakthroughs without some risk. Great thinking happens outside of our comfort zone.

Sure fire ways to kick the procrastination habit

Procrastination is a great example of comfort zone thinking. No one procrastinates unintentionally; we do it because it keeps us snug in our comfort zone. Do any of these things sound familiar?

- You do the quick and easy things first to get them out of the way. Then have no time left to tackle the big jobs.

- Even though you are given sufficient time to complete a project, you only seem to get to it just before the deadline.

- Some days you just don't feel like doing certain jobs, so you put them off.

- You complete a piece of work only when you feel so guilty about not having done it yet that it's hard to focus on anything else.

- You miss deadlines constantly.

Caution

Do you ever think; "Strange, I was really busy all day but I didn't achieve anything significant"? An inability to prioritise decisions and commit to a daily agenda is a poor work habit. It can lead to low productivity despite being busy during the day and tired at the end of it.

Your Turn

Write down all the things that you have been meaning to do but never get around to. Grade them as nice to have, not important for the moment and important. Now, ask yourself what's stopping you from doing the really important things?

Did you say lack of time or poor time management? There really is no such thing as time management. Unless you are the God of Time, you can't control time. What you can control are the tasks that fill up your time. Not prioritising tasks or decisions properly is a major cause of procrastination.

I suggest you develop a clear daily, weekly and monthly plan. Spend at least 30 minutes once a month, 15 minutes once a week and 10 minutes every day on task scheduling – note your deadlines and what you need to achieve for the month, week and day. Remember to break big tasks down into bite-sized daily activities. Prioritise activities for each day, and make sure that you start with your top priority. This way, if you do nothing else for the day, at least the top job can be ticked off. If you are putting off a hard-to-make decision, remember that it will have to be made at some point. The sooner you make it, the sooner the pressure of it looming will be relieved.

Checklist for dynamic decision making

1. Find and use trusted, good quality sources of information, especially when browsing the the Internet.

2. Track your information diet and look for signs of information overload.

3. Don't try to remove emotions from your decision-making process, it can't be done.

4. Listen to your gut feel. It is an important part of how we process information and supplements signals from our brain's logical or thinking part.

5. Recognise what triggers your rogue emotions. This will allow you to anticipate and harness them before they land you in trouble.

6. Remember that comfort and habit are far greater influences on our ability to think creatively and critically than our legendary box.

7. Accept some discomfort. Nothing significant can be achieved by staying in our comfort zone and accepting the status quo.

8. Step out of your comfort zone by challenging old ways of thinking about and doing things. This will put you on a path to success.

9. Foster a creativity process that includes a creative environment and immersion in the subject.

10. Break away from traditional brainstorming and ensure that everyone prepares for a brainstorming session so that not only are lots of ideas generated but they are of good quality too.

CHAPTER 19

JUMPSTART YOUR CREATIVE POTENTIAL
Using creativity to solve problems and
generate useful ideas

by **Titus Yong**
Director, Ingenio

Titus Yong's first careers included working on offshore oil platforms and in jungles as well as consulting corporations on business processes. He subsequently became a private equity investment professional during the dot com era before becoming an entrepreneur and an adjunct faculty member of Singapore Management University.

In 2005, Titus founded Ingenio, a venture that develops innovative educational programmes and interactive technologies. The programmes have been featured on Primetime news on Channel News Asia and TV news in four languages. Ingenio and Titus were awarded the 'Excellence in Innovation Award' in Mumbai in 2008.

Titus has been conducting courses for Fortune 500 companies and schools, and delivering presentations at thinking/creativity conferences throughout Asia Pacific. He has served on the judging panel for entrepreneurship and innovation-related competitions.

A graduate of Harvard University, Titus continues to learn from great minds and regularly meets or interviews innovative luminaries from various domains: Nobel laureates, billionaires, and creative producers. Through these interviews, working in different industries and travelling to over 35 countries, he was struck by the universal importance of innovation as a strategic competitive advantage as well as a source of fulfilment at work.

Find out more about Titus at: **www.fulfilling.us**

Contact Titus at: **yong@post.harvard.edu**

NAVIGATING EFFECTIVELY IN an increasingly complex world will require creativity. This is the conclusion of the IBM 2010 Global CEO Study involving over 1,500 Chief Executive Officers from 60 countries and 33 industries worldwide; and creativity has been selected as the top crucial factor for future success.

Whether you are a leader looking for new ways to create more value, an entrepreneur looking for fresh business opportunities, a marketer finding more interesting ways to brand your product, an employee trying to solve a problem in your project, or just feeling bored and waiting for inspiration to appear, creativity will be your ally.

But is creativity an innate trait, or is it as elusive as waiting for the muse to appear? Do you sometimes wish you were born a visionary like Steve Jobs or Richard Branson?

Let's take another trait for success — leadership. Fifty years ago, there were hardly any leadership courses. Many people assumed that leadership could not be learnt. Either you were born a leader or you were not. Here's the empowering news: creativity, similar to many other crucial skills, can be practised and learnt.

In this section, Titus Yong will demystify the concept of creativity and share useful ways to help you hone the relevant skills that will build your innovative capabilities. In this competitive world, your ability to solve increasingly more challenging problems and create new, useful ideas will be viewed positively as exhibiting successful leadership potential.

You will also learn shortcuts to get new ideas quickly, discover what type of creative person you are (in the context of the creative process), and how you can become a more inspiring and creative person.

⚷ Secret 73
CREATIVITY CAN BE LEARNT AND PRACTISED

Creativity that is useful for success at work refers to the skills of solving problems in a new way and the ability to generate new and useful ideas. My research and interviews of successful creative people have shown that there are a series of skills that can be learnt and honed over time.

In this first secret, I shall share two powerful skills that you can start practising right away that will help you become better at creative thinking.

1. Sharpening your power of observation

This is one of the most fundamental skills. Many successful executives and entrepreneurs are able to see trends, opportunities and solutions. By observing, let's not limit to seeing with your eyes, but also hearing and feeling what your customer needs.

In our fast-paced world, people often walk around listening to their mobile phones or media players and are oblivious to the things happening around them. Many discoveries in business and science are a result of paying attention to the things happening around you, and sometimes a great idea may surface. Discoveries such as Post-It notes, microfinance, thin film displays on mobile devices, elliptical cross training equipment, antibiotics, and the microwave oven were the result of observations.

One useful way to hone your skill of observation is to carry with you a camera and a notebook — either a hardcopy or electronic note-taker or tablet. When you see something interesting, you can take a picture or video of it, and then replay later and analyse it in greater detail.

Hot Tip

For recording ideas, a useful software is Evernote (www.evernote.com) or OneNote (www.onenote. com) – you can take notes on the go, even on your mobile devices.

Some suggestions on photos to take are: captivating advertisements, news headlines, interesting food (and guess the ingredients as you taste them), nicely renovated show flats, product launches, crowded events (you can analyse who goes to these events and what draws people to them), and importantly, nature (animals, plants, natural phenomenon, etc). These are rich sources of observations. Why not adopt an attitude of a traveller going on a holiday when you walk or drive out of your house? Life would be much more interesting and fun too!

Another way to use observation is to listen for opportunities. Even when you listen to people complaining, these are useful sources of business opportunities or suggestions for improvement. Complaints give perspectives of the gaps in the product features or new services that you can offer. For example, many people used to complain about expensive international phone calls – then Skype capitalised on the Internet to provide free Internet calls!

2. 'Flexibility' in thinking: Search and spot the similarities

When you were a child, did you enjoy playing the 'Spot the Difference' puzzles? In those two pictures, the backgrounds are similar but certain elements are different.

A useful skill to learn for improving creativity is 'Spot the Similarities', except that the backgrounds are different. Background in this case can mean geographies, or industries, or nature. For example, if a solution may be available in other countries, you can adapt the solution for your local context. Let's look at the example of AirAsia. Its founder, Tony Fernandez, studied the successful business models of Southwest Airlines in USA and Ryan Air in Europe. He then adapted the model for Asia, which at that time did not have a prominent budget airline. In the process, he became a successful billionaire in the span of ten years.

Another useful skill is to learn useful best practices from other industries or nature and apply them to your own industry. For example, you can use the best ideas from the advertising industry (eg: billboard, website design) to inspire your own project report cover or PowerPoint or Keynote presentation. Alternatively, if you run out of ideas for your workspace, why not study the colour schemes from the nature or autumn foliage to apply to certain parts of your office renovation?

Flexibility in thinking involves being able to see things from different contexts, perspectives, industries and applications. To hone this skill, try to move out of your comfort zone to experience other cultures, read a magazine or book that you would not normally read, learn some new software, observe the workings of another industry.

Does observing and flexible thinking lead to good ideas? Yes, but there's a catch. Linus Pauling, a two-time Nobel Prize winner, provided this advice: "The best way to get a good idea is to have lots of ideas". This quotation provides interesting insight and hope.

Caution

Among the "lots of ideas", many of them would be average ideas, some downright useless ideas, and finally, one of them will be good. So don't feel bad that most of your ideas are not spectacular. This is a numbers game!

Consistent with honing your observation skill, record your observations from a variety of sources and practise flexible thinking. Come up with lots of ideas without censoring yourself. After you have generated a long list of ideas, you and your colleagues can play the devil's advocate and decide which one is the gem among the stones.

Secret 74
INTERNAL MOTIVATION IS THE MAIN DRIVER FOR CREATIVE SUCCESS

Great creative ideas come forth with much passion. Let's explore how motivation affects our creative output.

There are two types of motivation — external and internal:

1. **External motivation**: This is largely linked to accolades and rewards such as awards, bonuses and job promotion.

2. **Internal motivation**: If you are working on something because it is meaningful to you and for the love of it, this is likely an indication of internal motivation. My professor at Harvard Business School found that this type of motivation is more likely to result in creativity. This section is about harnessing your internal motivation.

Work on something that you love and that you do well. I once met Warren Buffett, the legendary billionaire investor. He shared with us that he "tap dances to work" even though he was then in his 70s. He observed that some people chose to take up jobs that make more money; and after working a few years here and a few years there, they think they can finally change to a job that they truly love. His point here was that people wait and wait until they start doing something they really love to do. He joked that this mentality is similar to "saving sex for old age"!

What does this mean for you if you are working for an employer? I suggest that you evaluate your current job function and decide if you are truly passionate about your work or is there another job function that you can become competent in, one you would enjoy more? Very often, young working people cycle through a few jobs before they truly understand themselves, and then pick the job or industry that they love. In my case, I worked in several vastly different industries before deciding on the education and training sector.

Assuming that you are doing the job you love, what's the secret to greater creativity? You need to find your creative inspirations — people or products or services that you admire. They will form the beacon and reference point for your creative pursuits. You can learn a lot from studying the footsteps of these creative ideals.

My creative inspiration is a person from Bangladesh. What comes to your mind when you hear the word Bangladesh? Typically it is perceived by many as a backward country. I have a photo taken with Professor Mohamed Yunus, the 2006 Nobel Peace Prize winner. The photo is the wallpaper of my mobile device. Professor Yunus observed the plight of his countrymen and wondered why hardworking people can be stuck in poverty. From careful observations, he came to the conclusion that lack of capital is the limiting factor. Who would have thought that an idealistic professor from a third world country could impact millions of lives around the world?

Let me share another example from Singapore. Prominent music composer and creative director Dick Lee shared with me that his creative inspiration was Walt Disney. When he was a child, he admired Disneyland and created a miniature version of Disneyland's Main Street. Fast forward a few decades, and in recent years, Dick designed the Christmas lights along the shopping belt of Orchard Road.

Your Turn

Who is your creative inspiration and role model? Read the biography of the person you admire. Or perhaps your inspiration is a product or service that you love. What can you learn from it?

Attitude is also important

Besides having creative inspirations, having the right attitude is equally important for fostering creative ideas.

An important attitude is resilience — perseverance in the face of difficulty. Thomas Edison and his team tested over one thousand combinations of gases and filament materials before finding the combination that worked and enabled him to create a sustainable light bulb. This is consistent with 'quantity of ideas' explained in the first secret of this chapter. Edison's prescription was one per cent inspiration and 99 per cent perspiration! My interpretation is to let your creative inspiration lead the way with the first step. For the remaining 99 steps of dogged determination, try out as many ideas (quantity) and explore as many different angles as possible (flexibility).

Another useful attitude is 'fail often in order to succeed sooner'. In certain cultures, failure is a taboo word. Co-workers and superiors who accept that failures are a part of the process of innovation are crucial to fostering an innovative culture. The key is not to take the failures personally as an indication of a lack of creativity or entrepreneurship, but to treat them as useful lessons that help to lead you to the right answers.

Caution

Do not cling on to ideas that obviously do not work well even after repeated tweaking. Let the average ideas die quickly so the best ideas can flourish.

Secret 75
A PROCESS APPROACH CAN MAKE CREATIVITY HAPPEN

Do you sometimes wish that useful ideas would appear when you need them, as easy as switching on the magical light bulb over your head? Or does a well-conceived creative plan follow a step-by-step process?

Researchers found that creative problem solving or brainstorming that leads to actionable plans in the workplace usually involves a four-stage process:

1. Clarifying the problem

In the workplace, either the challenge/problem has already been determined or you are the one to determine the goal. The people who are likely to be impacted by the solution — the customers, suppliers, distributors — can shed some light on the nature of the problem. Very often, we tend to stick to our own pet ideas rather than observe the customers' actual needs. Once you have more insights into the nature of the problem, step back to ensure that you have defined the goal properly. Write down the desired outcomes.

2. Ideating (generating the ideas)

This is often considered the brainstorming phase, whether you are doing this by yourself or in a group. Resist the impulse of leaping into the ideating phase without first becoming crystal clear about the problem and desired outcomes. Many people get stuck at brainstorming because the initial clarifying stage has not been done effectively. During this phase, the ideas can be totally new or modified from other ideas. Study successful case studies in other industries as a springboard for your own ideas. List as many possible ideas as you can. Don't stop at the first few obvious ideas.

3. Developing the solution further (selecting and strengthening the solutions)

This stage can be broken down into a few actions:

- determining the essential criteria or factors that you would consider in making the decision.
- pruning the less promising ideas.
- looking at the ideas from multiple angles.

- exploring several different scenarios and fleshing out the details of the selected ideas.

4. Implementing the ideas according to the action plan

Here's where we delve into the actionable details. Develop a clear timeline and deliverables, and get the buy-in from everyone in the team. 'Implementation' or 'action' is the all-important link between ideas and results. Poor implementation is one of the most common reasons why projects fail. Do ensure that you have the right people doing the right jobs.

Some people prefer one particular stage of the process more than other stages. Which stage do you prefer? Do you need to be good at all the stages?

This questionnaire is a quick way to know your preferences. Give a score – any number between 1 and 5. 1 for 'least like me', 2 for 'a little like me', 3 for 'moderately like me', 4 for 'fairly often like me', 5 for 'very much like me'.

a. I like to ask the 'why' questions or to be clear about the heart of an issue. ☐

b. It is important to me that I determine the objectives of the problem or project. ☐

c. I like to come up with new ideas that others may not have thought about. ☐

d. I can think of many solutions to a problem or challenge. ☐

e. It is my nature to look into the details to improve the ideas. ☐

f. I like to contribute to strengthening the solutions. ☐

g. I like to formulate action plans with clear tasks and deadlines. ☐

h. I can't wait to implement the ideas! I experience great satisfaction when I complete the action plans. ☐

Add up your score for:

a and b (*clarifying stage*): ☐

c and d (*ideating stage*): ☐

e and f (*developing stage*): ☐

g and h (*implementing stage*): ☐

The stage in which you scored the highest is your top preference. The stage in which you scored the lowest is your least preferred stage. If you have the same score for more than one stage, this means an equal preference for the stages.

Caution

You don't need to attempt to master all stages of the creative process. Mastering all the stages takes too much time and effort.

In the creative process, how then should you handle your weak spots? Many of your successes in life will not depend on improving the areas of your weaknesses, but in growing your strengths and leveraging on the strengths of others. For example, perhaps your strength is in 'developing' and improving ideas and your weakness is in 'ideating' new approaches or 'implementing' them. You can co-opt team members who can cover the other stages of the creative process.

Your Turn

To get a better idea of your strengths in the creative process in your team, ask the people you work with to score the above questionnaire based on what they see as your value-add to the project or company. Do the same exercise for them. Discuss how you can re-allocate tasks to capitalise on each other's strengths.

Secret 76
YOUR PEOPLE NETWORKS ARE YOUR GREATEST CREATIVE RESOURCE

In the previous secret, you learnt that if you are not able to generate the good ideas by yourself, you have the option of turning to your colleagues, or even close friends or family members. Collectively, these are known as your 'strong networks' because you meet them often and have close, strong social bonds. They can be valuable in lending their ardent support for your ideas.

People usually feel comfortable approaching others in their strong networks who think like them. However, are these people the best sources for giving you ideas that are radically different from yours and providing critical challenges to your thinking? From my experience, the answer is typically 'no'.

This leads to the idea of building multiple 'weak ties' or 'weak networks' — people who are not in your immediate circle and with whom you do not interact frequently. They can be from another company, industry or country. They may be your friends' friends, the contacts of your business associates, ex-classmates from your school, people you meet at conferences, or acquaintances built from your networking efforts.

Caution

Multiple, diverse 'weak networks' are useful to get different ideas quickly. Having just one or two 'weak networks' may not be effective in garnering enough new ideas or connections to the relevant people.

In the work context, people are typically familiar with networking for business opportunities or meeting head hunters with the hope of getting a better job. Another good reason for building weak networks is to seek validation or constructive feedback for our ideas and to get new ideas.

Studies reveal that there are only up to six degrees of separation between any two people – this means that in six or fewer connections, you can be introduced to almost anyone on earth. It is possible to network your way to the expert or person who may be able to provide you with useful pointers or ideas. Therefore, 'weak networks' are very useful for building your creative capacity.

Chances are you have an account on Facebook, which can be a very cost effective way to solicit for ideas. For example, I know a TV news host who posts questions to her Facebook contacts to come up with ideas for a TV show.

You may be equally familiar with professional networking websites such as LinkedIn (www.linkedin.com) or Plaxo (www.plaxo.com). I recommend using any of these sites to build up both strong and weak professional networks. You can request, through someone in your network, to be introduced to relevant people. LinkedIn also shows you the degree of separation between you and the intended person, and who among your contacts know him/her.

These sites are useful for sourcing relevant interest groups. There are a wide range of special interest groups that you can join, and these can be sources of new contacts, ideas and business opportunities.

If you are new to building your professional network, a good place to start is your college or university alumni groups or organisations where you have previously worked. Search for current or ex-classmates/colleagues and invite them to be linked to you. Networking with people outside your interests and industry helps to build 'flexibility', which is an essential skill described in Secret 73.

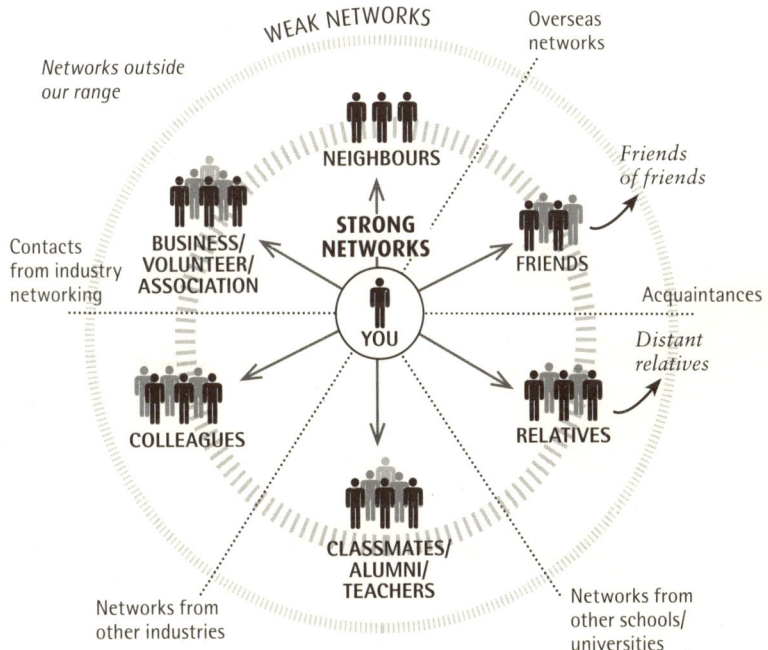

Weak networks can be a useful creative resource.

The principle of reciprocity (ie: give and take) is important in social interactions. It is a great idea to volunteer to provide feedback or ideas to contacts in your weak networks. When you need to ask for ideas, it is more likely that they would then reciprocate, i.e. return your favour by answering your queries or referring you to someone else who may be able to offer the help you need.

Hot Tip

When you approach your weak networks for solutions or ideas, most of them would not be able to spend a lot of time to give you long answers to many general questions. It is much better that you craft a specific question and seek short, targeted answers or validation for your ideas. This increases the likelihood that your weak networks would respond in a timely manner.

This secret is a shortcut to additional creative ideas. Creativity is such a strategic skill that you should not rely entirely on others for good ideas. Invest in my first three secrets, and then use this final secret to supplement your creative capacity.

Checklist to jumpstart your creative potential

1. Hone your powers of observation by capturing ideas on a camera or physical/electronic notepad.

2. Listen to others as they describe their experiences, problems and wishes. These are sources of opportunities and possible emerging trends.

3. Get interested in other topics and industries. Spot similarities that may be useful to your own projects.

4. Be patient to brainstorm for a long list of different ideas before deciding on the suitable ones.

5. Select your creative inspiration/role models and learn their factors for success.

6. Choose the work that you have a passion for and that you can be competent in. Have fun succeeding in your work!

7. Understand yourself: which stage of the creative process do you prefer the most and the least?

8. Invite your team mates to take the Creative Process questionnaire to understand each other's preferences. Take this data into consideration when you determine how to allocate tasks.

9. Select colleagues, associates or employees who complement you with their preferences in the other stages of the creative process.

10. Expand multiple 'weak networks' through networking events and professional networking websites. These acquaintances can help you with feedback, idea validation, new ideas or useful connections to relevant people who have the solutions that you need.

SECTION 8

Management, Leadership and Teamwork

CHAPTER 20

THE CORPORATE JUNGLE
— Is it a Jungle or a Zoo?

by **Benjamin Cheng**
(MEd, B. Eng)

Benjamin Cheng helps organisations with business strategy to penetrate new and emerging markets, improve corporate internal/external communication for greater synergy, and implement effective management for efficiency and productivity. He is well-known for his interactive, humorous and engaging style of speaking and training. As a bilingual (English and Mandarin) speaker, trainer and business consultant, Ben has travelled around the world including USA, Russia, UK, Ireland, Hungary, Belgium, Sweden, China, Dubai, Abu Dhabi, Australia, India, Malaysia, Mongolia, Thailand, Vietnam, Philippines, Indonesia, Hong Kong and Taiwan, speaking to more than 50,000 people.

Ben is currently the Senior Vice President of Training and Development for a US-based holding company, VP of Market Development (Far East) and Executive Director of HR for the Singapore subsidiary.

Ben is an internationally certified trainer in Neuro-Linguistic Programming (NLP). He graduated from NUS with a Bachelor of Electrical and Electronics Engineering Degree, holds an Advanced Certificate in Theology and a Masters of Education (Leadership, Policy and Change). He is a past President of APSS and was one of the Founding Members. He was also the co-chair for the International Convention Action Team organising the first Global Speakers Summit held in Singapore.

Ben is an active Toastmaster (ATM-S) and was the first speaker in District 80 to be the double district level Champion in Humorous Speech Contest (2004) and Table Topics Contest (2006).

Find out more about Benjamin at: **www.benjamincheng.com**
Contact Benjamin at **ben@benjamincheng.com**

WHAT ARE SOME of the words you think about when the term 'office politics' is mentioned? Common words often heard are, 'horrible', 'bad', 'backstabbing', 'victim', 'bully', 'bootlicker', 'boss pleaser'. These words are not very positive or empowering.

Instead of 'office politics', we could substitute the term with 'office dynamics' or 'communication matrix'. Interactions and communication are really the dynamics of how people talk to each other. Everyone is trying his or her best to excel in their work, impress higher management and contribute to the greater good of the company. The inner intentions are to survive better, to earn more money, and to provide a better life for themselves and their love ones. However, in the pursuit of wanting more popularity, achieving better results and climbing higher up the corporate ladder, some people take certain actions that others do not agree to. These actions and reactions are the root cause of so-called 'office politics'.

As much as we do not like certain people's actions, how many times do we look into the mirror and reflect on our own actions? Could it be possible that colleagues may label some of our actions in the office as 'office politics'?

In this chapter, based on his observations from the corporate world and working adults, Benjamin Cheng will share with you how to survive and do well in the corporate world.

Secret 77
GETTING TO KNOW YOUR COLLEAGUES' ANIMAL-LIKE CHARACTERISTICS CAN HELP YOU AT WORK

Human interactions in the workplace are very complex and dynamic. In the past, many people worked in the same company for decades. Working with the same people for so long made it is easier to know their characters, personalities and working styles. These days, many stay in a job for two to three years, so we need to get to know and understand our colleagues much faster. A new colleague normally takes between six to nine months to get up to speed in work tasks and relationship building.

When you observe the behaviours of your colleagues, you will see different characteristics manifested by each individual. In this secret, I'm going to show you how we can draw a parallel to the animal kingdom by looking at certain animal-like characteristics (ALC). You will find that in different situations and towards different people, the same person may display a totally different trait or a combination of them.

Animal-Like Characteristics

These are 12 out of the full list of animal-like characters we can find in the office environment.

1. The Puppy

Friendly, likable and tries to please everyone.

These people act like puppies in front of senior management, which makes them very well-liked, and sometimes draws jealousy from other colleagues. Although a very obedient worker, a puppy sometimes tries too hard to please everyone. Puppies also have the danger of being labelled a 'pet'.

2. The Cat

Unpredictable, aloof and practical.

Cats generally act very aloof and classy. When it comes to meal times, they can be very nice. However, watch out for their claws if they sense any danger. Even if you are its owner, you risk getting clawed. Loyalty swings to where there is food (advantage).

3. The Snake

Slithers, strikes fast, with a painful bite followed by wrangling or injecting venom.

When there is a fault, snakes wriggle their way out of trouble and get away by blaming others. They are like negative colleagues spreading negativity and gossip works just like venom spreading in your mind and body, paralysing your work performance and the company.

4. The Ox

Hardworking, stubborn, with no political agenda.

These people are hardworking and do not join any political affiliations within the company. At times, they still run the risk of being isolated or drawn into fights, as they do not want to offend anyone or any group. Do not offend an ox-like character, as they can be dangerous when provoked to defend themselves.

5. The Scorpion

Hidden, dangerous, with a venomous sting at the back.

Scorpions are nocturnal and are not normally found in the open. Just like some people, you have no idea when, how, what or who struck you until it hits you. These backstabbers generally strike when they find a weakness in your work or character.

6. The Hyena

Noisy, cowardly scavengers who can also be pack hunters.

Hyenas talk a lot and make a lot of noise to hide their insecurities. They love to talk about their achievements, take credit as their own, with no regard, regularly recruiting others into their gang and acting like Indian chiefs representing a pack (union).

7. The Peacock

Loud, obnoxious and show-offs.

Peacock-like people love to dress up, talk loudly, and can be quite annoying with their showing off. They tend to be good-looking, which they use to their full advantage. Some peacocks who are not as physically attractive are very good at using dressing and make-up to enhance their peacock-like persona.

8. The Sloth

Slow, steady, yet a competent swimmer.

Sloths are slow in everything they do at work, but it is hard to tell whether they do it naturally or intentionally. In water, sloths swim well. Some sloths display a different speed outside the work environment. Being steady can be good, but at times colleagues can get frustrated due to the slowness of their work.

9. The Chameleon

Master of camouflage.

Just like a chameleon, these people can change colours and blend in with every political group. When there is additional work to be done, they are nowhere to be found. They do not stand out in the group, yet they are very good at survival and hunting for food.

10. The Mother Hen

Protective, caring and nosy.

The hen seems to know everything that is happening within the organisation. A very caring and protective person, if you are one of her chicks (group), she will be quick to defend you if she feels you are being attacked.

11. The Geococcyx (Roadrunner)

Fast, busy and overly-excited.

A wonderful fast worker who always seems to be busy. When the roadrunner believes a situation to be a crisis or emergency, they will tend to be overly-excited and nervous. You just wish they would calm down a little and maintain a cool head to resolve issues.

12. The Monkey

Naughty, active and unable to keep still.

Monkeys love to play pranks even when it is not appropriate. As they have an active mind, they are not able to keep still, always needing to be on the move. Some are quite funny, which adds life to the boring working world, but some are plain naughty and can be quite a nuisance.

Caution

Please do not give your colleagues nicknames after any of these animals. They are merely displaying characteristics similar to a certain animal and they may not be aware of this. Instead, use this as a guide to help you to understand others better. Be nice to people, because what goes around, comes around.

Secret 78
FOR A HEALTHY WORKING ENVIRONMENT, YOU NEED TO HAVE A BALANCE OF JUNGLE AND ZOO

In the corporate world, the fight to outperform and outshine others in order to get promoted can sometimes be quite bloody and brutal. Extreme behaviours include sabotage, backstabbing, slander, gossip, nicknaming, group attacks, and many other battle strategies. You may have been a victim of such attacks. When I was a young engineer working for a UK MNC, I was reporting to a project director in managing different projects. When he fell out of favour with the senior management and was asked to leave, his successor brought in his own group of people to take over every position. All of us who had been hired by the previous director were ostracised and either fired or asked to resign. It was the most hostile purge I experienced in my working life.

The corporate jungle is the common name given to the working world. In a real jungle, in order to survive, animals need to be fast, strong or smart. They need to find food and they must avoid being eaten – unless of course they are lucky enough to find a place where there are no natural enemies, with an abundant supply of food so there is little or no hunting required. In the corporate jungle of the past, it was common for people to find a job and stay in the same company their whole life with pension benefits. These days, such employment benefits and people willing to stay for years in the same job are hard to find and close to extinction.

Jungle survival skills

In the jungle, each animal will have different survival skills. This is true in the corporate jungle too. Let's take a look at some of these survival skills:

1. **Hunting:** Many animals depend on speed and strength to hunt for prey. In the corporate world we need to be fast to pick up the latest technological developments and adapt to new environments. The world is now a global marketplace where inventions and discoveries are being rolled out at the speed of thought. We also need to be mentally and emotionally strong to take on both the internal competition and external challenges to succeed in the workplace.

2. **Defending**: In the animal kingdom, there are various defence mechanisms, including out-running the predator, camouflaging, distracting, setting up a decoy, relying on group defence, hiding, displaying stealth, among others. It is similar in the corporate world. People who are unable to keep up with the better performers will have to opt for a defensive strategy. Some will avoid doing work that makes them look bad, others will form an alliance with other people to launch attacks, while a group will hide and wait for their turn to strike.

If your corporate environment is like a jungle with people who are hungry for success, that is a good thing. If you are a leader managing these people, it is important to manage the dynamics of the group, unite them to a common goal, and channel their energy to fight the outside competition. Failure to manage these people will result in everyone turning inwards and tearing each other apart.

The corporate zoo

Let me introduce you to the idea of the corporate zoo. In the initial stages of many companies, it is often a struggle to survive. People are more motivated to do well to ensure the company reaches a certain level of success. However, when a company is doing relatively well, with sufficient cash reserves, many of the top management and employees begin to slow down their pace and let their guard down. When business is good they become complacent, even though they are not so intense and competitive. The system has already been set up for sales to continue, and business is in autopilot. In this situation, the environment within the company has the risk of becoming a corporate zoo.

Look at the animals in the zoo. There is no need for them to go hunting as food is readily available. Now confined in a cage, the animals cannot choose their territory, their own mate or roam freely. Slowly but surely, they will start to lose their ability to hunt and their hunger for success, and some will become very lazy. Does any of this sound familiar?

Some companies that have enjoyed prosperity for an extended period of time are in danger of slipping into a corporate zoo mentality. By observing the attitude of some civil servants and the inefficiency of some government ministries, you can tell whether the company is hungry for success or has become complacent.

Caution

Whatever is not growing is dying! Nations, political parties, companies and organisations rise and fall. Many times it is the founding fathers who have the vision and fighting spirit to build up.

Choosing the right team with the desire for success will ensure continuity and growth to leave a lasting legacy; a written record in history books.

The challenge to top management

Do not be fooled by the lion or tiger in a cage in the zoo, thinking that they no longer posses the animal instincts. Even though they may not be able to hunt like those in the wild, they still have the thirst for blood. If you try walking into the enclosure, these beasts will still attack. It is their inborn nature. The cobra will still strike with venom even in captivity.

The immediate challenge of top management leaders these days is to balance the organisation somewhere between the corporate jungle and the corporate zoo. We do not want our employees to focus on fighting each other. We need them to have the hunger for greater success, motivation and a desire to fight the competition in the outside world, yet we also need them to feel a sense of security and certainty.

Holy Moly!

Now I know I need to have the hunger for success and if I am complacent, I may end up like an animal in the zoo.

Secret 79
BEING LIKEABLE AND POPULAR IS EASY WHEN YOU KNOW HOW

Working in a company sometimes seems like a popularity contest, doesn't it? Let's take a look at some of the elements that will help you to be likeable and popular at work. However, remember that to be the most popular, you will need combinations of all these elements and a lot of effort.

1. Be nice to people

No one likes to be around a grumpy, negative person. A few small kind gestures go a long way. Be on the lookout for occasions where you can offer a little help. People will appreciate these small things. It's important to avoid being inward looking or to keep asking "What's in it for me" or saying, "No one cares about me." Whatever you want to receive, give! Acts of kindness will come back to you when you are kind to others. Get to know what your colleagues like. A small gift or a friendly gesture can cheer up anyone's day.

2. Be wise in knowledge

No one likes to talk to a dumb person, and neither do we like an empty vessel who brags about how much he or she knows. Read widely, learn as much as you can and be equipped with general knowledge. You will be a more interesting person to talk to during tea breaks and lunch hours. People like to be around knowledgeable people. They will learn a lot more just by spending time with you. The more we share, the more we will receive knowledge from others.

3. Be good at your work

When you are good at your job, people will like you and want to learn from you. However, when you are good at what you do, there is the risk of jealousy or being given more task and projects. The more efficient you are at work, the higher the likelihood of promotion when the higher management notice. Your colleagues will applaud and respect that promotion when it comes, because they know you deserve it.

4. Be presentable in your dressing

You do not need to dress like you are going to formal dinner every day. The minimum standard is to be presentable. Groom your hair, wash your face, shave, dress appropriately for the occasion, iron your shirt, match your blouse colour with your dress colours, clean your shoes regularly, take care of body odour, smell good, walk tall — and guys, please, trim your nose hair!

5. Be a good listener

We were all created with one mouth and two ears for an obvious reason – to talk less and listen more. Nothing can be more irritating than having a conversation with someone who does not listen and just keeps talking. If you want your colleagues to like you, be a good listener. Just hearing is not enough. You may hear what they say, but it is more important to listen to what they say and remember what they say. Listen with your eyes and your mind.

6. Be kind with your words

Think before you speak. There are people who put their mouths before their brains. In some situations, silence is golden. A careless comment may get you into big trouble. An appropriate comment delivered in the wrong way is equally bad, Give feedback only when necessary. Not everyone wants to know his or her mistakes. And please, choose the right timing to give feedback. It's never a good idea to point out someone's mistake in front of others.

7. Be generous in praise

The sweetest sound in anyone's ears is praise. Notice the good things your colleagues do, and give them some encouragement by praising them. Genuine praise goes a long way, so give credit where credit is due. Don't take it to the extreme though by praising every little thing, and do not exaggerate. The effect will be just like sugar – a little of it is nice, but too much is just overpowering.

The wrong route to popularity

Let me share a quick story of an ex-colleague who took the 'shameless' route to popularity. This colleague was well-liked by his 'gang' of followers. He was also well-hated by his non-followers. The elements he combined were:

- **Thick-skinned:** He claimed affiliation to every credit and took the credit even when it was not his work.

- **Blame-shifting:** Whenever he made a mistake, he always pushed the blame to others, including his subordinates.

- **Sucking-up:** He praised loudly when the boss was right and kept quiet when the boss was wrong. He followed the boss everywhere and followed every action including his bad habits.

- **Hero-stories:** Every time he told a story it always revolved around how good and popular he was, how hard he worked to solve problems and how important he was to the company.

- **Favouritism:** He strategised to make sure everyone bowed down to him, and those who did received special favours. Those who did not were ostracised. He continued to work on those who had not been bought in to his 'gang'

I know he did not ask, but if he did, my suggestion for him would be: If you want to be more popular; you must share more glory and credit with others. You must talk less about yourself and listen more to others. You must win the hearts of your non-followers by being nicer to them. If you do all this, and exercise a sweeter tongue, you could be invincible.

Your Turn

How many of these elements are you currently practising in your working environment? How many of these elements do you need to work on?

Secret 80
YOU NEED MORE THAN LUCK TO GO BEYOND SURVIVAL TO SUCCESS

The majority of people in the working population are in the survival mode. How wonderful would it be if you could move beyond survival to success?

When you get promoted into a higher position, if you are not prepared for it, you will have a tough time ahead. It should be a confirmation that you truly deserve that position. To be successful, you need a little bit of 'luck'. According to Lucius Annaeus Seneca (Roman philosopher, mid-first century AD), "Luck is what happens when preparation meets opportunity." To prepare for success, here are some things you need to be mindful of:

1. Be well-connected

What you know is important, of course, but something even more important in your career will be who you know. Your professional network will play a big part in helping you to climb the corporate ladder. You need to be well-connected within the company and with other top players in the same industry. It's also important to work towards having the right authority and government connections.

Hot Tip

Who you know will be essential for survival, but it is who knows you that will be the key to your success.

2. Be hungry for success

Les Brown said, "You gotta be hungry." He brings the message of desire, persistence and hunger for success to the world. If you want to be successful, you need to be hungry for success. You need to turn on your natural instincts to hunt for success like the animals in the corporate jungle. Once you turn off those instincts, you will start turning into someone within the corporate zoo.

3. Be credited for your work

Give credit where credit is due. If you deserve the credit, accept it! Why give it to others? Some Asians really overdo the humility, sometimes in a way that is not beneficial to themselves. When you compliment them for what they have done well, they go into this mode of self-denial and keep repeating the minor mistakes and saying, "No, no, no, I don't deserve it." Don't do that. Take what you deserve! Using the animal kingdom as an example, if you have just hunted for meat and leave it on the ground, the next passing predator will take it and enjoy all your hard work. People around you will claim the credit if you do not. Next time, when someone compliments you, just say "Thank you!"

4. Be politically-wise

You may not like office politics but politics will come knocking on your door. I advise everyone to be politically-wise, to know when to join in and when to stay away. I used to make all the right but unpopular decisions and another colleague always made the popular decisions even though they were not necessarily 'right'. He became much more popular with the staff. Now, I will still make the right decision. But in situations where right or wrong is not so straightforward, I may choose to take the more popular decision. Some amount of flexibility helps you take better control of situations.

Your Turn

When faced with a difficult situation and have to make a tough decision, you can't have both. Do you make the right decision or the popular decision?

5. Be a problem solver

If the company faces a problem, who would the management trust and call upon to solve it? Whoever is chosen will become a very important asset to the company. If you are able to be a proven problem solver, you will go far in your career. Companies will headhunt you to join them. The bigger the problems you are able to resolve, the higher you will climb up the corporate ladder.

6. Be very good in timing

In the animal kingdom, whether in attacking or defending mode, timing is everything. For a cheetah, the right timing to start the run and make the tackle will mean it gets a meal. For the gazelle, the right timing to turn and evade means saving its life. Be aware and sensitive of the season, tide and timing of the world economy, local economy, industry, company and department you are in. Position yourself to be the right person at the right place and, more importantly, at the right time.

7. Be willing to take a calculated risk

No man has ever discovered new territory and virgin land without first having the courage to sail out from the safety of the shores. At times, you may need to take on a new project, change your job, and relocate to a new country, change company or even enter a new industry. If you are creative, visionary and courageous, you may even create a brand new industry. A single lioness will never attempt to take down a herd of elephants by herself. Calculate the cost of taking any action that is perceived to be risky. Don't be hasty. Think carefully, and if the odds are in your favour, go for it courageously. Nothing spectacular has ever been accomplished without a little risk, a little insanity and a lot of uncertainty.

8. Be prepared for success

Many people want success but when success arrives, they lose it fairly quickly. Other than planning and working towards your success, you need to be mentally prepared and set goals for what will happen after the success and financial breakthrough arrives. Set up to keep and sustain your success. Success is not a destination; it is a lifelong journey.

The ultimate secret is not to be any 'animal'; but to be a zookeeper. Every 'animal' will be under your care, protection and most importantly, they will be yours to keep. That will bring you ultimate success.

Checklist for succeeding in the corporate world, be it a jungle or a zoo

1. Know the different animal-like characteristics. Decide what desirable actions to take and undesirable actions to avoid.

2. Learn to be a great communicator. Listen more, talk less. When speaking, let your words come out like nuggets of wisdom.

3. Be hungry for success. Are you still on the hunt or do you have mentality of a caged animal?

4. Do all the right things to be well-liked and popular in your company.

5. Be well connected in your company and industry. Continue to expand your circle of influence.

6. Be flexible in your approach.

7. Be nice to people, and generally they will be nice to you.

8. Be politically-wise.

9. Go beyond survival to success.

10. Be ready to sustain and retain success when it comes.

CHAPTER 21

TIMELESS MANAGEMENT
Improving leadership effectiveness by taking time
to reflect and renew

by **Bob Feldman**
*Corporate Trainer, Executive Coach
and Professional Speaker*

Bob Feldman choreographs his speaking, training and coaching engagements to heighten people's self-awareness and activate their personal presence to speak and communicate with credibility, believability and cross-cultural sensitivity. A mime artist and actor born raised in Chicago, Bob has also lived and worked for lengthy periods on two other continents, primarily in Germany and Singapore, where he has made his home for the past 12 years. He holds a Bachelor's Degree (B.A.) in Movement, Psychology and Education and a Masters Degree (M.Ed.) in Adult and Continuing Education from the University of Illinois.

Bob's expertise in stress management and effective relaxation methods has helped people keep a balance and holistic perspective on life. He is a certified massage therapist as well as a practitioner of the Feldenkrais Method, a gentle way to relieve tension in the body. In the management arena, Bob is a Personal Efficiency Program (PEP) Consultant and also Managing Director of a successful arts conservation and restoration business. He works as a corporate trainer and executive coach throughout the Asia-Pacific region.

Find out more about Bob at: **www.bobfeldman.net**
Contact Bob at: **mail@bobfeldman.net**

MAYBE WE HAVE it all wrong. While there is much information about the need for good time management – setting priorities, managing interruptions, dealing with procrastination, not over-scheduling and creating a 'do it now' attitude – what may be surprising and underestimated is the ability to have good 'timeless' management.

Timeless moments are those in which time disappears, the space between the millions of moments that make up our time-filled day. Managers who take time for quiet timeless breaks for self-reflection report less stress, better sleep, improved health, not to mention enhanced well-being and wiser decisions. To be an effective leader, timeless management adds value to your leadership role as you find innovative ideas that reverberate throughout the organisation and increase productivity.

In this section, Bob Feldman offers suggestions on how to create the space you need to reflect, relax and refresh your mind and body, including simple breathing exercises to calm the mind.

You'll learn how to create the opportunity for timeless moments rather than continuing to be overwhelmed by the whirlwind of endless meetings, phone calls, emails, presentations and troubleshooting, becoming breathless. Bob will help you create the space to breathe – the timeless space – and to feel more in control.

Secret 81
YOUR BEST IDEAS DO NOT COME IN THE BOARDROOM

Where are you when you get your best ideas? Are you sitting at your computer rushing to complete work for the next deadline? Are you in the midst of your weekly team meeting? I don't think so. If you are like most people, you probably get your best ideas while resting in bed, walking in nature, listening to music in the car or taking a shower. All of these activities reflect a sense of solitude. This was the finding of Michael Gelb, who asked these question to thousands of people and reported in his book *How to Think Like Leonardo da Vinci:*

Seven Steps to Genius Every Day. Da Vinci knew that his most creative insights came when he was alone. Even Einstein has been quoted as saying, "Why do I get my best ideas while shaving?" These are breakthrough moments, when you let go of your control and allow the subconscious to work to your advantage.

By stepping 'outside of time' into timeless space, you remove the pressure. You are able to see more clearly, increase your productivity, and find solutions to the difficult problems you are facing. This doesn't mean running away from responsibilities, nor does it mean escaping into some fantasy world. Timeless space is very real! Two paradoxes can illuminate this idea.

1. Slow down to speed up

This is one of the great paradoxes of time. Think about how it feels when you are really immersed in something: a fascinating novel, a challenge at work, your passionate hobby, or even watching children at play. What happens? You look at your watch and are shocked how much time has passed. When you are deeply involved in what highly interests you, your internal clock slows down.

An awareness scan during the day can help this process of slowing, allowing your attention to expand.

Your Turn

Sit comfortably in your chair. Notice your breath. Shift your attention to the parts of your body in contact with the chair. Notice the position of your hands, your fingers, your elbows. Are your feet touching the floor? Become aware of your knees, hips, the tilt of your head. Shift attention to your breath again. How do you feel?

2. Let go to let come

This paradox is drawn from the work of researcher and theorist Otto C. Scharmer, who noted that a key shift in awareness comes when we are willing to let go — of old habits, resistance, prejudices and blocks — and then be open for what comes next, the future that is waiting to emerge. It takes courage to step into this apparent void, to develop "the capacity to operate from the nothingness of the now, the ability to discern and take the next step in situations where old structures have broken down and new structures haven't yet emerged." Scharmer feels that this may be the most important core capacity for the 21st century.

For timeless management to succeed, we must break away from our habitual contexts. The 'breakout principle' is a means for managers to enhance performance, increase productivity and avoid burnout by tapping into their own creative insights. The term 'breakout principle' was coined through research conducted by William Proctor and also Dr. Herbert Benson of the USA-based Mind/Body Medical Institute, known earlier for his pioneering work at Harvard Medical School in the mid-1970s on eliciting the relaxation response to reduce stress.

While stress can be positive and motivating, at the tipping point it becomes the negative phenomenon we know so well: faster heart rate, higher blood pressure, increased breathing rate leading to the fight-or-flight response. Their latest findings show that if you work only up to the tipping point and then completely let go of your problem by applying certain triggers, the brain will rearrange itself to allow the hemispheres to communicate better. "By bringing the brain to the height of activity and then suddenly moving it into a passive, relaxed state, it's possible to stimulate much higher neurological performance than would otherwise be the case." A 'calm commotion' develops as the brain quiets down and creates a focused increase in activity associated with attention, space-time concepts and decision-making.

The breakout sequence has four steps:

1. Struggle with a difficult problem, task or project – and stop when you start feeling stressed and unproductive.

2. Break out and walk away from the problem and do something completely different that produces a relaxation response in the body for at least 10 minutes (i.e. focus on your breathing, take a nap, do some relaxation exercises, play some music - or go to the art museum, take a hot shower, go to the gym, take a walk, or simply find a quiet place away from the office).

3. The breakthrough occurs when you gain a sudden insight, sometimes referred to as 'being in the zone' or 'flow' or 'peak experience,' leading to increased self-confidence.

4. Finally, you return to this 'new-normal' state in which the sense of self-confidence continues.

Breaking away can also be done by a conscious move into timelessness through 'braindorming,' adding the Latin 'dormire' (to sleep) to traditional brainstorming. Close your eyes, relax and breathe, place your concern before you, and then let the ideas emerge without struggle. Try it. You'll be surprised at the positive results!

Secret 82
TO BECOME A MINDFUL LEADER, YOU NEED TO SHAPE-SHIFT

Cultivating mindfulness

Are you distracted throughout the day with thoughts about what you have to do, haven't done yet, wish you hadn't done? If so, you're not alone. These mindless meanderings are inefficient time wasters. Why not choose to become a mindful leader instead?

Mindfulness is a Buddhist concept that refers to being in the present with your full attention, a non-judgmental awareness from moment to moment. Mindfulness is a timeless capability. There is only the present moment. You need to create the intention to give full attention first to yourself, and then it will expand to the individuals and groups you speak with. If you practise time-urgent gestures that indicate you want to be somewhere else, they will negate being 'with' others.

Cultivating mindfulness can be practised through shape-shifting, a term used in Native American Indian culture to describe the ability to seemingly disappear as a human being by transforming oneself into the form of an animal. You can shape-shift to appear invisible to others, yet still be very present.

Quiet breaks for reflection

If you want to rejuvenate and rescue yourself from exhaustion, you can shape-shift and disappear with your eyes closed. This will also stimulate creative thinking. The Sleep Research Centre at Loughborough University (UK) reported that a ten-minute nap in the afternoon is more effective than two extra hours of sleep to keep you alive and alert during the day. I change that to ten minutes of simply closing your eyes - a nap, breathing exercises, relaxation techniques, meditation – whenever you feel the need. You disappear for ten minutes and use that time for yourself, uninterrupted. Enter that timeless state of being to calm the mind, let go of your controls, look for a solution to a problem or just to find a joy and energy that will leave you refreshed throughout the rest of the day.

You can also shape-shift with your eyes open. Business executive Karen Salmansohn developed 'do-nothing' relaxation exercises with the same results. Her first 'exercise' emerged when she noticed (as did her co-workers) a dynamic positive flow throughout the day after five to ten minutes alone just 'being with' her morning coffee: really smelling it, feeling the heat of the cup, the taste, the liquid down her throat, the whole context. There really is something to be said for the phrase 'the pause that refreshes.' This is mindfulness in action.

We have circadian rhythms in the body (from the Latin 'circa diem' meaning around the day) which regulate our balance between the waking hours and sleep. We need to get horizontal to allow our bodies to recover from the day, to allow all our hormones and inner systems to come to a homeostasis and prepare us for a new day. Seven to eight hours of sleep is the recommended average. Six hours per night and you dramatically increase your likelihood of having high blood pressure. Five hours per night and you double your risk of heart attack. Whether you are working in one place or travelling during the week, do not sacrifice your sleep!

Psychologists note that due to our ultradian rhythms (from the Latin 'ultra diem' meaning many times during the day), the body needs short recovery periods during the day after every 90 to 120 minutes of work. You are draining your body if you continue to work non-stop. Just a walk to the pantry, a chat with your colleague or a look out of the window may be enough. The busy executive often skips these breaks because they consider them to be unproductive time. Wrong! Take your breaks to become more productive. Taking care of yourself takes care of your colleagues. You become more available.

Holy Moly!

I will become more productive if I take my breaks with mindfulness, because I will return to work more energised and focused.

The open and closed door

You can also shape-shift with the door closed. Many executives pride an open-door policy that leads to transparency, trust and open communication. However, there are times when it is best to protect your boundaries. By closing your door you indicate that you do not want to be interrupted. If you are to be effective at your job, you need time for planning and reflecting, and your staff will understand this. You can even put a note on your door indicating that if it is urgent you can be interrupted but otherwise please wait until a particular time as you are in planning mode. You will find that your effectiveness and productivity as a leader in your organisation will dramatically improve. You will feel more prepared and therefore more confident and refreshed. When you are refreshed, you can carry this attitude and be more mindful in your interaction with associates. Stress is like a virus that is contagious in the office. If you lead with mindfulness, this is the attitude that will spread.

Making yourself invisible will increase your visibility. Take control by shape-shifting into a timeless space.

Secret 83
ENHANCE YOUR PLANNING EFFECTIVENESS BY FINDING 'ISLANDS OF PEACE'

The hideaway outside the office

You can run and you *can* hide. You just have to decide you want to do that. Emotional intelligence authors, Robert Cooper and Ayman Sawaf, suggest we should create 'islands of peace' in the midst of all the daily demands that compete for our attention and energy. For some managers it is the nearby coffee shop, for others a hotel lobby, or even the gym or a spa. Schedule a longer time for your meeting so you have 30 minutes or more to go somewhere else where you will not be seen by your staff. When I proposed this to some managers, they felt incredibly guilty the first time they did this, as if they were cheating, like a school child playing hooky. However, eventually they found that in these moments of 'stolen' time, creative impulses and ideas emerged. This happened because they found a timeless moment to relax their controls and think without interruption. It could work for you too!

Caution

Keep your hiding place to yourself, otherwise you will soon be joined by colleagues and friends, which will defeat the original purpose!

In Robin S. Sharma's fable *The Monk Who Sold His Ferrari*, the enlightened former-lawyer says "Taking your time to renew yourself is the most important thing you can do. Ironically, taking time out from your hectic schedule for self-improvement and personal enrichment will dramatically improve your effectiveness once you get back into it." Take the chance and let the surprises spring forth.

As a corporate executive coach, I have met CEOs and Managing Directors in the privacy of their homes. Away from the office in their own space, the executives could experience a freedom to experiment and express themselves in a way that would have been awkward in the confines of their organisational context.

Take a retreat to renew and refresh

A group retreat is often an effective team building event for your staff, but what I mean here is a self-retreat. And it's not just for 10 or 20 minutes. You need a full day – or at least a morning or afternoon. It really is a treat. 'Re' means 'again.' So you treat yourself again. My wife and I like to go as day guests to a particular spa with an outdoor pool and spend the entire day in a sense of timelessness, alternating between reading, talking, swimming, sleeping, daydreaming, reflecting, writing. You get the picture?

A remarkable idea was set in place by Geshe Michael Roach, an American Buddhist monk who was instructed by his abbot to get a job in the business world and apply Buddhist principles. Written in his book 'The Diamond Cutter,' Roach took a Tibetan elders process of Weekly Circles and got the owners of the diamond business to agree that he would not work on Wednesdays. This would break the corporate mindset and routine cycle of the week and allow him time to plan, reflect, seek inspiration and take care of his health. He arranged the day so he was in silence until 2 PM, with no interruptions. The afternoon was for study and hobbies that were enjoyable and not related to the job. In the evening, he would go out and help someone, to be in service. Light meals and exercise were sprinkled throughout the day, and in the evening some silent reflection to review the activities and discoveries of the day. Through this practice he added irreplaceable value, saving the company millions of dollars from the ideas that emerged from this time alone.

To be an effective leader, these ideas of timeless management are essential. The more you value effective timeless management, the more you will add value to your leadership role in your organisation. You cannot afford not to. From the energy this provides, you will feel renewed and refreshed, leading to new and fresh ideas that will reverberate throughout the organisation.

Imagine yourself as Nataraj, Shiva with his four arms, the Hindu lord of dance who controls movement and the flow of time in the cosmos. What we mortals could do with four arms! In his book *Life of Pi*, Yann Martel writes that Nataraj "dances on the demons of ignorance, his four arms held out in a choreographic gesture, one foot on the demon's back, the other lifted in the air. When Nataraj brings his foot down, they say time will stop."

It's time to put your foot down.

Create a culture of innovation

The islands of peace idea could permeate across your corporate culture. It is well-documented that 3M Corporation allows, actually requires, their employees to devote a certain amount of time each week for creative thinking. This leads directly to innovative ideas that can be implemented in the company. Many offices have 'casual Fridays' with no suits, no ties, no high heels. Corporate wellness programmes provide courses in yoga, relaxation and fitness, encouraging a healthy workplace and taking time and care for oneself. Lucasfilm Animation has flexible start/end times and no dress code. Google employees can enjoy short retreats in special audio-tuned swinging cocooned chairs. The best companies to work for are those where the employees are motivated to work hard because their work/life balance is supported and respected.

⚷ Secret 84
RELAXATION METHODS CAN INCREASE PERSONAL AND PROFESSIONAL EFFECTIVENESS

Back in 1975, Dr. Herbert Benson, Associate Professor of Medicine at the Harvard Medical School, researched techniques used in the East and the West to help people reach the 'relaxation response,' the state that dissolves stress-producing and controlling thoughts, reduces tension, lowers the heart and breathing rates, slows down the metabolism and increases the alpha brain waves.

From his research Benson found that you can get to the relaxation response most effectively when the following four elements are in place:

- A quiet environment with minimal external distractions and a calm atmosphere.

- A mental device on which to focus in order to deepen concentration, such as a word, phrase, sound or image. When 'mind wandering' occurs, one simply returns to the repetition of the chosen device to help eliminate other thoughts and quiet the mind.

- A passive attitude, allowing one to empty all thoughts and distractions from one's mind, neither worrying about how well you are doing the technique nor about what is right and wrong.

- A comfortable position so there is no undue muscular tension.

The benefits of eliciting the relaxation response are numerous. You will relieve fatigue, cope better with your anxieties, relieve the stress that can lead to high blood pressure and hardening of the arteries, heart attack and stroke, and you will be more alert so you can focus on what is really important. Let me share with you some breathing exercises that are easy to learn, can be done anywhere, and have no dangerous side effects.

Ten breathing exercises to calm the mind

Much can be written about the background and variations of these exercises. To be practical, I will simply describe how to do them (and where they come from) and leave it to you to research further if you wish. So find a quiet space, be present, get comfortable, and begin.

Hot Tip

If you practise one or two of these exercises regularly, they will seep into your subconscious and emerge when you need them.

1. Conscious deep breathing (Yoga)

Close your eyes, inhale slowly while expanding the belly or tan t'ien (about two finger widths below the navel). Count to four as you inhale through your nose, hold the breath for four counts, then exhale through the nose counting to four and again hold the breath for four more counts. Repeat the process until calmness sets in.

2. Four-direction breathing (the Feldenkrais Method)

Slowly breathe forwards eight times, bringing awareness to your rib cage, chest, belly and tan t'ien. Breathe backwards eight times, bringing awareness to the movement of the muscles along your back. Combine these two directions for a count of eight, expanding as you inhale. Bring your attention to your right side as you breathe. Now breathe into the left side, noticing any differences. Breathe simultaneously sideways eight times, allowing both sides to expand on the inhale. Now combine these four directions with each breath, expanding on the inhale forwards, backwards, left and right, then returning to the beginning.

3. Tonglen (Tibetan Buddhism)

Inhale and imagine taking in the suffering of all people. Exhale and imagine giving happiness and success to all. This receiving/sending develops loving-kindness and compassion to others, and helps reduce selfish attachment to our personal problems. Buddhists say it involves all of the Six Perfections: giving, ethics, patience, joyous effort, concentration and wisdom.

4. Fire breath (Sufism)

Inhale through the mouth and imagine light filling up the body, from head to fingertips to toes. Then imagine the warmth in your heart, and as you exhale through the nose, give that warmth back out to the universe.

5. Watching your breath (Buddhism)

As you inhale, say to yourself "now I'm breathing in." As you exhale, say to yourself "now I'm breathing out." Naming what you are doing is an excellent way to stay in the present moment. Repeat this many times.

6. Breathing with a mantra

The Sanskrit word 'mantra' comes from 'man' (the mind) and 'tra' (an implement of), meaning an implement of the mind by using repeated words to empty the mind of its clutter. Originating with meditation in India, the word became secularised with business mantras, advertising mantras, sports mantras — and relaxation mantras. Repeat the words "I am calm" or "Peace" with your breath. As thoughts appear, let them fade away by continually repeating the words.

7. Percussive breaths (theatre training)

Inhale smoothly through the nose, exhale in percussive breaths through the mouth, as if you were blowing out a candle numerous times. Then reverse the process, percussive inhale and smooth exhale.

8. Hissing (theatre training)

Make a hissing 'ssssss' sound and hold the exhale for as long as possible for a good release of tension and anxiety.

9. Breathing until the last drop (the Feldenkrais Method)

Somewhat like a percussive exhale, breathe out and out and out again, and even more, and then more, until you absolutely must inhale. Then let the full breath enter your body and enjoy the uplifting feeling.

10. Squeezing the lungs (theatre training)

Inhale as fully as possible, then feel like a sponge as you squeeze the air out. Another simple stress relief exercise.

How do you feel? I hope these simple yet profound breathing exercises will lead you into the delicious space of timelessness and perhaps to a place deeper inside: a knowing, a longing, an awareness of something greater than yourself. I wish you well on the journey into timelessness.

Checklist for timeless management

1. Slow down to speed up. When you immerse yourself in a project, time disappears paradoxically.

2. Let go of old habits, resistance and prejudice that block change to allow for a new future to emerge. Let go to let come.

3. Struggle with a problem until just the tipping point of stress, then break away from it.

4. Use braindorming visualisation to allow solutions to problems and new ideas to emerge.

5. Cultivate mindfulness by being present, in the moment, with what you are doing and with whom you are talking.

6. Take quiet breaks for reflection. Your energy and productivity increase after you devote some time simply to 'not doing'.

7. Close your door to protect your boundaries. Make yourself unavailable for periods of time to enhance your focus. This will be understood and respected by your staff and clients.

8. Create 'islands of peace' outside the office. Find a special hideaway where you will not be disturbed, where you can think, plan, dream and envision.

9. Take a retreat to renew and refresh. Your good health is critical for you, your family and your job responsibilities.

10. Choose to use breathing exercises to calm the mind. Awareness of breath is a hidden treasure for well-being.

CHAPTER 22

MAXIMISING TEAM PERFORMANCE

How to achieve greater team success through leadership
and performance management

by **Ken Wong**
CEO and Leadership Coach
ProActive Training & Education

Ken Wong is the CEO and Leadership Coach of ProActive Training & Education, a regional training and management consultancy, based in Singapore. He is a certified management consultant, seminar speaker, professional trainer and business entrepreneur, with more than 15 years of corporate training and consulting, speaking and business development experience in Asia.

Ken is fluent in English, Mandarin and Cantonese, and that makes him one of the most versatile multi-lingual trainers and seminar speakers in Asia. He specialises in the areas of leadership and supervisory management, performance management, learning and development and customer service. He has trained many participants from USA, Germany, Japan, Korea, India, Australia, South Africa, Hong Kong, Taiwan, Philippines, Vietnam and Myanmar. They have benefited greatly from his highly engaging, fun and consultative training style.

Ken holds an MSc in Training and Performance Management from the University of Leicester, United Kingdom and a Bachelor of Business Administration (Passed with Merit) from the National University of Singapore. He is a Certified AEM-Cube Consultant and a Certified Emergenetics Associate.

Ken is a regular contributor to *The Straits Times* Recruit, with his articles on supervisory management, customer service, sales, entrepreneurship, HR development and secretarial skills. He has also been interviewed by 938LIVE on management and secretarial topics.

Find out more about Ken at: **www.ProActiveTrg.com**
Contact Ken at: **ken@ProActiveTrg.com**

LEADING AND MANAGING a team is never an easy task. It comes with its own set of issues and challenges. As the saying goes, "With greater power comes bigger responsibilities". The team leader has a big responsibility to ensure that he/she can lead the team towards greater success.

In this section, Ken Wong will share insights and important lessons on leadership to help you achieve greater team success. He will highlight tips and pointers on how to manage your team to reach better team performance and also care for their well-being.

Ken will also help you to understand performance management better, especially how to conduct fair and constructive performance appraisal discussions. You'll learn to coach and correct your team members for improved work performance and desirable behaviours.

Secret 85
IF YOU WANT TO LEAD YOUR TEAM MORE, YOU NEED TO MANAGE THEM LESS

I enjoy observing people in the workplace, especially managers and supervisors. I have seen many of them managing their employees but not leading them towards the key performance indicators or other measurements of work success. During my leadership workshops, I had many learners asking me the question, "What are the key differences between managers and leaders?" Let me share my answer with you here.

Warren G. Bennis, a university professor and founding chairman of the Leadership Institute at the University of Southern California, said "Managers do things right, leaders do the right things." This captures the essence of the key differences between managers and leaders. Managers and leaders think differently. Managers usually think in a more incremental manner, whereas leaders tend to think more radically. For example, managers solve work problems in a systematic and sequential manner similar to walking up the stairs to reach the top of a building. Leaders think 'out of the box' to solve work problems, even exploring taking a helicopter to reach the top. I like to think that managers are more like administrators at the workplace – they understand company rules and regulations and get employees to follow them. On the other hand, leaders are more like innovators and rule breakers – they look at new ways of doing things and they break existing rules to suit that.

Managers versus leaders

Let's make a brief comparison of the manager and the leader here:

Managers have subordinates

- Managers use an authoritarian, transactional style in managing employees. They direct the employees in what they need to do, sometimes even telling them how they should do their work. They like employees who listen, obey and execute their instructions. The relationship they have with their employees is more of a manager/subordinate working relationship where a subordinate needs to follow what the immediate superior says. Where the employees deliver good results, the manager rewards them with promotions, salary increments, performance bonuses and other perks to motivate them further.

- The manager's focus is work, work and more work. Managers believe that employees need to be supervised closely and managed effectively to deliver the desired results. Managers are results-oriented and they want employees to get the work done efficiently within the specified time frames. This is evident in their ongoing communication with employees where any conversation is always about work, work updates and progress.

- Managers take comfort in the status quo. To them, big radical changes are no good and disruptive for work. They are comfortable with steady and incremental improvements for their work and that of their employees. They do not encourage creativity and innovation in work among employees, as this would mean new ways of doing things.

Caution

Try not to spend too much time managing your employees. You do not have to manage them on every aspect of their work and solve all their problems.

Leaders have followers

- Leaders adopt a charismatic, transformational style in managing their employees. People are attracted to them because of their charisma and dynamic personality. Employees love working for these leaders because it is fun, challenging and inspiring. The relationship between them is that of a leader-follower, an informal arrangement as compared to the formal arrangement of a manager-subordinate.

- The main focus of leaders is people. Work results are important too, of course, but people are equally important to them. Leaders spend time developing their employees, equipping them with the necessary skills and knowledge to do their jobs well. They pay close attention to the well-being of their employees, and ensure that they are happy and healthy at work. Regular communication with the employees will usually cover more than just work.

Leaders enjoy risk and like to discover new ways of working. They go for quantum leaps to improve the work processes and subsequently much better team performances.

Many managers manage their employees and few lead them. It would be greatly beneficial for managers to master leadership skills and start to lead their team towards greater work success. That would also generate better work relationships between managers and employees and a happier work environment for all.

Holy Moly!

If I lead my employees more and manage them less, I could get better and faster results from them. They would also feel more appreciated at work.

○ *Secret 86*
WE CAN LEARN FROM INEFFECTIVE LEADERS TOO

I would like to share two of my favourite quotations on leadership with you:

> *"If you treat a person as he is, he will stay as he is; but if you treat him as if he were what he ought to be, he will become what he ought to be and could be."*
>
> — Johann Goethe

This quotation, in my opinion, shows the significance and the responsibilities that managers and supervisors carry in leading their employees well. If they see their employees as potential star employees and treat them that way, the employees would gradually become that. Managers and supervisors could identify the hidden potential in them and set about to develop their individual bests.

"Leadership: The art of getting someone else to do
something you want done because he wants to do it."

— Dwight D. Eisenhower

I find this quotation insightful because it shares a deeper meaning of leadership, ie getting employees to do what you want them to do willingly. Here, the leader is able to influence and persuade the follower to achieve goals because he is committed to do that himself.

Hot Tip

Quotations contain words of wisdom that we can tap on and learn from the past experiences of others. Choose your favourite ones carefully and use them as good reminders in leading teams.

Leading employees effectively is a huge challenge for managers and supervisors. Most of us learn how to lead and manage employees from attending relevant workshops, reading books and gathering real work experience ourselves. It would be wonderful if we have role models and mentors who are effective leaders. In observing them in action, we shorten our own learning curve and master the knowledge and skills of effective leadership in double quick time.

What happens if we are unlucky and we only have ineffective leaders at our workplace? Does it mean that we cannot learn anything from them to become effective leaders? Not true – we can always learn from the mistakes made by ineffective leaders.

Mistake 1: Leaders who do not listen

There are some leaders who believe that they possess all the knowledge and skills necessary to run their business well. They may have been very successful for a long time and they believe their success formula will last. They will not listen to anyone else except themselves. They do not trust that their followers are smart enough to share valuable input and feedback. Some of them pretend to listen but do not take the feedback seriously. As time passes, because these leaders do not listen, the followers give less feedback and eventually stop giving any at all.

Lesson 1: Listen to all employees and take their feedback seriously

No one has a monopoly of all the knowledge and skills needed in the business. Effective leaders learn to listen to their followers because they are in constant contact with the customers. There may also be changes in market conditions, so the leaders need to know these to implement plans to counter the changes.

Mistake 2: Leaders who instil fear in others

In the course of my work, I often come across managers and supervisors who share with me that they lead their teams with fear. They tell me that when their employees are fearful of them, they work much faster and harder. They feel more powerful when they are feared by others.

Lesson 2: Instil authority, not fear

The problem with having too much fear at the workplace is that employees are afraid of making mistakes and end up not trying hard enough. They also would not take initiative because they are scared they would be heavily penalised if they make mistakes. Also when mistakes are made, the employees may just cover it up or pass the buck to others. Effective leaders instil authority in their teams and encourage joint problem solving among followers.

Mistake 3: Leaders who use favouritism

Some leaders give certain employees preferential treatment and practise favouritism at the workplace. For employees that they like, the leaders are more likely to overlook their mistakes and reward them, even though they did not perform well.

Lesson 3: Treat all followers fairly

The fastest way to break a team is preferential treatment and favouritism by the leader. An effective leader treats all followers fairly. Capable employees who perform well should be rewarded even if they are not well-liked. Performance appraisals must be conducted in an objective and fair manner focusing on work performance, not personalities.

Your Turn

Find a partner and spend five minutes telling him or her about your observations of ineffective leaders at the workplace. What are some of the lessons you learnt from them? Then change over and let your partner do the same.

Secret 87
BE FAIR AND CONSTRUCTIVE IN MANAGING PERFORMANCE

During my performance management and appraisal workshops, managers and supervisors like to ask me how they could motivate their employees to deliver their best performance at the workplace. They shared with me that the employees are simply doing the bare minimum required for the work and are not motivated to do better. And some of these employees were much better performers in the past. I would like to share some of my insights with you here.

When employees first join organisations, they are usually full of energy and highly motivated to do their best. They work harder than other employees and even volunteer to take on additional work or new projects. They display a strong desire to perform well, and in return want to be recognised and rewarded for their great performance. If they get the recognition and reward, they would continue to be motivated and deliver their best. Sadly, more often than not, they would not get the correct recognition and rewards. Even if they do get the recognition and rewards, it would be after a long period of time, long after they have forgotten about it.

I have spoken to new employees, mature employees and other experienced managers and supervisors about this. Based on the discussions and through my own work and coaching experience, it seems that Asian managers and supervisors are not generous in lavishing praise and compliments when employees have performed well. A few superiors even possess the mindset that great work is expected from employees, but mistakes are not forgivable and definitely not forgotten. Some employees told me, "The 100 great things they have done for the company are never praised and remembered, but that one tiny mistake they have committed is never forgiven and forgotten by their superiors!"

I find it very sad that, instead of highlighting the great performance displayed in the past and recognising that, the superiors focus on the employees' mistakes and use them for negative demonstrations during meetings. I believe that managers and supervisors should focus their attention on the track records of their employees, not missteps in their careers.

Hot Tip

Remember to recognise employees for their great work performance through appropriate praise and compliments. Never take their performance for granted.

Conducting fair and constructive performance appraisal discussions

Performance appraisal discussion is not a form-filling, documentation or scolding session. It is a time where the superiors give feedback to their employees on their past performance and inspire them to do even better in the future. Performance appraisal discussion must be conducted in a fair and objective manner to benefit employees, managers and the organisation. Setting shared key performance indicators (KPI) and using them consistently throughout the assessment period is fair for both managers (appraiser) and employees (appraisees). The manager should measure the performance of the employees against the stated KPI and avoid making any last minute changes to the KPI. Also the manager should measure employees with similar job functions with the same yardstick and not deviate too much. Otherwise, the employees may complain that the manager is appraising their performance using different yardsticks and is not fair to all of them.

To fully optimise the performance appraisal discussion, it is important for the manager to know exactly what employees want. Generally, employees desire to have:

- A clear understanding of what's expected of them
- Information about how they have performed so far
- An assessment of their strengths and areas for development
- A sense of their relationship with their manager

⚷ Secret 87
BE FAIR AND CONSTRUCTIVE IN MANAGING PERFORMANCE

During my performance management and appraisal workshops, managers and supervisors like to ask me how they could motivate their employees to deliver their best performance at the workplace. They shared with me that the employees are simply doing the bare minimum required for the work and are not motivated to do better. And some of these employees were much better performers in the past. I would like to share some of my insights with you here.

When employees first join organisations, they are usually full of energy and highly motivated to do their best. They work harder than other employees and even volunteer to take on additional work or new projects. They display a strong desire to perform well, and in return want to be recognised and rewarded for their great performance. If they get the recognition and reward, they would continue to be motivated and deliver their best. Sadly, more often than not, they would not get the correct recognition and rewards. Even if they do get the recognition and rewards, it would be after a long period of time, long after they have forgotten about it.

I have spoken to new employees, mature employees and other experienced managers and supervisors about this. Based on the discussions and through my own work and coaching experience, it seems that Asian managers and supervisors are not generous in lavishing praise and compliments when employees have performed well. A few superiors even possess the mindset that great work is expected from employees, but mistakes are not forgivable and definitely not forgotten. Some employees told me, "The 100 great things they have done for the company are never praised and remembered, but that one tiny mistake they have committed is never forgiven and forgotten by their superiors!"

I find it very sad that, instead of highlighting the great performance displayed in the past and recognising that, the superiors focus on the employees' mistakes and use them for negative demonstrations during meetings. I believe that managers and supervisors should focus their attention on the track records of their employees, not missteps in their careers.

Hot Tip

Remember to recognise employees for their great work performance through appropriate praise and compliments. Never take their performance for granted.

Conducting fair and constructive performance appraisal discussions

Performance appraisal discussion is not a form-filling, documentation or scolding session. It is a time where the superiors give feedback to their employees on their past performance and inspire them to do even better in the future. Performance appraisal discussion must be conducted in a fair and objective manner to benefit employees, managers and the organisation. Setting shared key performance indicators (KPI) and using them consistently throughout the assessment period is fair for both managers (appraiser) and employees (appraisees). The manager should measure the performance of the employees against the stated KPI and avoid making any last minute changes to the KPI. Also the manager should measure employees with similar job functions with the same yardstick and not deviate too much. Otherwise, the employees may complain that the manager is appraising their performance using different yardsticks and is not fair to all of them.

To fully optimise the performance appraisal discussion, it is important for the manager to know exactly what employees want. Generally, employees desire to have:

- A clear understanding of what's expected of them
- Information about how they have performed so far
- An assessment of their strengths and areas for development
- A sense of their relationship with their manager

Managers should treat performance appraisals seriously and make all the necessary preparation and time for the session. Likewise, the employee who is going to be appraised needs to make some preparations too. The performance appraisal discussion should be an interactive, two-way communication between the manager and the employee.

To have a constructive performance appraisal discussion, managers need to do the following:

- Encourage the appraisee to do more of the talking.

- Allow scope for reflection and analysis.

- Analyse performance, not personality — concentrate on what appraisees have done, not the sort of people they are.

- Keep the whole period under review, not concentrating on isolated or recent events.

- Adopt a 'no surprise' approach — performance problems should have been identified and dealt with at the time they occurred.

- Recognise achievements and reinforce strengths.

- End the meeting positively with agreed action plans and an understanding of how progress in implementing them will be reviewed.

Holy Moly!

If I am fair and appraise the performance of my employees in a constructive manner, they will be happier and more driven to deliver their best.

♀ Secret 88
COACHING EMPLOYEES IS AS SIMPLE AS LEARNING ABC

Coaching is the process of helping people enhance or improve their performance through reflection on how they apply a specific skill and/or knowledge in the business. In my supervisory workshops, I share with my learners these four different purposes for coaching. They are:

- Coaching to correct and align behaviours at work on a day-to-day basis.

- Coaching for skills and competence.

- Coaching for deficient work performance.

- Coaching for long-term growth and development of our subordinates. This can actually take the form of mentoring.

For the first purpose, I often highlight that how the employees behave at the workplace is primarily dependent on their superiors. Some managers disagreed and told me that the employees have been misbehaving for a long time and they are simply like that. They told me there is little they can do as these employees have been with the organisation for a long time — they are the old timers! As a result, the managers just kept quiet and 'close one eye' to whatever these old timers are doing, even though they disagreed with those behaviours. I shared with the managers that silence meant consent. If they do not voice their unhappiness and disagreement, the employees would assume that the managers have given them implicit approval and continue to behave in that manner. Pretty soon, the bad behaviours became a norm and subsequently a departmental culture. We should not condone bad behaviours such as being late for work, bullying, skiving, etc. We need to correct them on their bad behaviours and coach them on the desirable behaviours to display at the workplace.

To deal with discipline issues, I would advise managers to take these practical approaches:

- Understand possible reasons for an employee's bad behaviour.

- Pinpoint unacceptable work practices.

- Give a reasonable time frame to see improvement.

- Highlight the consequences of non-compliance.

Caution

Do not keep quiet when you see employees misbehave. To them, your silence means your consent for their bad behaviours.

Coaching for skills, competence and performance improvement

The manager or supervisor plays the role of performance coach and provide his team members with opportunities to fine-tune their skills, gives feedback on good moves, and points out where adjustments to action plans need to be made. It's important to develop and motivate your staff with a 'make it happen' attitude. Here are my seven steps to coach effectively to improve the skills, competence and performance of your employees:

1. Observe work performance.

2. Identify the performance gap.

3. Demonstrate how to do it.

4. Let the individual do it and provide feedback.

5. In case of error at any step, re-coach to correct.

6. Confirm that the performance meets standards.

7. Review — weekly, monthly, then quarter-annually, and yearly.

Coaching forgetful and stubborn employees remains a big challenge for managers and supervisors. For forgetful employees, you may want to tell them to write down the steps for doing the new task. They can refer to that when they forget and they do not have to keep running to you. You can jokingly tell them that if they forget how to work, one day finance division may forget to pay them their salaries. For stubborn employees, let them know that their methods are outdated and insist that they follow the way that you have coached.

Your Turn

Find a partner and use the seven-step coaching process to coach him or her on a new task. Did you display clarity and sufficient patience? Now change over and let your partner coach you on another task.

Checklist for achieving greater team success through leadership and performance management

1. Lead employees more, manage them less.

2. Do not micro-manage the work of your employees.

3. Choose your favourite leadership quotes and use them wisely to lead your team.

4. Learn from the mistakes of ineffective leaders.

5. Recognise employees for their great work performance through appropriate praise and compliments.

6. Conduct performance appraisal discussions fairly and constructively.

7. Measure the performance, not the personality, of your employees.

8. Recognise achievements and reinforce strengths during performance appraisals.

9. Correct bad behaviours when you see them — do not keep quiet.

10. Coach employees to improve their work performance.